CONTEMPORARY ENGLISH
BOOK 1

Ardith Loustalet Simons

with Kathleen Santopietro Weddel

CONTEMPORARY BOOKS

a division of NTC/CONTEMPORARY PUBLISHING GROUP
Lincolnwood, Illinois USA

With grateful thanks to Steve, whose kindness and patience have made so much difference.—Ardith

In gratitude for my teachers of spirit: Sue, Susan, Dot, and Elizabeth.—Kathleen

ISBN: 0-8092-0707-9

Published by Contemporary Books,
a division of NTC/Contemporary Publishing Group, Inc.
© 1999 NTC/Contemporary Publishing Group, Inc.,
4255 West Touhy Avenue, Lincolnwood (Chicago), Illinois 60646-1975 U.S.A.

890 VL 0 9 8 7 6 5 4 3 2 1

Contents

Scope and Sequence: Literacy

Unit	Topic	Culture Focus	Literacy Skills	Functions	SCANS Competencies
Unit A	Preliteracy		Shape recognition, directionality, recognizing, tracing, copying uppercase letters		Foundation Skills
Unit B	Preliteracy		Shape recognition, directionality, recognizing, tracing, and copying lowercase letters; matching uppercase and lowercase letters; numbers 1–10		Foundation Skills
1	Human Relations: Greetings	Greetings at school and work	Interpreting and identifying ideographs signifying male and female; sight word recognition	Greetings; stating one's name	Foundation Skills
2	Numbers	Counting	Recognizing, tracing, and copying numbers; matching numbers and quantities; understanding numbers 1–20	Repeating words for clarification	Foundation Skills
3	Home and Neighborhood: Home	Filling out forms	Understanding simple street addresses; identifying name, city, and address on a simple form; matching words and pictures; copying and writing phone numbers and addresses	Identifying; requesting information	Foundation Skills
4	Transportation and Travel: Directions	Getting to know your town	Understanding simple directions and spatial orientation; sight word recognition; matching numbers and quantities; identifying room numbers and sequence on a simple diagram; understanding numbers 21–30	Identifying; asking for clarification; requesting information	Foundation Skills
5	People and Machines: Time	U.S. attitudes toward time	Understanding time and reading clocks; reading signs with business hours indicated; reading analog clocks; understanding numbers 31–60	Showing gratitude; telling time	Foundation Skills
6	Home and Neighborhood: Family	Sharing family information	Understanding words for family members; identifying family members and talking about family; reading simple biographical information forms; copying personal information onto a simple form; numbers in the tens, from 10 to 100	Identifying; demonstrating	Foundation Skills
7	Employment and Opportunity: Jobs	Mini-résumés	Understanding job titles; identifying job titles, times, and phone numbers in simple job ads; sight word recognition; reading the year in figures; recognition of work signs	Expressing state of being	Foundation Skills
8	Consumer Economics: Money	Shopping	Reading prices and price tags; reading symbols for dollars and cents; identifying amounts on coins and paper money; relating prices to coins and bills; adding and subtracting amounts of money	Requesting information; expressing gratitude	Foundation Skills
9	Healthy Living: Food	Groceries	Identifying food items; reading names of food items; reading labels and ads for food; writing prices	Requesting information; giving information	Foundation Skills

Scope and Sequence: Book 1

Unit	Topics	Culture Focus	Functions	Grammar	SCANS Competencies
Introductory	Numbers; alphabet	Missing people	Greetings; taking leave; asking for information	Simple commands	Foundation Skills: listening, speaking, reading, writing
1	Human Relations: occupations; place of origin; filling out forms; giving personal information	Family and relatives; a family tree	Asking for information; introductions; giving personal information	*Be*: present affirmative and negative statements and contractions; subject pronouns; *be + from*	Work with cultural diversity; interpret and communicate information
2	Employment and Opportunity: applying for a job; jobs and activities	Supervisors and levels of organization; organization charts	Expressing needs; asking for information, giving answers; making offers	Present of *be*, yes/no questions, short answers; singular and plural nouns; *this* and *that*	Understand systems; organize and maintain information
3	Community Services: school and community; drugs in schools; U.S. drug, alcohol, and nicotine use	Volunteer and community workers	Telling about people; expressing wants	Possessive adjectives; prepositions of place; affirmative and negative commands	Teach others; allocate human resources
4	Home and Neighborhood: neighbors; helping people; child care and babysitters; child care coops	Neighbors helping each other	Refusals; telling about activities; asking for clarification	Present continuous statements and yes/no questions, short answers	Allocate time; negotiate
5	Healthy Living: healthy food; the food pyramid; fast food; planning healthy food	Fast food in the United States	Expressing likes and dislikes; ordering; expressing disagreement; expressing needs	Simple present, affirmative and negative; yes/no questions and short answers	Improve and design systems; participate as a member of a team
6	Transportation and Travel: travel by car; road signs, colors of cars; car maintenance	The importance of cars in the United States	Expressing likes and dislikes; apologizing; asking for information	Wh-questions with *be*; introductory *It*; information questions with simple present	Allocate money; interpret and communicate information
7	Consumer Economics: paying bills; job experience and office skills; wages, salaries, and raises	Minimum wage in the United States	Asking for suggestions; making suggestions; talking about ability and inability	*Can*, affirmative, yes/no questions and short answers; prepositions of time	Allocate human resources; exercise leadership
8	Arts and Entertainment: sports; cable and network television; amount of TV people watch per week	Cable and network television	Giving information and asking for information about the past; speculating about the past; expressing dissatisfaction	*Be*, past, affirmative and negative statements, yes/no questions and short answers	Acquire and evaluate information
9	History and Geography: famous women in U.S. history; Susan B. Anthony; voting	Mary Lyon, who founded Mt. Holyoke	Complimenting; talking about past activities	Simple past (statements, yes/no questions, short answers, information questions)	Organize and maintain information; understand systems
10	People and Machines: phones and phone cards; ATM cards; international calls	Smart cards with computer chips	Talking about plans; expressing necessity; making suggestions; talking about possibility	Future with *going to*: statements, yes/no questions, short answers, information questions; compound sentences	Monitor and correct performance; teach others

Scope and Sequence: Book 2

Unit	Topics	Culture Focus	Functions	Grammar	SCANS Competencies
1	Human Relations: school, company-sponsored training; elementary school, adult education	Asking for clarification on the job	Asking for and giving information; asking for and giving directions; introductions	Present of *be* in affirmative / negative statements, questions; past of *be*; possessives	Work with diversity; sociability, understand organizational systems
2	Arts and Entertainment: relaxation and leisure; going to the zoo; activity schedule, being busy, stress on the job	Stress on the job	Comparing and contrasting; giving advice; talking about preferences; talking about plans; arguing pros and cons	Simple present; verb + infinitive; adverbs of frequency	Allocate time; manage self
3	Home and Neighborhood: community problems; neighborhood; neighborhood security	Security guards	Offers, requests, and warnings; discussing problems	*There is, there are, there was, there were*; past regular and irregular verbs; prepositions of location	Solve problems; teach others
4	Employment and Opportunity: success and successful people in the United States; successful immigrant Americans	Teamwork and leading a group	Asking for and giving information	Simple past in yes/no questions and negative statements, past time expressions	Exercise leadership; monitor and correct performance; participate as a member of a team
5	Healthy Living: health, exercise, risk factors for heart disease; missing work because of illness	U.S. concerns about dieting and losing weight	Comparing and contrasting; asking for and giving advice	Direct object pronouns, future with *going to*, count and noncount nouns	Acquire and evaluate information; make decisions
6	Home and Neighborhood: renting an apartment; daycare; mortgage rates; renting vs. buying	Operating a home daycare business	Asking for and giving information	*How much/how many*; future with *will*; wh-question words	Serve clients or customers; negotiate and arrive at decisions; evaluate information and make decisions
7	Transportation and Travel: transportation; accidents and accident reports; trains and buses; buying a car	Driving rules and responsibilities	Asking for and giving directions; expressing necessity; reporting something	*Need to, have to*; present continuous; *could* and *would* for requests	Allocate money; demonstrate responsibilities
8	Community Services: libraries and community services; getting a library card; freedom of speech	Feedom of speech	Telling what one should and shouldn't do; apologizing	*Should* and *shouldn't*; demonstrative pronouns; demonstrative adjectives	Select technology; apply technology to task; apply problem solving skills
9	Employment and Opportunity: job search; interview tips; what employers want of new employees	Job search, interview tips, what employers want of new employees	Expressing ability and inability; making suggestions; giving advice	Meanings of *can* and *can't*; compound sentences, *must* and *must not, must* and *have to*	Organize and maintain information; sociability
10	Consumer Economics: shopping; discounts; bargains	Using coupons to save money	Complimenting; comparing and contrasting	Indirect objects; comparative adjectives; meanings of *could* and *couldn't*	Allocate money; participate as a member of a team

Scope and Sequence: Book 3

Unit	Topics	Culture Focus	Functions	Grammar	SCANS Competencies
1	People and Machines: business machines; the Internet	Machines and where they are used	Explaining; expressing needs; making suggestions	Adverbial clauses with *because* and *so*; two-word verbs	Select technology; apply technology to a task
2	Arts and Entertainment: U.S. jazz; music and clubs	Music festivals in the United States	Expressing likes and dislikes; asking for and giving information	Verbs with reflexive pronouns; *each other*	Work with cultural diversity; social skills
3	Home and Neighborhood: decorating one's home; colors; weddings; jobs in construction and design	Cultural connotations of color	Expressing needs and desires; complimenting; describing	Order of adjectives; prepositions of location	Creative thinking; acquire and evaluate information
4	Healthy Living: health, fitness, insurance; good and bad habits; longevity	Americans living longer	Giving strong advice; expressing possibility; predicting consequences; expressing obligation and necessity	*Should, have to,* and *might; either . . . or; must, must not*	Acquire and evaluate information; monitor and correct performance
5	Human Relations: family, personal relationships; Larry King; childcare	Changes in the American family	Sympathizing; expressing surprise; expressing agreement and disagreement	Past participles; present perfect with *ever* and *always*; object pronouns	Social skills; interpret and communicate information; acquire and evaluate information
6	Consumer Economics: food, ingredients, cooking; regional food products	Regions and the foods they produce	Expressing dissatisfaction; talking about plans; sympathizing; making requests and commands	Inseparable two-word verbs; count and noncount nouns; quantifiers	Social skills; acquire and evaluate information
7	Employment and Opportunity: job benefits, days off; work and home responsibilities	Companies and benefits	Comparing and contrasting; explaining; asking for and giving information	Comparatives; superlatives	Decision making; acquire and evaluate information
8	History and Geography: immigration to the United States; ethnic groups	Ethnic groups and their occupations	Expressing worry; congratulating; complimenting; promising; predicting	Past continuous; past with *used to*; future with *will*	Interpret and communicate information; acquire and evaluate information; work with cultural diversity
9	Community Services: animals and people; pets; types of dogs	Pets in the United States	Making suggestions; asking for advice	*Ought to, should, have to, must*	Responsibility; acquire and evaluate information; creative thinking
10	Human Relations: nonverbal communication; shaking hands; relationships with co-workers	Shaking hands American style	Expressing unhappiness; expressing desires; expressing possibility; expressing obligation	Verbs with gerunds; sentences with *and*	Social skills; self-management; acquire and evaluate information

Scope and Sequence: Book 4

Unit	Topics	Culture Focus	Functions	Grammar	SCANS Competencies
1	Employment and Opportunity: networking; writing résumés and cover letters; preparing for interviews	Job skills for the future	Asking for and giving information; giving advice; introductions	Present perfect; present perfect continuous with *for* and *since*; simple past; present perfect; and present perfect continuous	Acquire and evaluate information; identify human resources; understand systems
2	Transportation and Travel: transportation announcements; vacation requests; accident reports; travel costs	U.S. emphasis on driving	Discussing problems; asking for and giving information; reporting something	Reported speech; present perfect; past perfect	Interpret and communicate information; think creatively; solve problems
3	Home and Neighborhood: natural disasters; volunteer organizations	Volunteer work	Asking for and giving information; offers, requests, and warnings	Passive voice; present conditional, conditional with *would*; conditional	Participate as a member of a team; organize and maintain information
4	Healthy Living: medical insurance coverage and claims; nutrition; non-traditional medicine	Alternative medicine	Asking for and giving information; comparing and contrasting	Gerunds and infinitives	Acquire and evaluate information; solve problems; self-manage
5	Employment and Opportunity: citizenship requirements, forms, and exam; undocumented immigrants	INS rules	Giving advice; expressing necessity; making suggestions; arguing pros and cons	Modals of advice and necessity; short answers, tag endings	Acquire and evaluate information; socialization, participate as a member of a team/negotiate
6	Arts and Entertainment: opinions; arts programs; family plans; entertainment expenses	Dance in different cultures	Comparing and contrasting; describing	Present participles as adjectives, past participles as adjectives	See things in the mind's eye; make decisions; teach others
7	History and Geography: small business; job retraining; overfishing; protecting natural resources	Water pollution	Talking about preferences arguing pros and cons	Relative clauses with *who*; relative clauses with *which* and *that*; word order in relative clauses	Interpret and communicate information; participate as member of a team
8	Consumer Economics: banking; small business loans; budgets; saving money in the United States and around the world	Employee benefits	Asking for and giving information; comparing and contrasting	Direct and indirect objects, embedded questions and embedded yes/no questions with infinitives	Acquire and evaluate information; identify and allocate resources (money); interpret and communicate information
9	Community Services: community resources; community college courses; single parents in the United States	Parenting strategies	Asking for and giving advice; asking for and giving information	Time clauses; clauses of cause and effect; clauses of opposition	Acquire and evaluate information; solve problems, reasoning (cause/effect and opposition)
10	People and Machines: telephone bills; using answering machines and voice mail; technology in school	Technology at home and work	Asking for and giving information; comparing and contrasting	Future conditional; phrasal verbs and separable phrasal verbs	Participate as a member of a team; understand systems; acquire and evaluate information

Introduction

Program Components and Philosophy

Contemporary English is a five-level interactive topic-based English-as-a-Second-Language series for adult learners ranging from the beginning-literacy level to the high-intermediate level. The series includes

- Student Books for classroom use
- Workbooks for independent use at home, in the classroom, or in a lab
- Audiocassettes for individual student, classroom, or lab use and
- Teacher's Manuals, with reproducible activity masters and unit progress checks for assessment. These materials were correlated from inception to the California Model Standards for Adult ESL Programs, the MELT Student Performance Levels, and the SCANS (Secretary's Commission on Achieving Necessary Skills) Competencies.

Unique among adult ESL series, *Contemporary English* presents high-interest topics as a framework for developing a wide variety of language, thinking, and life skills. In addition to focusing on listening, speaking, reading, and writing skills, *Contemporary English* integrates work on language structures; problem-solving, critical-thinking, and graphic-literacy skills; and—increasingly important—work-related skills.

Contemporary English empowers students to take charge of their learning and to develop strong communication skills for the real world. For example, each unit in Books 1–4 falls under one of the following broad topics: Home and Neighborhood, People and Machines, Employment and Opportunity, Human Relations, Consumer Economics, Community Services, Transportation and Travel, Healthy Living, History and Geography, and Arts and Entertainment. (The lowest-level book, *Contemporary English* Literacy, addresses all of these topics except History and Geography and Arts and Entertainment.) In short, the series addresses topics of interest and concern to adult learners.

Contemporary English presents engaging and meaningful situations that provide a context for grammar structures, listening activities, and an emphasis on the world of work. Within this framework each unit offers a wealth of pair and group activities, often with designated team roles, and frequent individual and group presentations to the class. This approach mirrors the team organization characteristic of today's workplace and reflects the recent influence on education of the Department of Labor's SCANS report.

Teaching Suggestions

In general, keep the following suggestions in mind when you introduce activities from this series.

1. Rather than direct the classroom, try to manage or facilitate learning and encourage your learners to take active roles, even at the lowest levels of instruction.
2. Model activities before learners do them so that learners have a clear idea of how to work with a partner or a group.
3. Whenever possible, use students or classroom objects and people in your models. For example, say, "I am a teacher" or "She is a student." Move around the class and use gestures to convey meaning.
4. Review the directions orally and ask learners if they have questions.
5. Monitor learners as they do the activities.

6. Provide follow-up activities in some of these ways:

- When appropriate, post learners' work on the classroom walls for them to read.

- Have pairs or small groups share role-played conversations with the rest of the class.

- From time to time, have learners informally reflect on their participation by asking themselves questions such as these: "How well did I understand the activity? Was I a good listener? How much did I participate?"

As you progress through the units, always try to consider the book as a meaningful whole. Whenever possible, review aspects of content, language, vocabulary, and workplace skills, and incorporate them into each new unit. In this way, the process of recycling—a strong feature of this series—can be customized to meet the needs of your class.

General extension activities can be used in all units. In Book 1 you can use TPR (Total Physical Response) activities quite successfully as extension. True role-playing can be used especially from Book 2 on up. Improvisation can be used in Books 3 and 4. Strip stories can be created from the readings at all levels. Higher-level students can be asked to read or find newspaper and magazine articles related to unit topics. And for classrooms or programs with technological capability, the Internet, word-processing, database, and even spreadsheet activities related to series topics—such as job-search and citizenship issues—can be highly motivating and also practical, as students can list this experience for employers in their job-skills summary.

Use of monolingual English dictionaries is appropriate in Books 3 and 4, and bilingual native-language dictionaries can be used at all levels.

Dictations

You may want to do a dictation activity every time the class meets. Dictation is a good way to practice several English skills simultaneously, as learners listen, write, and read sentences in English. You can choose two sentences from one of the Scenes or a short section from one of the readings. Follow these steps.

1. Tell learners to listen to the first sentence but not write it.

2. Repeat the sentence. Tell learners how many words are in it.

3. Give learners time to write the sentence.

4. Repeat the sentence again if needed.

5. Show learners where to find the sentence in the book.

Language Experience Stories

At the lower levels of the series, you may also want to use learner-generated language experience stories in your teaching approach. If you are not yet comfortable using language experience stories as a whole-class activity, the following steps may be helpful:

1. Ask the class to look at a photo or illustration related to the content of the unit.

2. Have learners talk about the visual.

3. Write what they say.

4. Read their words to them.

5. Ask if they want to make any changes or corrections, but keep the emphasis on the connection between spoken and written language, not on correct grammar.

6. Read the story aloud while learners follow along.

7. Point to words and sentences and have learners read them to you.

8. Have learners practice reading the story as many times as they show interest in doing so.

Journal Writing

You may want to have higher-level students keep journals to improve their written English. If you have not monitored journal writing before, try following these suggestions:

1. Give learners a formal or informal schedule on which you will review the journals.

2. Tell them to write about anything they are interested in learning about that day or week. Low-level students or those who have little practice writing may need to write just one sentence every day at the end of class.

3. After reading each journal, write several sentences or questions about the entries.

4. Don't make corrections unless the individual learner asks you to do so.

5. Discuss journal entries with their student authors.

Bringing the World to the Classroom

1. Ask learners to look in magazines or newspapers for stories related to the unit. An alternative is to bring periodicals to class yourself and look through them together.

2. Listen to the radio or television for stories about topics related to those in the units. Ask learners if they have heard or seen the stories.

3. Talk about the stories in class and relate them to the unit.

Always encourage learners to take active roles, even at the lowest levels of instruction. One way in which you can move learning in a more active direction is to have students ask the questions provided in the unit-specific notes in this Teacher's Manual. You can write the questions on 3 x 5 inch index cards, hand them to students, and let them direct their own and one another's learning. Higher-level students can add a question of their own to the cards, and students can exchange cards. The possibilities for encouraging active learning with *Contemporary English* are unlimited.

Graphic Organizers

These useful tools for organizing individual or collective thinking and writing play a central role in *Contemporary English*. Graphic organizers such as Venn diagrams, idea maps, T-charts, and Johari windows can be used successfully in the learning process. Graphic organizers are particularly helpful in developing higher-level thinking skills, and the visual aspect of these tools makes them ideal for visual learners.

Even among experienced teachers and teacher trainers, there is surprising variation among terms used to identify certain procedures and techniques for language learning, so the following definitions may be useful to you in working with graphic organizers. Although you may already be familiar with the definitions, consider presenting them to your class and explaining that you will be using certain organizers throughout the term. In the student materials themselves, efforts have been made to provide very brief definitions in context so that students will feel comfortable with the designated organizers for their level even when working independently.

Johari window. A square divided into four parts; a four-paned window. While Joharis can, of course, compare four different things, they are most commonly used to compare and contrast two things in this way:

panel 1: A has/does/etc. this

panel 2: B has/does/etc. this

panel 3: Both A and B have/do/etc. this

panel 4: Neither A nor B has/does/etc. this

T-chart. A two-column chart (in the form of a T), used to compare or contrast.

Venn diagram. Two overlapping circles, also used to compare and contrast. Properties of two things or concepts are written in the outer portions of the circles. In the overlapping section, shared properties are written.

Idea map. An organizer used to brainstorm ideas and gather information. The map has a central circle with a topic word, phrase, or sentence and connected circles surrounding it in which related or subordinate ideas or examples are written.

Time line. Even at the lowest levels of English instruction, the time line is a useful tool for teaching sequencing skills. As your students do the time line activities related to the content of their books and workbooks, you can guide them, whenever appropriate, to create their own time lines for different stages of their lives. This process involves gathering data and subsequently organizing it and presenting it to an audience.

The Student Book

Before you begin the first **Scene,** discuss—or explain with words and gestures if necessary—the meaning of the title, which can be a springboard to understanding the central issues. You also may wish to bring in photos, illustrations, and/or realia that illustrate the content and the concept. At more advanced levels, ask students themselves to predict what the unit is going to be about.

Ask questions that encourage students to contribute general information and personal information related to the topic (for example, "Fatima, do many people have big families in your country? Juan, do you have brothers?").

Write some of the questions and answers on the board or provide a handout.

You may wish to have students ask and answer some of the same questions in pairs.

Scenes

Each unit is divided into two parts, each of which begins with a **Scene** that presents, in comic-strip format, incidents from the lives of newcomers to the United States or aspects of U.S. culture that students encounter regularly. Lively, humorous, and dramatic, the **Scenes** engage students in the unit topics—usually by presenting typical problems in the lives of average people. A series of discussion questions proceeds from factual comprehension of the **Scene** to personalization and, in Books 3 and 4, problem solving. For example, at the highest level the sequence is *Facts* (comprehension questions), *Feelings* (inference), *And You?* (application), *Comparisons* (often between the students' native countries and the United States), and, finally, the *Action* problem-solving questions—for example, *What should ___ do?*

Here are some techniques to enhance class work for each **Scene** with lower-level learners:

1. Write the conversation on the board.

2. Read or play each line of the conversation twice and ask the class to repeat it. Whenever possible, emphasize a holistic approach. In other words, try to have learners deal with whole chunks of language, rather than breaking language down word by word.

3. Read the language that learners have difficulty pronouncing and ask them to repeat words and phrases as a class as often as necessary. As soon as pronunciation improves, work with repetition of the entire line again.

4. Ask individual students to repeat the line.

5. Have students do a final choral repetition. Then move to the next line.

6. As each new line is practiced, add it to the previously learned section of the Scene. Continue this way until students can repeat the entire dialogue. At higher levels you may wish to have learners read the cartoon in groups of twos or threes.

7. Review new or difficult vocabulary.

8. Say the words and have learners repeat them.

9. Elicit definitions of the words. Check comprehension. If students cannot define the words, you can provide definitions or examples.

10 Extend the **Scene** by doing some or all of the following activities:

- Have learners spell the words (on the board or aloud).

- Use the words in two or three sentences.

- Ask learners to use the words in sentences.

- Have students practice in pairs as you move around the classroom, checking pronunciation.

- Have learners take roles and read the dialogue aloud. Allow several pairs or groups of students to present each **Scene** for the class.

- Have partners take turns dictating the conversations. Student A can dictate while Student B writes the conversation in his or her ESL notebook.

- Write three to five sentences on small paper strips and hand these to individual learners. When prompted, each learner can read his or her sentence. You can then write each on the board or on an overhead transparency. Lower-level classes can copy the sentences. The class can then order the sentences chronologically by assigning a number to each one.

- Read a summary of the **Scene.** Then write it on the board or an overhead transparency, or provide it on a handout. Remove the summary and have learners write their own.

- After learners answer the questions under the **Scene,** have each one write one or two additional questions to ask other learners.

- Have students retell the story and write about the pictures in their own words.

These activities are particularly useful with multilevel classes. The **Scenes** introduce students to the topic of the unit, give them a context for the grammar, get them interested and involved in the story, and build a context for the unit.

Sound Bites

After each opening **Scene** comes **Sound Bites,** a focused listening task that includes prelistening and postlistening work. **Sound Bites** presents target content and language structures through lively conversations and other samples of natural speech, such as telephone answering-machine messages and transportation announcements.

For any **Sound Bites** activity, you can follow these steps:

1. Read the directions aloud.

2. Model the directions.

3. Tell students what kind of conversations or passages they will listen to.

4. Read or play the tape for each individual **Sound Bites** item several times. Speak at a normal speed. Remember that learners don't need to understand every word to get meaning.

5. Model the appropriate written response.

6. Let students listen as often as they want.

At lower levels let students direct their learning by frequently asking them questions such as "Do you need to listen again?" and teaching them to ask clarification questions such as "Can you repeat number six?" At higher levels you may wish to have students take notes as they listen.

You can provide repeated active-listening experiences for all levels of students by assigning a different focus for each one. For example, play **Sound Bites** the first time and ask students, "Have you heard anything like this before? Where were you?" Then play the tape again and have students listen for vocabulary. A third time they can listen for something else—perhaps to complete the task or to listen for specific questions you provide, such as "What kind of person is Jerry?" Encourage students to compare answers. As an extension activity, later in the unit, you may wish to make the **Sound Bites** into a cloze exercise, for example, by leaving out the examples of the grammar point throughout.

Vocabulary Prompts, Your Turn, and In Your Experience

Vocabulary Prompts, Your Turn, and **In Your Experience** occur within the units at the point of need, rather than in a fixed or unvarying part of each unit. **Vocabulary Prompts,** for example, serves to isolate challenging vocabulary before a listening or reading task. **Your Turn,** a follow-up to reading, listening, or structure practice, serves as a participatory task. **In Your Experience,** an activity drawing on students' prior knowledge and personal lives, allows learners to personalize the topics and relate them to their own experience.

In Book 1, before students actually open their books to one of these vocabulary sections, you may want to prepare them by doing the following:

1. Show related pictures, maps, and realia.

2. Provide clear pronunciation models and ask students to repeat each word or term several times.

3. Provide additional explanations and examples as needed and use people and objects in the classroom whenever possible.

4. Finally, preview the **Sound Bites** tape and ask learners to listen for the words in the **Vocabulary Prompts** box.

A way to maximize learners' opportunities to practice oral communication in the **Your Turn** and **In Your Experience** sections is to use three-way interviews. These proceed in the following way: Students 1 and 2 talk to each other; Students 3 and 4 talk to each other. Then 1 and 3 talk, and 2 and 4 talk. Finally, 1 and 4 talk, and 2 and 3 talk. You can then assign all students with one number to report their results to the class. This procedure allows everybody plenty of opportunities to talk.

Spotlight

Throughout *Contemporary English*, grammar structures are first contextualized in the **Scenes** and listening activities, and then presented, practiced, and applied on follow-up **Spotlight** pages. Appearing two to four times in each unit, the **Spotlight** pages model target structures in contexts related to the unit topic. Special **Spotlight** feature boxes present the target structures schematically and provide brief, straightforward explanations when necessary. Exercises following the structure presentations allow students to manipulate the structures in meaningful contexts, such as stories or real-life situations. **Spotlight** pages usually end with a **Your Turn** and/or an **In Your Experience** activity providing communicative application of the new structures.

To present the **Spotlight** structures most effectively to learners using Books 1 and 2 of the series, try the following sequence of steps:

1. Ask questions that either lead into the target structures or contain the target structures. For example, to lead into the target structures, you can ask questions that would normally take an answer with the target structure. You can then elicit the correct structure or, if students are unable to produce it, provide a sentence containing the structure. In this way, you will establish an appropriate context for the target structure from the beginning.

2. Guide students through the language forms in the **Spotlight** box.

3. Elicit and answer any questions learners may have.

4. Provide oral practice for correct pronunciation of the sentences containing the forms.

5. Read any rules that follow the example sentences, and then return to the sentences to demonstrate those rules.

With learners using Books 3 and 4, the following suggestions may help:

1. Ask questions that either lead into the target structures or contain the target structures. For example, to lead into the target structures, you can ask questions that would normally take an answer with the target structure. You can then elicit the correct structure or, if students are unable to produce it, provide a sentence containing the structure. In this way, you will establish an appropriate context for the target structure from the beginning.

2. After you have elicited or provided several examples of the target structure, try to elicit rules from learners. Many may have encountered the structures before or may actually have studied them formally.

3. You may wish to put sentences on the board for students to complete with the target structures. You can continue in this way until the class begins to get a feeling for the new structure.

4. Draw two faces. Write a conversation in speech bubbles for them but leave blanks. Say, "Just shout out the missing part. What should it be?" (For example, "I want to _____." or "I need to _____.")

5. Have students open their books and look at the **Spotlight** box. Depending on the level and ability of the class, have students read silently, prompt different learners to read parts of the box, or read to learners.

6. Ask, "Do you have questions?" If no one has a question, ask students to do the exercises as suggested in the sections that follow.

Spotlight Exercises

Follow these steps with the **Spotlight** exercises:

1. Whenever possible, have learners do the exercises with a partner or a small group. This allows for interaction and speaking practice. Assign partners or, if the class interacts well without prompting, allow students to choose their partners. If some learners prefer to work alone, at least have them check their answers with a partner.

2. Read the exercise directions aloud to students and point out the completed example.

3. Model the activity and ask if learners understand.

4. Check answers by asking one student from each pair to read that pair's sentences to the class.

5. Allow for differences. Some students may be especially interested in learning forms and may want you to create charts of language forms on the board, on an overhead transparency, or on handouts.

Person to Person

Listening and speaking skills are developed further in the **Person to Person** activities, which present recorded two-person conversations exploring the unit topics in natural, colloquial language. Students listen to conversations, practice them, and work in pairs to complete a final open-ended dialogue. Students can then present their new conversations to the class.

Have students listen first, rather than read, in order to focus on the meaning of each conversation. Read or play the tape for each conversation separately. Ask learners if you should repeat the conversations or replay the tape. Ask some general questions (such as "Who are the speakers?") to check comprehension. Have learners practice words and phrases after you. You may wish to avoid having them read at this point.

Have students practice each conversation in pairs. Then ask for volunteers to role-play each conversation. Reluctant students will be more likely to participate after eager volunteers have done so.

Some students may not want to do the final, creative conversation, and it is better not to force the issue. Instead, you may wish to have learners again volunteer to perform conversations for the class.

Try to check the conversations learners create before they present them to the class so that errors are not internalized by listeners. Of course, even after you check the conversations, presentations will quite likely have some errors, but resist the temptation to correct as learners speak. A better approach is to take notes on the errors and provide these to students later, along with positive comments on their performances.

To extend the **Person to Person** activities, have learners record their conversations on an audiocassette player. Then play all the conversations for the class. Also, you may wish to have learners write their final conversation. You can then put all the papers into a box and ask each pair of learners to draw out a conversation, practice it, and perform it for the class. If appropriate, ask listeners to try to guess the authors of each conversation based on content clues.

Reading for Real

Contemporary English helps students develop their reading skills and become motivated readers of English through **Reading for Real,** a page in each unit that provides stimulating authentic or adapted texts. With passages and realia that typically relate directly to the lives of characters in the **Scenes, Reading for Real** includes such real-life documents as a winning job résumé, instructions for office voice mail, biographies of real people, advice from the local police, and listings of music festivals around the country. Follow-up activities (such as **Your Turn** and **In Your Experience**) extend and personalize the reading.

Before beginning **Reading for Real,** try the following:

1. Prepare students by asking them to look at the pictures and the realia on the page.
2. Have them glance at the reading and ask questions such as the following:
   - What is this? (a bill? a résumé?)
   - Have you ever seen anything like this before?
   - Have you ever gotten one of these?
   - How does it relate to what we've been doing?
   - Why are you looking at this?
   - What will you read to find out?

Continue with the following steps:

Books 1 and 2

1. Read the text aloud.
2. Check students' comprehension.
3. Encourage the class to talk about the topic by asking questions.
4. Record ideas on the board or a flipchart.

Books 3 and 4

1. Ask learners to scan for specific pieces of information. With less advanced students you may wish just to call out words and have students circle them.
2. Tell students to read silently without stopping.
3. After they read, ask them to check a maximum of three words they don't know. Tell them you will talk about the words as a class later.
4. Emphasize to learners that things can—and should—be read more than once. Tell them that even the best readers don't remember everything the first time and that those readers reread difficult sections automatically.
5. Finally, stress that they don't have to worry about not being able to pronounce all the words at the beginning.
6. After **Reading for Real, Your Turn,** and **In Your Experience,** extend and personalize the reading. For example, after reading a brief résumé prepared by one character, students, with the help of a partner, use the model provided to write their own résumés. Partners then meet with another pair, exchange résumés, and make suggestions or corrections.

Culture Corner

Culture Corner provides further work on reading skills by focusing on the useful inside information about U.S. life that students love. Presented as brief readings typically paired with charts, graphics, or artwork, **Culture Corner** gives students the information they need to adapt to a culture that can often be confusing and difficult to understand. Interactive follow-up activities help students integrate cultural knowledge with their language skills.

The following steps will be useful in implementing **Culture Corner:**

1. Have students look at the illustration or diagram.
2. Ask questions that encourage thoughtful guessing. If some students are advanced enough to ask others questions, encourage them to do so.
3. Have learners read the short text silently on their own.
4. When students finish, read the text aloud to them and check their comprehension.
5. Ask learners to create one or two questions about the text and ask a partner those questions.
6. If possible, have the pairs of students write their questions and answers.

As an extension activity for the **Culture Corner,** you may wish to do the following, at least in some units: Draw a simple T-chart or Venn diagram on the board or distribute copies of one of these generic organizer masters as a handout. Then ask students to compare some aspect of life in the United States to life in their native countries.

Scene 2

The second half of the unit begins with a second **Scene,** which usually reintroduces at least one character from the previous **Scene.** This is followed by a second, smaller **Sound Bites** that recycles the **Scene's** language and content. Next comes one or more **Spotlight** pages.

To recycle language effectively, before you start work on Scene 2, revisit the first page of the unit and retell the story in the first **Scene.** This recycling is especially important in situations where attendance is sporadic or where open-entry/open-exit policies are common practice.

Based on this rereading, ask learners to make predictions about **Scene 2.** Read the speech bubbles, look at the pictures, and follow the steps suggested for **Scene 1** on pages xii and xiii.

The second, smaller **Sound Bites** (which appears in Books 2–4) recycles the language and content of **Scene 2.** It differs from the first **Sound Bites,** which serves as an initial introduction of the unit topic in that there are no picture cues and students need to take notes on what they hear.

Get Graphic

Graphic literacy is the focus of **Get Graphic,** a feature that offers practice in reading charts, graphs, diagrams, and time lines—skills that are crucial in the workplace and for preparing for the GED. **Get Graphic** provides high-interest stimuli related to the unit topics and characters while it incorporates or recycles target language structures. A typical feature of this page is a follow-up activity in which learners develop their own simple graphs or charts and share them with partners or groups. The activities on this page help students learn to read, interpret, and use information in a graphic format.

Follow the steps below to ensure learners' success with chart and graph work:

1. Try to introduce the activity through something in the classroom. For example, if the graphic in the student book is a pie graph, use the board or an overhead transparency to draw a very simple pie graph for the class population with information about students from different countries, students' native languages, different eye colors, and so on. Explain what the graph is and what it shows.
2. Check students' comprehension by asking if there are questions. Also, ask questions about the information on the graph. If students demonstrate comprehension, move into the graph in the book.

3. Have students quickly look at the graph. Ask, "What is this? What is the title? What do the numbers on the sides mean?"

4. Ask if students have seen a graph like this before and, if so, where? Was it at work? in a newspaper or magazine? in a math class?

5. You may wish to discuss and demonstrate the meaning of words such as *axis*, *fraction*, *decimal*, and *time line.*

6. Finally, read the directions, point out any examples, and model the activity.

7. Encourage work in pairs and small groups. If students work alone, try to have them check their answers with a partner or a small group.

Issues and Answers

Problem-solving and critical-thinking skills are developed further in **Issues and Answers.** This feature typically presents two opinions—often in direct opposition—in formats such as advice columns or letters to the editor. **Issues and Answers** contains short, humorous texts with views of U.S. life from a variety of perspectives, including those of immigrants and their "cultural advisors"—the experts who help to orient the newcomers as they bridge the gap between their native and adopted countries.

Here are some ways to implement **Issues and Answers:**

1. Before your students read, have copies of newspaper advice columns available for them to look at.

2. Prepare them for the reading by pointing out the column format. Show them that in the advice-column type of **Issues and Answers** found in some units of their books, the letter on the left asks a question that the letter on the right answers.

3. Encourage silent reading first because **Issues and Answers** is a reading activity. With lower-level students follow the silent reading by reading the text aloud.

4. Check students' comprehension by asking questions.

5. Have a class discussion about the topic.

6. Record students' ideas on the board or on a flipchart.

Wrap-Up and Think About Learning

In Books 2–4 the last page of each unit contains a **Wrap-Up,** a project in which students use a graphic organizer such as a T-chart, a Venn diagram, an idea map, or a time line to brainstorm and organize ideas and then talk or write in a group. Following **Wrap-Up** is the self-assessment activity **Think About Learning,** a final reflection task that asks students to evaluate the quality of their own learning on the major content points, life skills, and language structures in the unit. Students can thus assess what they have learned and provide feedback to the teacher, all of which helps to build a learner-centered classroom.

At the very end of each unit in Book 1 is **Think About Learning.** In every even-numbered unit of Book 1, this activity follows **Wrap-Up.** In odd-numbered units **Think About Learning** follows **Issues and Answers.** In each case, **Think About Learning** provides a way for students to assess what they have learned and provide feedback to the teacher, all of which helps build a learner-centered classroom.

Before administering the unit assessment, or **Progress Check,** always take time to study learners' responses to **Think About Learning** and systematically review points that need further work, ideally working both with the whole class and with individual students or small groups.

Unit Follow-up

After learners have recorded their progress, you may wish to talk about the following in class:

- what students thought was the most important thing they learned in the unit
- what part of the unit they enjoyed most
- other situations in which they could use the same skills and strategies
- other previously mastered skills and strategies that could relate to the content of the unit just studied

In the beginning some of this may be difficult for students. Remind them to continue using previously introduced strategies and skills as they add new ones. As they progress through the book, they will expand their repertory of learning strategies.

Finally, before moving to a new unit, ask learners if they would like to do anything different the next time. Try to respect these wishes by tailoring the instruction for your learners, thus giving them a real sense of directing their own learning. The learning process will be more dynamic if these possibilities for building on experience and creating positive change can flourish in the classroom.

The Workbooks

The *Contemporary English* Workbooks are designed for individual independent study as well as for classroom work. In the Workbooks, as in the Student Books, a predictable sequence is maintained.

For ease of use, the essential information in the **Spotlight** boxes of the Student Books is reproduced in the Workbooks. Each **Spotlight** is followed by a series of contextualized practice exercises, progressing from simple fill-ins to more challenging activities that ask students to use the target structures as they write answers to real-life questions about themselves. Answers to all Workbook activities can be found in the Teacher's Manual.

The **Read, Think, and Write** pages at the end of each Workbook unit for Books 2–4 synthesize skills presented and practiced in the unit in an engaging multistage activity. The reading is supported by pre- and postreading questions. After the reading, one or two activities ask learners to organize the information, usually with the same type of graphic organizer used in **Wrap-Up** in the Student Book. The final problem-solving activity challenges learners to apply the content to their own lives. Each unit closes with a brief questionnaire, similar to **Think About Learning** in the Student Book, in which students note what was most enjoyable and helpful in the Workbook.

Using a Problem-Posing Approach

Contemporary English stresses problem-solving and critical-thinking skills. Many teachers, however, may want to go beyond this framework to use a problem-posing approach, which focuses specifically on the lives of students and their own special concerns. While all of the topics in *Contemporary English* are applied to students' lives, using problem posing may help to make the connection with students' real concerns even stronger. The questions on the first page of each unit are an ideal place to begin problem posing, which involves the three following stages:

1. listening for students' concerns and issues
2. having a dialogue in which the class thinks about these issues
3. thinking about changes that people can make in their situations and suggesting a course of action

Key to this whole process is to make the discussion as learner centered as possible, so that students' issues and concerns—rather than the hypothetical or imaginary situations of characters in the text—become the focus of discussion. The text, however, can serve as a springboard for exploring students' problems since it brings into focus situations in which students and newcomers to the United States typically find themselves. Of course, students' concerns will often go beyond the context of life in the United States; and if you use problem posing, you will want to explore all of these concerns, to the extent that students find them important.

The Audiocassettes

All key listening components of each unit are available on audiocassette. These include the **Scenes**, **Sound Bites**, **Person to Person** conversations, and the **Listen** component of the **Progress Check**.

The Teacher's Manuals

The Teacher's Manuals give teachers additional tools to enhance learning and create an active, dynamic classroom. These include the general Introduction you are now reading for suggestions on using the approach successfully as well as unit-specific pages with teacher-friendly suggestions for preparing for, presenting, and extending activities. For ease of use, the unit-specific directions for a particular activity refer to a page of the general suggestions in this introductory unit. Many content questions that you can ask students at various points in the unit (to check comprehension and encourage application and synthesis) are also included in the unit-specific notes.

In addition, the Teacher's Manuals contain a variety of suggestions for adapting activities to the needs of multilevel classes. These suggestions are listed as Options, and they are signalled in the text by the following icon, placed in the margin:

At the end of this general introduction are two special sections: "Maximizing Results in the Multilevel Classroom" and "Creating a Work-Oriented Classroom." Written by teachers whose classroom and administrative experience makes them experts in those issues, these sections provide valuable information on using *Contemporary English* effectively in a variety of classroom settings.

Assessment

Flexible two-page **Progress Checks** allow a program or teacher to assess learning systematically. The four sections of these tests—**Speak or Write, Listen, Language Structures,** and **Content**—can be evaluated quickly to determine readiness to move to the next unit. The **Progress Checks** are largely self-explanatory and need no special instructions here apart from a word of caution on the **Listen** section. It is best not to read the listening script slowly to accommodate learners' developing listening skills. Rather, it is better to read each passage two or three times—but always at a normal rate of speed.

Activity Masters

Two reproducible **Activity Masters** extend each unit's learning still further. One is an interactive activity—a strip story, game, sequencing activity, or information gap—that practices language structures and reinforces content. This master can also be effective as a team-building, cooperative-learning activity. The other master— usually an additional reading or a graphic literacy activity to be completed individually or in pair or team situations— can also be used as part of the **Progress Check**.

Here are a few practical classroom management suggestions for using the **Activity Masters:**

1. Explain the general purpose of the handouts to learners. Tell them that the handouts will give them more language and vocabulary practice and allow them to share information and ideas with other learners.

2. If possible, copy the handouts on card stock so that they will be more durable and will last longer.

3. Store the masters in labeled envelopes or in a small standing or hanging file.

4. Handouts that need to be cut have dotted lines and scissors icons. Rather than cut apart your masters, whenever possible, have learners cut their individual copies. This will give them a more active role, and it will decrease your preparation time.

An additional tool for each unit is the Workbook Answers page, also on a reproducible master so that you can copy it for students if you wish them to check their own homework or one another's.

Maximizing Results in the Multilevel Classroom

by Elizabeth Minicz, Harper College, Palatine, Illinois

Everyone who has taught adult ESL classes is aware of the phenomenon of multi-level classes. The causes—among which are varying levels of education, disparate skill development, and open-enrollment policies—are further complicated by other factors which affect language learning, such as hemispheric dominance, personality, and sensory modality preference. Given all the challenges of a multilevel class environment, can ESL teachers rise above them to teach effectively and even enjoy the process? The answer is a resounding yes—if they have some practical tips and tools to help them perform the job.

First, recognize and accept the fact that you cannot always be all things to all students. That said, allow yourself the freedom to experiment with the techniques, methods, or "tricks of the trade" that experienced multilevel teachers discover through trial and error, and give yourself permission to fail from time to time. Some years ago, Tom Peters cautioned people in the business world to make mistakes quickly. This is sound advice for ESL teachers too; if something isn't working, try something else—immediately!

Below are some tried and true ways for you to use the realities of multilevel classes to your advantage. As you read them, you may have an occasional "Aha!" reaction—Aha, I can do that! Aha, I've done that! Aha, so that's why that works! In the end, there really is no magic answer to what to do about multilevel classes. You need to decide what works best for you, feels most comfortable, and best promotes learning. These things will always vary from teacher to teacher and class to class. Here are several approaches you should consider in using your students' variety of abilities to advantage.

Approach 1: Use a Variety of Grouping Strategies

How are grouping strategies in multilevel classes different from grouping strategies in homogeneous classes? Actually, the techniques are the same, but the purpose or intent is different. Using various grouping strategies in any class enhances learners' opportunities for practice. In multilevel classes, however, variations on grouping structures allow you to manage learner differences and abilities better. For example, separating learners according to language groups is a general grouping strategy, as are separating by gender, age, or interest. In multilevel classes, learners' abilities—which may vary according to the skill area targeted—also determine groupings. In multilevel classes, higher-level learners may be grouped together for one activity, and in another activity they may be grouped with lower-level learners.

In multilevel classes, whole-class activities can help learners develop a sense of community as they help one another succeed. They foster the "We're all in this together" feeling that temporarily overcomes individual differences. In addition, whole-class activities are confidence builders. Shy or timid learners can watch, listen, and "silently practice" until they feel comfortable participating more actively. More assertive learners can serve as role models, mentors, or tutors.

Despite these advantages of whole-class activities, if you always keep your class together, you can "miss" two-thirds of your learners because the activities are often too easy for one-third and too difficult for another third. It is important, then, to plan whole-class activities in which everyone can participate according to their individual abilities and to follow up with individual, pair, and group practice opportunities.

In *Contemporary English,* for example, the whole class looks at the pictures in a **Scene,** listens to **Sound Bites,** or reads silently. Such activities are followed by pair or group work, subsequent debriefing for the whole class, and, later, workbook activities completed at home or, if time permits, individually in class. Although in the **Scene** or **Sound Bites** all learners receive the same stimulus, individual responses will vary according to ability.

You will want to vary the pairings or groupings of learners from unit to unit, page to page, class session to class session. In homogeneous classrooms the purpose of varying groupings is simply to "mix up" the learners to avoid predictability and routine. In multilevel classes the purpose is to accommodate learner ability differences. Less able learners should have ample opportunity to work with more able learners, but not all the time!

Think through the purpose of pairings or groupings before directing your learners to work together. Arranging by categories or by assigning numbers or colors is common practice in both homogeneous and multilevel classrooms. But in homogeneous classrooms the results are random, while in multilevel classrooms you will want to determine the *who* and *why* of the groupings ahead of time. And sometimes you will want to let learners decide for themselves who they will work with.

If you are especially motivated or fond of challenges, you may have decided to use more than one level of *Contemporary English* in your class. If so, it's a good idea to begin each session with whole-class activities. Then plan to meet for 15 to 20 minutes with learners assigned to one level of the text while learners assigned to the other level(s) do pair, group, or individual work such as reading or writing. Finally, end by bringing all learners back together for a final whole-class activity. Although teaching from three levels of the series in your multilevel class is possible, two levels are undoubtedly more manageable.

Approach 2: Adapt the Textbook Pages for Different Proficiency Levels

This approach requires more planning time than Approach 1, in which—with the exception of using two or more levels of the series in the same class—the stimuli are the same for all learners, but responses vary according to individual abilities. In Approach 1 it is your standards that must change or adjust. However, in Approach 2 the stimulus itself varies according to ability level. This means you must create or adapt tasks according to the learners' proficiencies. For example, if learners have difficulty generating language to talk about the **Scenes,** you might pose a series of yes/no, either/or, or wh-questions for them to answer first orally and then in writing.

Another way to adjust the textbook materials up or down a notch is to look closely at the tasks learners are asked to do. For example, in some **Sound Bites** activities, learners listen and write a word or phrase. You may instead want give your lower-level learners several choices and ask them to circle or check the answers—since checking or circling are easier tasks than writing words or sentences. You can also limit the number of items lower-level learners hear or, conversely, increase the number of items for higher-level learners. When in doubt, let learners decide which level of activity to complete.

Here are some additional ways to modify activities for learners' differing abilities. For the **Person to Person** activities, you can assign more advanced learners all four conversations to practice and role-play. You can ask lower-level learners to listen to all four but have them choose only one to practice and role-play. Or higher-level learners may need the additional challenge of writing more than one original conversation in **Your Turn,** whereas lower-level learners may need to have the **Your Turn** structured more tightly, with specific questions and responses that you provide.

On the **Spotlight** pages have lower-level learners work together to complete the exercises but let higher-level learners work alone. Also, you may want them to act as your aides by helping you spot-check other learners' work.

As you teach from the series, you will discover on your own more ways to add to or reduce the language load for learners.

Approach 3: Structure Activities So That All Proficiency Levels Can Participate

Several kinds of activities can be particularly effective in multilevel classes. For example, you can provide learners with grammar practice by writing sentences and questions from **Spotlight, Reading for Real,** or **Issues and Answers** on sentence strips. Cut the strips into individual words, phrases, or clauses. Clip the words from each sentence together or put each sentence in a separate envelope. Give learners the sentences to unscramble according to their ability levels, with longer sentences going to higher-level learners and shorter ones to lower-level learners. These strips are worth the time you take to make them because they can be used over and over again. To increase the longevity of the strips, use cardboard or laminate them.

Activities involving sorting or categorizing and variations on vocabulary bingo are easy to prepare and provide meaningful practice for learners in multi-level classes. For each new unit copy **Activity Master 8-2** from the Book 1 Teacher's Manual, write the vocabulary words for the unit in the bingo squares and duplicate the page for learners' independent, pair, or group work. Then give learners scissors and have them cut out the word squares. Have them use these words for several sorts: words they know how to pronounce, words they know the meanings of, and words they can use in sentences. Otherwise, they can also use the words for alphabetizing practice. Or learners can scramble the words, put them in a pile, and take turns turning over a word, spelling it, or using it correctly in a sentence. The variations are endless.

Traditional vocabulary bingo uses an enjoyable format to provide learners with scanning practice. To play vocabulary bingo, use the same generic reproducible master mentioned above. Make the game challenging for different levels of learners by having higher-level learners pronounce, spell, and give definitions. Have lower-level learners simply say or spell the words.

In short, to maximize the effectiveness of *Contemporary English* in multilevel classes, you will need to be creative and flexible, and once you have found new ways to implement activities, share your innovations and successes with your colleagues!

Suggestions for Creating a Work-Oriented ESL Classroom

by Jan Jarrell, San Diego Community Colleges

In the last decade, modeling and practicing workplace tasks and situations have become increasingly important components of the adult ESL classroom. This trend—together with the related tendency toward increased accountability—has been prompted by three interrelated societal shifts: (1) welfare reform, (2) governmental pressure on educational institutions to link funding to outcomes, and (3) the changing nature of the workplace as described in the 1992 Secretary of Labor's Commission on Achieving Necessary Skills (SCANS) Report.

Brief Background and Description of SCANS

In the late 1980s the United States found itself playing catch-up with two booming economies: Germany's and Japan's. Comparisons of work practices in these three countries became commonplace, and as a result, many U.S. companies switched to Japanese-style management practices known as Total Quality Management (TQM). This approach coupled an emphasis on teamwork with quality control at the level of the individual employee. In response to these dramatic changes on shop floors as well as in boardrooms, the U.S. Secretary of Labor organized a national commission to identify what the new high performance workplace demanded from workers.

The fruit of this Commission was the SCANS report, which identified two tiers of essential workplace know-how: foundation skills and workplace competencies. Foundation skills include basic communication and math, as well as higher-level thinking, decision making and learning-how-to-learn skills. Personal qualities such as positive attitude, self esteem, and individual responsibility are also considered foundational. The higher-order workplace competencies include understanding and effectively using resources, technology, information, and systems. In addition, workers need effective interpersonal skills so they can work on teams, teach others, negotiate, serve customers and collaborate on the job with people from diverse backgrounds.

Continued study of workplace needs and trends since 1992 has confirmed the relevance, indeed the necessity, of integrating the SCANS competencies into the curriculum at every educational level. In order for ESL students to get and keep jobs even at the entry level, teaching the SCANS is no longer optional. Many ESL programs in states with significant second-language populations have partially or completely integrated SCANS competencies into their curricula to meet these new challenges.

Promoting Teamwork in the Classroom

Of all the SCANS competencies, learning to work effectively in teams is perhaps the most pivotal. Teamwork either directly or indirectly drives most of the other SCANS skills, and yet many ESL students have had very little experience working in teams in their own countries—either in the classroom or on the job.

The most obvious and pedagogically familiar way of promoting teamwork in the classroom is by integrating cooperative-learning structures into your lessons. According to Johnson, Johnson, and Smith (1991), cooperative learning can be distinguished from other pair or group work because it includes five key elements:

- **Positive Interdependence:** The success of each team member and that of the team in general depends upon the effectiveness of all team members. By promoting activities such as jigsaws, which, because no student has all the information, encourage sharing of knowledge and resources, and by assigning group roles, you can allow work in teams to emerge naturally in your classroom.
- **Individual Accountability:** Structure activities so that all students must contribute. Assessing both individuals and groups assures that all learners must participate.
- **Group Processing:** Regularly provide time for team reflection and evaluation.
- **Social Skills:** Through your explicit teaching, modeling, and reinforcement, your learners can learn to lead, build trust, make decisions, and deal with conflicts.
- **Face-to-Face Interaction:** If you physically arrange learners to facilitate active involvement with one another as they discuss, teach, encourage, solve problems and negotiate, you will enhance team spirit in your classroom. In cooperative learning jigsaw activities, for example, students master content in expert groups, and then return to home groups to teach the content they have learned and also to learn new content from their teammates. As such, positive interdependence, new social skills, and face-to-face interaction are built into the activity. Later, you can assess individuals on all the content and ask the different groups to evaluate the strengths and weaknesses of their group interaction. This allows you to build in the other two elements: individual accountability and group processing.

Team Roles

In the work-centered ESL classroom, you can assign individual team members workplace roles. For example, in a group task, each team can be comprised of a manager or leader, a secretary, a supply clerk and a timekeeper. The manager must make sure that everyone participates and may also present the group's findings to the whole class. The secretary records and reports the group's answers. The supply clerk makes sure each group member has the necessary materials and also collects and returns texts and papers at the end of the task. The timekeeper keeps the team on task by reminding members how much time remains for completing each activity. You can assign some or all of these roles on a class-by-class basis, or they can continue over a period of time. If students take roles for one or two months, you can periodically have "managers' meetings" in which assignments or problems can be discussed among the team managers who then report back to their respective teams.

Just like roles in the actual workplace, these roles are flexible, and the titles or jobs that learners assume can vary by project and possibly by geographical area or by preparation of learners for a particular sector of the economy. Having a secretary may be meaningful when many learners will be pursing an office skills track; similarly, the roles of recorder and reporter may be relevant for later involvement in community service projects. The choice of roles really depends upon you and the specifics of the business environment in your area.

Using the Reality of the Classroom

As SCANS and the workplace become more of an influence on classroom instruction, ESL instructors are often pleased to find that daily operations of the ESL classroom provide many opportunities for students to gain actual work experience. These tasks shift responsibility for the ESL class away from you and toward students themselves. In the workplace-centered classroom, you as the instructor become a facilitator rather than a performer or directive manager.

Classroom Management. You can assign many classroom maintenance tasks to student teams. Team members can check signatures on the sign-in sheet, welcome new students, erase boards, and straighten chairs. They can distribute, count, and collect textbooks and set up and test equipment such as overhead projectors and audiocassette recorders. You can ensure that this work is shared and completed by posting work schedules that indicate which teams are responsible for classroom maintenance tasks on any given week or day.

Students as Trainers. You may wish to identify classroom procedures that students can teach new members of the class. Examples of these procedures are explaining class rules, showing newcomers how to fill out registration cards, and demonstrating for them how to turn on a computer or load a software program. Peer revision is another excellent example of how all students can function as trainers for one another.

Solving Classroom Challenges. It's a fact that certain challenges arise all too often in the ESL classroom. Insufficient or uncomfortable work space, inappropriate first-language use in the classroom, teams' failure to fulfill their classroom duties—all of these may seem to be inevitable features of the adult ESL classroom. But instead of first defining and then solving these problems for learners, you can turn them into resources by involving your learners actively in the problem-solving process. School or classroom issues can be identified through an anonymous suggestion box or evaluation form. Then, in teams, students can list possible solutions to the problem, discuss positive and negative consequences of each solution, and finally choose one of these solutions, implement it, and evaluate the results either as individuals or in groups. After students implement the solution, the results can be evaluated either by individuals or in groups. As an alternative, try holding class meetings in which one representative from each team participates in a brainstorming session while the rest of the class observes and later offers feedback to the meeting participants.

Of course, other problems occur on an individual or personal level, and students need to be armed with strategies to handle them. When a technological problem such as a computer failure occurs, you can encourage students to troubleshoot by following an established procedure. You can also teach teams a process for dealing with interpersonal conflict without your intervention. For example, you can train students in a round-robin exercise procedure in which each team member has two minutes to talk without interruption about what he or she thinks the problem is. Sometimes simply airing problems in this safe way will significantly diffuse negative feelings. Following the round-robin, individual team members can also write their suggestions for solving the problem that has been identified, the team secretary or reporter can read the suggestions, and all members can then discuss them.

Emphasizing Accountability

Using Agendas. One easy way of keeping a class on track and modeling workplace procedures is to post an *agenda* at the start of each class. The agenda can be simply a numbered or bulleted list, or it also can indicate time frames for each activity. As each task is completed, you can check it off on the chalkboard and have students mark their ESL notebooks. At the end of class, you and your students can use the agenda to review what has been learned that day. Highlight any items that were not addressed and indicate when they will be included.

Checklists and Logs. Just as employees often need to account for how they spend time on the job, students can learn to monitor their own progress by marking checklists of skills, competencies, and objectives such as the **Think About Learning** chart at the end of each unit of the student books in this series. You may also wish to have students keep a daily or weekly log of what they study and accomplish.

Evaluation. Evaluation not only allows you to assess students' learning and interests, it also encourages critical thinking and decision making, two important SCANS skills. Evaluation can be formal or spontaneous, but it is an essential element of any work-centered classroom. It can be designed either to help the learner think about his or her own learning or to help the instructor quantify that learning.

On the formal end, instructors can prepare class evaluations in which students rate specific class activities on a scale. Students need to practice providing feedback because in the workplace they will often be asked to evaluate training they receive. Students can also grade themselves in mock performance self-appraisals. The **Think About Learning** component for each unit of this series can serve this purpose.

Less formally, you can also "check in" with students by simply distributing index cards at the end of a class period. On one side have students write what they found particularly helpful that day, and on the other side ask them to note what was unclear—or what they would like to study next. Finally, to raise students' own consciousness about the SCANS competencies, you may want to create a class poster of the SCANS using level-appropriate language or pictures. Then, at the end of each class, ask students which skills they practiced that day.

Classroom Incentives. Many businesses have an "Employee of the Month" award, typically for an exceptional worker, who gets his or her picture and biography posted on a special bulletin board. You can adopt this practice quite easily in the classroom by recognizing an individual student or a team each month. You may also want to present end-of-term certificates for attendance, punctuality, outstanding performance, "best suggestions," and so on. In addition, you can give letters of recommendation instead of, or in addition to, certificates. Students appreciate "to whom it may concern" letters that describe their strengths—such as being punctual or being a team player. These letters reaffirm the SCANS competencies, and students can actually use them to get jobs in the real world!

Workplace Language. All the suggestions outlined in this section provide students with learning experiences that can help them develop essential skills for the workplace. However, most of these strategies require systematic modeling and practice. For example, students need to be explicitly taught language to facilitate teamwork. They need to know how to agree and disagree politely, ask for repetition or clarification, and give instructions. For example, one of many employers' most frequent complaints is that employees do not let their supervisors know when they don't understand an instruction or procedure. As work-centered activities are implemented in the classroom, encourage students to use clarification strategies such as asking questions and paraphrasing instructions. By practicing the language that characterizes this new classroom environment, your learners will be actively preparing for the world of work. If you can help them to articulate these newfound skills to prospective employers, their chances of turning a job interview into a job offer can increase dramatically.

Organization of the Unit-Specific Materials in the Teacher's Manual

In the pages that follow, the teacher's material for each unit is arranged in the following order.

1. Overview

   A. Objectives

      • Skills and Structures

      • SCANS Competencies

   B. Realia

2. Unit-specific Activity Notes (with answers for student book exercises and indicators for when to use workbook pages)

3. Answers to **Progress Checks** and **Activity Masters**

4. Workbook Answers (provided on a separate, reproducible page)

5. Unit **Progress Checks**

6. Two reproducible **Activity Masters** (Note: teacher directions—in addition to the teacher and student directions that appear on the master itself—for some of the **Activity Masters** are provided in the teacher notes at the first point in the unit where the activity can be used).

Administering and Scoring the Placement Test

Allow 35 minutes for completion of the Placement Test. Use the Scoring Guide and the Answer Key below to score the tests.

Scoring Guide

Scores	Book	Level
0–3	Literacy	beginning literacy to literacy level
3–7	Book 1	low beginning level
8–17	Book 2	high beginning level
18–25	Book 3	low intermediate level
26–30	Book 4	high intermediate level

Answer Key

Part 1

1. d	2. c	3. b	4. a	5. c
6. b	7. c	8. a	9. a	10. b

Part 2

11. much	12. did
13. are	14. wasn't *or* was not
15. Where	16. were
17. Have	18. did
19. shouldn't *or* should not	20. am

Part 3

21. d	22. c	23. c	24. b	25. c
26. c	27. b	28. c	29. c	30. c

Name _____   Date _____

CONTEMPORARY ENGLISH PLACEMENT TEST

Examples

1. Complete the sentence. Circle the correct letter.

   What ___ you do in the mornings?

   a. do   b. does   c. are   d. am

2. Complete the conversation. Circle the correct letter.

   A: Are you from Algeria?

   B: Yes, I ___.

   a. is   b. are   c. am   d. be

Part I

1. Complete the conversation. Circle the correct letter.

   A: I took a vacation last week.

   B: Oh, really? ___

   a. Where did you went?   b. Where does you go?

   c. Where go you?   d. Where did you go?

2. Complete the conversation. Circle the correct letter.

   A: It was Alice's birthday last week.

   B: Oh, really? Did she get any interesting presents?

   A: Yes, ___

   a. Tom bought to her a beautiful lamp.

   b. Tom bought a beautiful lamp to her.

   c. Tom bought her a beautiful lamp.

   d. Tom bought a beautiful lamp her.

3. Complete the conversation. Circle the correct letter.

   A: Excuse me. ___ borrow your pen?

   B: Sure, no problem. Here you are.

   a. Do I   b. Could I

   c. Would I   d. Should I

4. Complete the conversation. Circle the correct letter.

   A: Can you help me? I need ___ box up there, but I can't reach it.

   B: Sure, I'll get it down for you.

   a. that   b. this   c. these   d. those

5. Complete the conversation. Circle the correct letter.

    A: My car is getting really old.

    B: I know. You ___ get a new one.

        a. would   b. may   c. should   d. need

6. Complete the sentence.

    Have you ever ___ any repair work on your car?

        a. did   b. done   c. does   d. do

7. Complete the conversation. Circle the correct letter.

    A: There are so many dresses here, and I like all of them. I don't know which one to choose.

    B: Oh, I think this one is the ___

        a. better   . b. good   c. best   d. well.

8. Complete the conversation. Circle the correct letter.

    A: Where are you from?

    B: I'm from Spain.

    A: Oh, I have never ___ to Spain.

        a. been   b. being   c. be   d. was

9. Complete the conversation. Circle the correct letter.

    A: How is your daughter doing in school?

    B: Oh, she's doing fine. In fact, she's ___ than many of the other kids in her class.

        a. better   b. best   c. good   d. well

10. Complete the conversation. Circle the correct letter.

    A: You should stop ___ those boxes like that.

    B: Why?

    A: You'll hurt your back.

        a. to lift   b. lifting   c. lift   d. lifted

Part 2

Example

Complete the conversation. Fill in the blank.

A: _____ *What* _____ is your name?

B: Maria.

11. Complete the conversation. Fill in the blank.

    A: How _____ coffee do you want?

    B: About a pound.

12. Complete the conversation. Fill in the blank.

    A: Where _____ you live in your native country?

    B: I lived in Mexico City.

13. Complete the conversation. Fill in the blank.

    A: What _____ you going to do tomorrow?

    B: I'm going to a movie.

14. Complete the conversation. Fill in the blank.

    A: Were you here yesterday?

    B: No, I _____ .

15. Complete the conversation. Fill in the blank.

    A: _____ do you live?

    B: I live in Miami.

16. Complete the sentence. Fill in the blank.

    What _____ you doing when you saw the accident?

17. Complete the conversation. Fill in the blank.

    A: _____ you ever worked in a bank before?

    B: No, I used to work as a cashier, but that was in a restaurant.

18. Complete the conversation. Fill in the blank.

    A: When _____ you talk to the boss about this matter?

    B: Only yesterday.

19. Complete the conversation. Fill in the blank.

    A: This letter says I've won a million dollars, but I have to buy some magazines to get the money. Do you think I should do that?

    B: No, you _____ .

20. Complete the sentence. Fill in the blank.

    I _____ never going to understand this tax form. It's too complicated.

Part 3

To answer questions 21 and 22, read the following ad.

SALE!!! SALE!!! SALE!!!
Peaches 10 cents each
Tomatoes 29 cents a pound
Red apples 5 cents each

---

21. You want to buy four peaches. How much will you pay? Circle the correct letter.

    a. 10 cents   b. 20 cents   c. 30 cents   d. 40 cents

22. You want to buy two pounds of tomatoes. How much will you pay? Circle the correct letter.

    a. 39 cents   b. 60 cents   c. 58 cents   d. 5 cents

To answer questions 23–25, read the memo and the story after it.

MEMO

TO: All employees

FROM: Mark

RE: Vacation time

Beginning in January of next year, Bestco Inc. will shift to the following vacation schedule.

Employees with up to 1 year of service:
1 week per year

Employees with 2–4 years of service:
2 weeks per year

Employees with 5 to 10 years of service:
3 weeks per year

Employees with more than 10 years of service:
4 weeks per year

Frank Malyszko started at Bestco at the beginning of this year. His friend Juan started two years ago. Right now, Frank has three vacation days, and Juan has a week.

23. How much vacation time will Frank have next year? Circle the correct letter.

    a. He will have one week.

    b. He will have two weeks.

    c. He will have three weeks.

    d. He will have four weeks.

24. How much vacation time will Juan have next year? Circle the correct letter.

    a. He will have one week.

    b. He will have two weeks.

    c. He will have three weeks.

    d. He will have four weeks.

25. How much vacation time does an employee get after 8 years? Circle the correct letter.

    a. one week

    b. two weeks

    c. three weeks

    d. four weeks

To answer questions 26 and 27, read the following memo.

MEMO

TO: All employees

FROM: James Ross

RE: Changes in Health Plan

Please note the following:

Those employees who now have REGNA Health Care will have to switch to a new company. Employees will be able to choose between HealthPrev Company, Keystone Health Maintenance, and Arbco Health. Here are the costs for each of these plans:

HealthPrev Company	Family Plan:	$205.00/month for a family with children
	Joint Plan:	$140.00/month for a couple without children
	Single Plan:	$105.00/month for a single employee
Keystone Health	Family Plan:	$180.00/month for a family with children
	Joint Plan:	$150.00/month for a couple without children
	Single Plan:	$90.00/month for a single employee
Arbco Health	Family Plan:	$200.00/month for a family with children
	Joint Plan:	$160.00/month for a couple without children
	Single Plan:	$80.00/month for a single employee

Employees who currently have the REGNA plan may wish to discuss it with other employees who already have one of the other three plans above.

---

26. Which of the plans is the cheapest for a single employee? Circle the correct letter.

    a. Keystone Health

    b. HealthPrev Company

    c. Arbco Health

    d. They are all the same.

27. Which of the plans is the most expensive for a family with children? Circle the correct letter.

    a. Keystone Health

    b. HealthPrev Company

    c. Arbco Health

    d. They are all the same.

To answer questions 28–30, read the following passage.

What do you need to do to stay healthy? Well, diet and exercise play an important role, but an important factor is avoiding things that can hurt your health. For example, if you smoke cigarettes, you have a much greater risk of heart disease and cancer than nonsmokers. Alcohol can also increase your risk for these health problems if you have several drinks each day, for example, and it can lead to liver problems also. Doctors are unsure about the risk of having only one drink a day. Drinking coffee presents some of the same risks as smoking, but smoking is worse for you. Doctors caution us to keep our consumption of caffeine low, but many Americans drink three or four cups of coffee a day, or more.

28. Which of the following health problems is not mentioned in the passage above?

   a. heart disease

   b. cancer

   c. diabetes

   d. liver problems

29. What are the health risks of having one drink a day?

   a. very serious

   b. heart disease

   c. unclear

   d. no risk at all

30. If "many Americans drink three or four cups of coffee a day, or more," which of the following is probably true?

   a. This is more of a problem than smoking cigarettes.

   b. This is not a problem for people who don't smoke.

   c. This is more than doctors think they should drink.

   d. There are no serious health risks in drinking coffee.

INTRODUCTORY UNIT

OVERVIEW

Objectives

Skills and Structures

Greet others

State one's name

Understand greetings

Write and spell one's name

Read numbers

Understand spoken numbers

Understand simple negative and affirmative commands

Understand time

SCANS Competencies

Foundation Skills:

Listening

Speaking

Reading

Writing

Realia

Photos of the following: a sunrise, a street scene on a sunny afternoon, an evening scene

A variety of clocks and watches, both digital and analog

Simple forms for students to provide personal information on

Short ads with telephone numbers and addresses

ACTIVITY NOTES

Page vii

Spotlight on Greetings

Refer to the general instructions on page xv in the Introduction.

Preparation

1. Greet the students in the class. Say *hello, good morning,* or something similar. Write the words or phrases on the board. Have students repeat after you.

2. Explain the word *greetings.*

Presentation

1. Have students read the comic strip silently. With the class discuss any words students do not understand. Ask for student volunteers to explain word meanings if necessary.

2. Tell students to listen carefully as you play the tape of the Spotlight.

Extension

1. Have students practice the comic-strip conversation in pairs.

2. With multilevel classes you may wish to choose among the following to continue with this activity:

Option 1: Students can copy the conversations and then perform the lines as written. You can assign pairs or let students choose their own partners. Students can act out the conversation (by getting up, sitting down, and gesturing, as in the comic strip, for example). You may wish to include special props (to simulate the desk and computer in the comic strip) to allow students to act out the conversation more effectively.

Option 2: Students can substitute their own names and practice the new conversation with this substitution. Students can act out the conversation (by getting up, sitting down, and gesturing, as in the comic strip, for example). You may wish to include props (to simulate the desk and computer in the comic strip) to allow students to act out the conversation more effectively.

Option 3: With the most advanced students, you may wish to explain that *hello* is more formal than *hi*. These students can ad-lib a continuation of the conversation in the Spotlight or imagine they are in the conversation with the characters in the Spotlight. As suggested in Options 1 and 2, you may wish to have students act out the conversation (by getting up, sitting down, and gesturing, as in the comic strip, for example). You may also wish to include props (to simulate the desk and computer in the comic strip) to allow students to act out the conversation more effectively.

5. If possible, have volunteers perform their conversation before the class.

Vocabulary Prompts

Refer to the general instructions on page xiv in the Introduction.

Preparation

Show photos to convey the idea of morning, afternoon, and evening. Write the words *morning, afternoon,* and *evening* on the board.

Presentation

1. Have students look at the Vocabulary Prompts box. Have the class repeat the phrases after you. Tell students which greeting is appropriate now.

2. Answer any questions students may have.

Your Turn

Refer to the general instructions on page xiv in the Introduction.

Preparation

1. Choose a student from the class. Say *hi* or *hello* and give your name. Have the student respond in the same way.

2. If you wish, have that student then model the activity by repeating the procedure with another student in the class.

Presentation

1. Have students work in groups of four to practice greeting each other and saying their names.

2. Circulate among the students and answer any questions they may have.

Spotlight on the Alphabet

Refer to the general instructions on page xv in the Introduction.

Presentation

1. Have students look at the Spotlight box.

2. Play the tape. Tell students to listen carefully.

3. After you have played the tape, read the letters of the alphabet and have students repeat after you.

Extension

Have students practice the comic-strip conversation in pairs.

Vocabulary Prompts

Refer to the general instructions on page xiv in the Introduction.

Preparation

Write your first, middle, and last names on the board. Introduce the words *first, middle,* and *last* by showing a series of objects in a row. You may also wish to have three volunteer students line up in front of the class. Then label the students *first, middle,* and *last.*

Presentation

1. Have students look at the Vocabulary Prompts box. Read the names on the form.

   Have students silently read the conversation in the Spotlight comic strip again while you read it aloud.

2. Answer any questions students may have.

Your Turn

Refer to the general instructions on page xiv in the Introduction.

Preparation

Model the activity by writing your name on the board. Then spell your first name and your last name. You may also wish to have a volunteer from the class spell his or her first and last names.

Presentation

1. Have students work in pairs to complete the activity. In a multilevel class you may wish to choose from among the following options for proceeding with the activity:

Option 1: Pair stronger students with weaker students to complete the activity if you think that the weaker students have sufficient literacy skills to attempt the activity.

Option 2: Pair stronger students together and pair some of the stronger students with some of the weaker students who can nonetheless handle the activity. Work with the weakest students in a single group and help them spell their names.

2. Circulate among the students and answer any questions they may have.

Spotlight on Numbers

Refer to the general instructions on page xv in the Introduction.

Presentation

1. Have students look at the Spotlight box.
2. Play the tape. Tell students to listen carefully.
3. After you have played the tape, read the numbers and have students repeat after you.
4. Read the social security number and the phone number from the comic strip. Then have students repeat those numbers after you. Read them digit by digit.

Extension

1. Have students practice the comic-strip conversation in pairs.
2. With multilevel classes you may wish to choose among the following to continue with this activity:

Option 1: Students can copy the conversations and then perform the lines as written. You can assign pairs or let students choose their own partners. Students can act out the conversation, and you may wish to include special props (to simulate the desk, the chairs, and the computer in the comic strip) to allow students to act out the conversation more effectively.

Option 2: Students can substitute their own names and social security numbers (if they have social security numbers) and practice the new conversation with this substitution. Students can act out the conversation, and you may wish to include special props (to simulate the desk, the chairs, and the computer in the comic strip) to allow students to act out the conversation more effectively.

Option 3: The most advanced students can ad-lib a continuation of the conversation in the Spotlight or imagine they are in the conversation with the characters in the Spotlight. As suggested in Options 1 and 2, students can act out the conversation, and you may wish to include special props (to simulate the desk, the chairs, and the computer in the comic strip) to allow students to act out the conversation more effectively.

5. If possible, have volunteers perform their conversation before the class.

Vocabulary Prompts

Refer to the general instructions on page xiv in the Introduction.

Presentation

Explain that the first three digits of the phone number in the comic strip are the area code. The area code corresponds to a city or a larger area. Point out the area code in the Vocabulary Prompts box.

Your Turn

Refer to the general instructions on page xiv in the Introduction.

Preparation

Tell students the area code of your school and write it on the board. Then give the school's phone number and write it on the board.

Presentation

1. Have students work in pairs to complete the activity. In a multilevel class you may wish to choose from among the following options:

Option 1: Pair stronger students with weaker students to complete the activity if you think that the weaker students have sufficient literacy skills to attempt the activity.

Option 2: Pair stronger students together and pair some of the stronger students with some of the weaker students who can nonetheless handle the activity. Work with the weakest students in a single group and help them spell their names.

2. Circulate among the students and answer any questions they may have.

Page x

Spotlight on Numbers

Refer to the general instructions on page xv in the Introduction.

Presentation

1. Have students look at the Spotlight box.
2. Play the tape. Tell students to listen carefully.
3. After you have played the tape, read the numbers and have students repeat them after you.
4. Read the address and the zip code from the comic strip. Then have students repeat those numbers after you. Read them digit by digit. Have a volunteer come up to the board and write the number for the address on the board.

Vocabulary Prompts

Refer to the general instructions on page xiv in the Introduction.

Preparation

1. On the board write the address of the school, along with the zip code. Read the numbers for the street number and the zip code. Introduce the word *zip code*.
2. Point to the city and state in the school address. Introduce the words *city* and *state*.

Presentation

Have students silently read the address, city, state, and zip code in the Vocabulary Prompts box as you read the items aloud. Then have the class read them after you.

Your Turn

Refer to the general instructions on page xiv in the Introduction.

Presentation

1. Have students work in pairs to complete the activity. In a multilevel class you may wish to choose from among the following options:

Option 1: Pair stronger students with weaker students to complete the activity if you think that the weaker students have sufficient literacy skills to attempt the activity.

Option 2: Pair stronger students together and pair some of the stronger students with some of the weaker students who can nonetheless handle the activity. Work with the weakest students in a single group and help them say their addresses.

2. Circulate among the students and answer any questions they may have.

Page xi

Spotlight on Commands

Refer to the general instructions on page xv in the Introduction.

Preparation

1. Ask for a volunteer from the class and tell that student to stand up. Ask the student to spell his or her name. Then ask the student to sit down. Use simple commands for each action.

2. Have another volunteer model the commands with another student.

Presentation

1. Have students look at the Spotlight box. Point out the negative form. Write *don't* on the board. Point to the No Smoking symbol in the Spotlight box. Tell students that this means "No Smoking." Write "Don't smoke" on the board. Explain that *don't* makes commands negative. The word *please* makes commands more polite.

2. Teach and practice a few commands that can be acted out using sounds or gestures, repeating them several times. For example, go to the classroom door and knock on the outside of it. Have the students say, "Come in." Gesture with your hands as a choral conductor would, for the students to stand up and sit down. As you gesture, have them say "Stand up" and "Sit down."

Reading for Real

Refer to the general instructions on page xvii in the Introduction.

Preparation

Have students look back at the comic strips on pages viii, ix, and x. In these cartoons Ted Omachi gives his name, address, telephone number, and social security number. Read the conversations or play the tape for these parts again.

Presentation

1. Have students read the form silently. Then read it aloud to them.

2. To check their understanding, make true or false statements. Have the learners indicate their comprehension by showing their red (*no*) or green (*yes*) index cards. Here are some examples:
   * Ted's address is 300 Bridge Street. (no)
   * Ted's social security number is 349-33-9956. (yes)

3. Answer any questions students may have.

Your Turn

Refer to the general instructions on page xiv in the Introduction.

1. Model the activity with a volunteer. Use one- or two-word questions to elicit answers: "First Name?" "Middle Name?" and so on. If you wish, you can have the volunteer model the activity with another student for the rest of the class.

2. Have students work individually to complete the form. Circulate among the students and provide any help necessary.

3. Have students work in pairs to ask each other for personal information. Tell them to use short one- or two-word questions, as you showed them earlier. (For "social security number" students will ask a three-word question.) This practice will help students learn to handle basic questions in routine administrative or bureaucratic situations.

Spotlight on Time

Refer to the general instructions on page xv in the Introduction.

Preparation

1. Point to the clock in your classroom, if there is one. Otherwise, point to an analog clock you have brought in specially for this lesson. Elicit the time from anyone who knows. Then say the time and write it on the board, in numbers and in words.

2. Show the class a digital clock. Explain that it shows the same time as the analog clock. (Make sure the clocks are synchronized.)

3. Put the following question on the board: *What time is it?* Have a volunteer come up to the board and write the correct time.

Presentation

1. Have students look at the Spotlight box and read the conversations.

2. Play the tape. Tell students to listen carefully.

3. After you have played the tape, read the times and have students repeat them after you.

4. Make sure students understand *a quarter after, a quarter to, half past,* and *-thirty.* In some languages the time *three-thirty* may contain the word *four* instead of *three.* For many students the term *quarter* will be difficult. You may wish to draw a circle on the board and then erase a quarter of it. You can then draw the missing quarter outside the circle. Elicit from students the word *quarter* for this part of the circle.

5. Look at your own clocks again. Ask the class, "What time is it?" Wait for the answer and write it on the board.

6. Have students practice the Spotlight conversation in pairs. With multilevel classes you may wish to choose among the following to continue with this activity:

Option 1: Students can copy the conversations and then perform the lines as written. You can assign pairs or let students choose their own partners. Students can act out the conversation (by getting up, looking at their watches, and going toward the door, as in the comic strip, for example). You may wish to include special props (to simulate the desk in the comic strip) to allow students to act out the conversation more effectively.

Option 2: Students can substitute their own names and practice the new conversation with this substitution. Students can act out the conversation (by getting up, looking at their watches, and going toward the door, as in the comic strip, for example). You may wish to include props (to simulate the desk in the comic strip) to allow students to act out the conversation more effectively.

Option 3: With the most advanced students, you may wish to explain that *good night* is something people typically say when they leave work (or a work situation) in the evening. They can also say *good-bye* or *see you tomorrow.* In the comic strip it is

5:30, which is already early evening. The most advanced students can ad-lib a continuation of the conversation in the Spotlight or imagine they are in the conversation with the characters in the Spotlight. As suggested in Options 1 and 2, you may wish to have students act out the conversation (by getting up, looking at their watches, and going toward the door, as in the comic strip, for example). You may also wish to include props (to simulate the desk in the comic strip) to allow students to act out the conversation more effectively.

5. If possible, have volunteers perform their conversation before the class.

Vocabulary Prompts

Refer to the general instructions on page xiv in the Introduction.

Preparation

Refer to the Spotlight on Numbers, page x. Review the numbers *ten, twenty, thirty, forty, fifty*. Show the class your analog clock again. Showing the numbers on the clock, count five minutes, ten minutes, fifteen minutes, twenty minutes, and so on. Explain that you can tell time in this way: five-ten, five-fifteen, five-twenty, and so on.

Presentation

1. Read the times for each of the clocks in the Vocabulary Prompts box. Have students repeat the times after you.
2. Show your analog clock to the class again. Ask, "What time is it?" Wait for the answer and write it on the board.

Your Turn

Refer to the general instructions on page xiv in the Introduction.

Presentation

1. Have students work in pairs to complete the activity.
2. Circulate among the students and answer any questions they may have.
3. Have pairs of students compare their answers.
4. Go over the answers orally with the class. Ask students what time they put down for the last clock. Have a volunteer or volunteers come to the board, draw a clock, and write the time underneath it.

OVERVIEW

Objectives

Skills and Structures

Read an application form

Make a family tree

Write a conversation

Read a pie graph

Tell what you think

Use subject pronouns

Use the present tense of *be* (statements)

Use the present tense of *be* (negatives)

SCANS Competencies

Work with cultural diversity: Student Book, Issues and Answers, page 10

Interpret and communicate information: Student Book, Culture Corner, page 6; Student Book, Get Graphic, page 9

Realia

A large map of the world

Pictures of people in various occupations, including mechanics, waiters, waitresses, cooks, construction workers, and teachers

A photo of a large extended family, preferably with three generations

An advice column from a newspaper, preferably with short letters and answers and the photo of the columnist

ACTIVITY NOTES

Page 1

Scene 1

Refer to the general instructions on page xii in the Introduction.

Preparation

1. Explain the meaning of the title of this unit before students talk about the pictures. Show pictures or drawings of your family or other families, especially those with mothers, fathers, sisters, and brothers. Elicit students' prior knowledge of the vocabulary. When necessary, provide these words: *mother, father, children, sister,* and *brother.*

2. Encourage students to talk about their own families, either by answering direct questions—such as "Do you have sisters?"—or, if your students are advanced enough, by responding to open-ended questions such as "Tell about your family."

3. Show pictures or drawings of friends in typical social situations. Make sure that the difference between family and friendly relationships is clear. Use direct questions or open-ended questions to encourage students to share information about their friends. Ask, "Do you have friends here?" or "Tell us about your friends."

Presentation

1. Ask questions about the pictures in Scene 1.
   - Which one is Ann?
   - Which one is Rita?
   - Where are they?
2. Have pairs of students read the directions and text above the pictures. Discuss any words the students do not understand.
3. Have students read the comic strip. With the class discuss any words students do not understand. Ask for student volunteers to explain word meanings.
4. Have students read the questions below the comic strip. Make sure students understand the questions.
5. Tell students to listen carefully as you play the tape of Scene 1.
6. Have pairs of students answer the questions below the comic strips, either orally or in writing. If necessary, replay the tape of Scene 1.
7. Call on pairs of students to share their answers with the class.

Extension

Have pairs of students practice the Scene dialogue for the class in one of several ways. Bring in props or costumes to make the activity more interesting.

Option 1: Students can perform the lines as written. You can assign pairs or let students choose their own partners.

Option 2: Students can make a simple substitution in some lines (by inserting their own names and countries, for example).

Option 3: More advanced students can ad-lib a conversation on the topic treated in the Scene or imagine they are in the conversation with the characters in the Scene.

Page 2

Vocabulary Prompts

Refer to the general instructions on page xiv in the Introduction.

Preparation

1. To introduce the vocabulary about families, sketch a tree on the board or on an overhead transparency showing parents (*mother, father*), children (*daughter, sister, son, brother*).
2. To introduce the vocabulary for occupations, write the words *teacher* and *student* on the board. Tell students, "I am a teacher." Then point or gesture to one of the students and say, "You are a student."

Presentation

1. Have students look at the words in the top row of the Vocabulary Prompts box. Then have students find an example of family photos on page 1. Ask a volunteer to stand up and point to the family photos that Rita and Ann are holding.
2. Ask students to give an example of a person who is *handsome*. Explain by giving an example of someone famous or showing a magazine photo of someone who is handsome.

3. Refer to the family tree you drew on the board and have students look at the pictures of family in the Vocabulary Prompts box. Have students match the pictures to the specific parts of the tree.

4. If you wish, have volunteers give the names of their family and write those names on the board in a family tree.

5. Have students look at the vocabulary for occupations and then point to the character on page 1 who is a waitress (Ann, on the left in the first frame of the comic strip). Then have students find the character who is a cook (Rita, on the right in the first frame of the comic strip). You may wish to have a volunteer stand up before the class and point to the pictures.

6. In a multilevel class you may wish to try some of the following options to extend the vocabulary presentation:

Option 1: Provide photos (or photocopies of photos) of families whose family relationships are clear. Have the lower-level students work in groups to label the pictures (with adhesive notes, for example) with the family members. If several groups have the same pictures, students can then compare their work. You can do the same with pictures for the occupations.

Option 2: With students who have greater vocabulary and reading skills, you may wish to discuss occupations further. Point to the mechanic in the Vocabulary Prompts box and have students point to the car. If students are ready, introduce the words *wrench* (seen at the bottom of the picture) and *engine*. Other vocabulary words that can be found in the drawings and that can be introduced with students who are able to handle the vocabulary load are the following: *apron, bowl, chair, chef's hat, desk, glass, headlights, plate, tray,* and *wheel.* You may also wish to include the words *dress, shirt,* and *shoes.* Students can copy these words into their notebooks.

Option 3: With the most advanced students in the class, you may wish to present all the vocabulary listed in Option 2, above, and have students write sentences using those words.

Sound Bites

Refer to the general instructions on page xiii in the Introduction.

Preparation

1. Have students look at the pictures. Point to each picture and ask questions to elicit the differences between the pictures in each pair:

   - Are Rita and Ann in a restaurant?
   - Does Ann have one picture or two?
   - Is Ann happy or sad?
   - How many photos does Rita have?

Presentation

1. Tell students that they will hear several sentences. Explain that you will play the tape three times and that they should try to match the pictures with what they hear. Tell them that they do not have to do anything the first time they listen; they will circle the correct answers when you play the tape the second time. When you play the tape the third time, they will check their answers.

2. Play the tape three times. When you play the tape the second time, students should mark their answers in their books. When you play the tape the third time, students should check their answers individually.

Listening Script

1. Ann is a waitress and Rita is a cook.
2. Ann has one brother.
3. I miss my brother in New York.
4. Rita has two brothers in Mexico.

Answers to Sound Bites

1. a   2. b   3. a   4. a

Your Turn

Refer to the general instructions on page xiv in the Introduction.

Preparation

1. Explain to students that they will listen again and repeat the sentences from Sound Bites. You may wish to model the activity with a volunteer.
2. Before the activity read or play the tape of the conversation between Ann and Rita from Scene 1 again. Have students read it silently as they listen.

Presentation

Read or replay Sound Bites. Ask students to circle the sentences they hear in the Sound Bites, and then have them compare answers with a partner.

Extension

1. Write the conversation on the board and omit words introduced in the Vocabulary Prompts. Write a blank for each omitted word in the conversation, as shown here:

   Ann: My _____ is in New York. I _____ him.

   Rita: I _____ my _____ in Mexico too.

   Ann: Rita, your _____ are _____.

2. Ask students to write the conversation in their notebooks and to fill in the blanks with the correct words. Model by completing the first blank (*brother*). Tell students that they may refer to their books if necessary.
3. Have students check their work by referring to the conversation in the book and making any necessary corrections.

Page 3

Spotlight on Subject Pronouns

Refer to the general instructions on page xv in the Introduction.

Preparation

1. Show the world map. Help students find their native countries or cities. Pronounce the names of these places clearly and ask students to repeat them several times.
2. On the map locate and introduce the following: the United States, Texas, Mexico, Thailand, Asia, Vietnam, Peru, Europe, South America, and Africa.

Presentation

1. Guide students through the art for subject pronouns in the Spotlight box. Give additional explanations and examples, as needed, before students begin the exercise.

2. Use the home countries of students in the class as examples for this practice with place names. Point to yourself and students to convey meaning. For example, say, "I am from California; she is from Mexico," and so on.

3. When students understand the meaning, ask them to repeat after you several times. Use the drawings in the book, as well as people and things in the classroom as your examples. Emphasize understandable pronunciation.

4. Give individualized help, as needed.

Answers to Exercise 2

1. He   2. You   3. She   4. It   5. We   6. They

Your Turn

Refer to the general instructions on page xiv in the Introduction.

Preparation

Model the activity with a volunteer from the class.

Presentation

1. Have students work in pairs to complete the activity.

2. Circulate among students as they work. Answer any questions they may have.

3. Go over the correct answers with the class.

Extension

Ask one student from each pair to read his or her sentences to the class. Put pins or other place markers on the world map to show the home countries they name.

Workbook

Workbook pages 1 and 2 can be assigned after students have completed page 3.

Page 4

Spotlight on Present Tense of *Be*

Refer to the general instructions on page xv in the Introduction.

Preparation

1. Write the words *student* and *teacher* on the board. Point to the word *teacher*, gesture to yourself, and say, "I am a teacher." Write the sentence on the board. Then point to the word *student* and choose a student in the class. Call that student by name and say, "You are a student." Write that sentence on the board.

2. Write the words *waitress* and *cook* on the board. Then point to Ann on page 1. Say, "Ann is a waitress." Point to Rita and elicit from a volunteer the sentence "Rita is a cook."

3. Write the sentences on the board. Then have the class repeat the sentences after you.

Presentation

1. Have students look at the sentences in the Spotlight box. Write the contractions on the board. Then write the sentences "Rita is a cook" and "Rita's a cook," with an equal sign between the two.

2. Write the remaining sentences (with the uncontracted forms) from the Spotlight box on the board. After the sentence with *am*, write the *is* sentences in one column and the *are* sentences in the next column. Then write *am, is,* and *are* above the respective columns.

3. Read the sentences and have students repeat after you.

Extension

1. Model correct pronunciation of the sentences in both their compete and contracted forms. Have students repeat the sentences several times.

2. Use index cards with alphabet letters on them to show how to form contractions. Replace omitted letters with apostrophes (also on index cards).

Exercise 3

Refer to the general instructions on page xvi in the Introduction.

Preparation

Model the exercise by writing the first sentence on the board, with the correct answers left out. Then fill in the blanks.

Presentation

1. Have students complete the sentences individually.

2. Circulate among the students and answer any questions they may have.

3. Go over answers orally with the class.

Option: In a multilevel class you may wish to have students pair up to compare their answers. Pair weaker students with stronger students. If there are not enough students to pair up effectively, try creating groups of three to four students of different proficiency levels.

Answers to Exercise 3

1. is, is   2. are, are   3. are, are   4. is, is   5. are, are

Person to Person

Refer to the general instructions on page xvi in the Introduction.

Preparation

Have students look at the picture. Then model introductions by introducing yourself to a student in the class. When that student says his or her name, model introducing the student to another student. Make sure to include the gesture shown in the illustration.

Presentation

1. Play the cassette. Have students listen and read the conversation silently.

2. Have students work in pairs to practice the conversation.

3. Circulate among the students and answer any questions they may have.

Your Turn

Refer to the general instructions on page xiv in the Introduction.

Preparation

1. On a world map review the names of countries that students are from.

2. Review the occupations already introduced on page 2.

3. Model the activity by writing the sentences on the board and having a volunteer from the class come up and introduce him- or herself. Then tell something about that student to a second volunteer. Complete the sentences as the first volunteer speaks or have another volunteer complete them.

Presentation

1. Have students work in groups of three to practice their own introductions. In order to start the process, one student has to talk about him- or herself. A second student should then introduce him- or herself to the first student and should then turn and introduce him- or herself to a third student and introduce the first student as well. Students should continue in a chain.

2. Circulate among the students and answer any questions they may have.

3. In a multilevel class you may wish to choose from among the following options:

Option 1: In a class with a high proportion of students who know very little English, you may decide not to have the weaker students—or any of the students at all—mention their occupations. You may also wish to use this procedure in a class in which few students are employed or in which most students do not know the words for their occupations.

Option 2: In a highly divided class with significant differences in proficiency levels among students, you may wish to group the stronger students separately from the weaker students if you decide to have students talk about their occupations. Take note of the occupations students mention and plan to have them report about their jobs at a later date.

Extension

1. Ask students to stand with others from the same country.

2. Take Polaroid photos or make drawings of individual students and also of the national groups.

3. Have students write captions for the pictures. For example, the captions might say, "They are from Vietnam. She is from Russia."

4. Hang the pictures with the captions in the classroom.

Workbook

Workbook pages 3 and 4 can be assigned after students have completed page 4.

Page 5

Reading for Real

Refer to the general instructions on page xvii in the Introduction.

Preparation

1. Prepare students by asking them to look at the pictures and the application. Match (or ask the students to match) the characters in the picture with the names on the application. Match the card and videocassette movie in the picture to the written vocabulary on the application.

2. Encourage logical guessing. Hand out red and green index cards. Each student should take one green card and one red card. On the board write the words *parent, children, sister, brother, father,* and so on. Point to one of these and say the name of a character. For example, point to *sister* and say *Adam*. Students should indicate lack of agreement with a match by showing their red cards, or agreement with a match by showing their green cards.

Presentation

1. Have students read the short text silently. Then read it aloud to them.

2. To check their understanding, make true or false statements. Have the students indicate their comprehension by showing their red (*no*) or green (*yes*) index cards. Here are some examples:

   - Tina Martin is 10 years old.   (no)
   - The family needs a card.   (yes)

3. Ask *or* questions. Have students indicate comprehension in a choral response of the correct choice. Here are some examples:

   - Is the parent Adam or Daniel?   (Adam)
   - Is the password have or hello?   (hello)

Exercise 4

Refer to the general instructions on page xvi in the Introduction.

Preparation

Model the exercise by writing the first item on the board, together with the answers. Have a volunteer come up and circle the answer.

Presentation

1. Have students do the exercise individually.

2. Circulate among the students and answer any questions they may have.

3. Have students work in pairs to compare their answers.

Option: In a multilevel class with a significant number of students with low literacy skills, you may wish to pair stronger students with weaker students to compare answers before you discuss the answers with the class.

4. Go over answers orally with the class.

Answers to Exercise 4

1. no   2. no   3. yes   4. yes   5. yes   6. yes

Talk About It

Refer to the general instructions on page xvii in the Introduction.

Preparation

1. Show students an example of a video rental card and a videocassette.

2. Ask students if they ever rent videos. Ask where they get them.

Presentation

1. Have students work in groups to discuss the questions in Talk About It.

2. Circulate among the students and answer any questions they may have.

3. You may wish to a few volunteers tell the class their answers.

Culture Corner

Refer to the general instructions on page xviii in the Introduction.

Preparation

1. Prepare students for the reading by having them look at the family tree. Encourage logical guessing. Talk about where the family might be from and where each of them might live now.

2. Talk about the meaning of the diagram showing parents at the top, children beneath them, and connecting lines that indicate marriage.

Presentation

1. Have students read the short text silently. Then read it aloud to them.

2. To check their understanding, make true or false statements. Have the students indicate their comprehension by saying yes or no. Here are some examples:

   • Chan Luong is from New York.   (no)

   • His wife is American.   (yes)

Exercise 5

Refer to the general instructions on page xvi in the Introduction.

Preparation

Model the activity by copying the first sentence on the board and having a volunteer fill in the answers.

Presentation

1. Have students work individually to complete the exercise.

2. Circulate among the students and answer any questions they may have.

3. Go over the answers orally with the class.

Answers to Exercise 5

1. Ming, Hang Doan   2. Thu, Duc, Hanh   3. Kim   4. yes   5. no

Your Turn

Refer to the general instructions on page xiv in the Introduction.

Presentation

1. Have students work individually to fill in the chart.

2. Circulate among the students and answer any questions they may have.

3. When students have finished, ask for a volunteer to put his or her chart on the board so that others can check their work by comparing. Make any corrections necessary.

Answers to Your Turn

Parents	*Brothers*	*Sisters*
Ming Luong	Duc Luong	Thu Luong
Hang Doan Luong	Chan Luong	Hanh Luong

In Your Experience

Refer to the general instructions on page xiv in the Introduction.

Preparation

Model the activity by drawing your own family tree on the board.

Presentation

1. Read the directions aloud.

2. Provide large pieces of chart paper and markers for the students to use. Use tape or thumb tacks to hang the family tree of each student as he or she shares it with the class.

3. Circulate among the students and answer any questions they may have.

Page 7

Scene 2

Refer to the general instructions on page xviii in the Introduction.

Preparation

1. Introduce the word *retired* by first showing pictures of workers of all ages and then showing pictures of senior citizens who are obviously beyond retirement age and relaxing at home. For example, point to the workers and say, "They work." Point to the senior citizens and say, "They are retired. They do not work."

2. Check for understanding by pointing to additional pictures. Provide red and green index cards for students to show you their *yes* (green) or *no* (red) responses as you ask questions.

   For example, ask, "Is he retired?" or "Does she work?"

Presentation

1. Ask questions about the pictures in Scene 2. For the first frame ask questions such as the following:
   - Who are the people in the photo?
   - Are they Ann's parents or Rita's parents?
   - Where are they?

2. Ask the same or similar questions about the photo in the second frame.

3. Have pairs of students read the directions and text above the pictures. Discuss any words the students do not understand.

4. Have students read the comic strip. With the class discuss any words students do not understand. Ask for student volunteers to explain word meanings.

5. Have students read the questions below the comic strip. Make sure students understand the questions.

6. Tell students to listen carefully as you play the tape of Scene 2.

7. Have pairs of students answer the questions below the comic strips, either orally or in writing. If necessary, replay the tape of Scene 2.

8. Call on pairs of students to share their answers with the class.

Extension

Have pairs of students role-play the Scene for the class in one of several ways. Bring in props or costumes to make the activity more interesting.

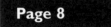 **Option 1:** Students can perform the lines as written. You can assign pairs or let students choose their own partners.

Option 2: Students can make a simple substitution in some lines (by inserting their own names and countries, for example).

Option 3: More advanced students can ad-lib a conversation on the topic treated in the Scene or imagine they are in the conversation with the characters in the Scene.

Activity Masters

Activity Master 1-1 can be introduced any time after Student Book page 7 has been completed.

Preparation

1. Make a sample interview grid like the one on the master or use a transparency of Activity Master 1-1. Read directions to the activity to students. Demonstrate how to complete the interview with a student or a volunteer. Record responses on your sample grid.

2. Have students interview three other students and write responses in the boxes.

Page 8

Spotlight on Present Tense of *Be* with the Negative

Refer to the general instructions on page xv in the Introduction.

Preparation

1. Write several false affirmative statements on the board. Make sure that these are statements to which students know the answers. For example, you might write about where students are from. You may wish to choose cities or states in the United States to avoid any possible antagonism over national identity. For example, "Pedro is from Texas. Irina is from California." Put about four to five sentences on the board.

2. Have students answer yes or no when you read each sentence. The answers should all be no.

3. Correct the first sentence by putting it in the negative. At this stage use the uncontracted forms. Then have volunteers come to the board to change the other sentences to the negative.

4. You may wish to have students copy the sentences in their notebooks.

Presentation

Have students look at the Spotlight box on page 8. Tell students that you add not after the verb to create the negative form. If students are ready, emphasize the contracted forms. With weaker classes you may wish to deemphasize the contracted forms at this point.

Exercise 6

Refer to the general instructions on page xvi in the Introduction.

Preparation

Model the exercise by copying the first item on the board and having a volunteer come to the board to circle the correct answer.

Presentation

1. Have students complete the exercise individually.
2. Circulate among the students and answer any questions they may have.
3. Go over the answers orally with the class.

Answers to Exercise 6

1. is not   2. are not   3. are not   4. is not
5. are not   6. is not

Person to Person

Refer to the general instructions on page xvi in the Introduction.

Preparation

1. Write the following conversation on the board:

   A: I'm from Colombia.

   B: You're from Columbus?

   A: No, I'm not from Columbus. I'm from Colombia.

2. Now write this conversation on the board:

   A: I'm from Texas.

   B: You're from Texas?

   A: Yes, that's right. I'm from Texas.

3. Explain that the question in each conversation is a good way to check understanding. Students basically repeat what they think they have heard (with a change of pronoun, if needed). If students understand correctly, the other person will respond with an answer like the one in the second conversation. If students understand incorrectly, the other person will respond with an answer like the one in the first conversation.

4. Model the conversations with volunteers or have volunteers model the conversations for the class.

5. Point to the picture. Tell students that Chan doesn't understand what Rita is saying.

Presentation

1. Play the cassette. Have students listen and read the conversation silently.
2. Have students work in pairs to practice the conversation.
3. Circulate among the students and answer any questions they may have.

Your Turn

Refer to the general instructions on page xiv in the Introduction.

Preparation

1. Copy the Person to Person conversation on the board and leave blanks for the names, occupations, and places. Have volunteers come up to the board and fill in the blanks.
2. Model the new conversation with one of the volunteers.

Presentation

1. Have students work in pairs to write new conversations. Emphasize that they should use their own information, and if the class is advanced enough, encourage students to use contractions if possible.

Option: With multilevel classes you may wish to pair stronger students with weaker students. You can have the stronger students take the longer parts. The weaker students can take the part that practices clarification (Chan's part in the model dialogue).

2. Circulate among the students and answer any questions they may have.

Extension

1. Ask for volunteers to perform their conversations in front of the class or on an audiocassette played to the class.
2. Alternatively, put a box in the middle of the room put the students' papers with their conversations into the box. Ask pairs to draw a conversation from the box and perform it for the class. Have listeners try to guess the authors based on the content.

Page 9

Get Graphic

Refer to the general instructions on page xviii in the Introduction.

Preparation

1. Introduce the concept of a pie graph by drawing a circle on the board to represent the total number of students in the class. Write the number inside the circle.
2. By a show of hands, find out how many countries are represented by members of the class. Write the country names and numbers on the board.
3. Erase the total number inside your circle and divide the circle into pie shapes to represent the number of students from each country. Write the appropriate number inside each piece of the pie.

Presentation

1. Have students read the short paragraph silently and then look at the pie graph. Then read the paragraph aloud to them.
2. To check students' understanding, make true-or-false statements. Have the students indicate their comprehension by showing red (*no*) or green (*yes*) index cards. Here are some examples:
   - Sixty-six students are single. (no)
   - One hundred fifty students are at Brown Adult School. (yes)

Exercise 7

Refer to the general instructions on page xvi in the Introduction.

Preparation

Show students the answer indicated provided for statement number 1. Have a volunteer find the answer in the second column of the exercise. Then have another volunteer find that number in the pie graph. (Two of the questions require that students subtract numbers provided in the pie graph from the total number of students in the school to find the answers.)

Presentation

1. Have students work individually to complete the exercise.

2. Circulate among the students to answer any questions they may have.

3. Have students work in pairs to compare their answers.

Option: In multilevel classes with some students who have low literacy skills, you may wish to pair stronger students with weaker students to compare answers.

4. Go over the answers orally with the class.

Answers to Get Graphic

1. 66   2. 84   3. 21   4. 6   5. 144

In Your Experience

Refer to the general instructions on page xiv in the Introduction.

Preparation

Model the activity by completing the first sentence on the board with your own information.

Presentation

1. Have students work individually to complete this activity.

2. Have students work in pairs to compare their answers.

3. Circulate among the students to answer any questions they may have.

4. Have volunteers tell the class about themselves or their partners.

Activity Masters

Activity Master 1-2 can be introduced any time after Student Book page 9 has been completed.

Preparation

1. Ask one or two students to write these words on the board:

   single   married   widowed   divorced

2. Demonstrate the instructions by putting a mark under your marital status. Then students who want to participate may put a mark under their marital status. Count the total numbers under each category. Write the total numbers next to the words.

3. Describe how to make a pie chart. If needed, refer to the page in the text where the pie graph is shown.

4. Students should make pie graphs in groups of three. Then they compare their charts with one other group.

Issues and Answers

Refer to the general instructions on page xix in the Introduction.

Preparation

1. Point to the pictures of Abdul (on the left) and Anita (on the right). Show similar advice columns in the newspaper (such as Dear Abby or Ask Ann Landers). Show the picture of the advice columnist if there is one.

2. You can explain that readers write letters to the newspaper and receive answers that are printed in the newspaper. Show the questions and answers in the newspaper and then show the question and answer in Ask Abdul and Anita.

3. Ask students if they have anything similar in their native countries.

Presentation

1. Have students read the letters silently. Then read them aloud to the class.

2. To check students' understanding, make true or false statements. Have the students indicate their comprehension by using green and red cards to indicate true and false answers. Here are some examples:

   - *Curious's* parents are still working. (no)
   - *Curious* is asking about adult parents and their children. (yes)
   - In the United States many adult parents do not live with their children. (yes)

3. Have students work in groups of three to answer the questions underneath the letters.

4. Circulate among the students and answer any questions they may have.

5. Poll students to find out what other answers they have come up with. Put the answers on the board.

Extension

Encourage students to talk openly about any other cultural differences they notice (and can express) in the United States. Record their ideas on the board.

Think About Learning

Refer to the general instructions on page xix in the Introduction.

Preparation

Explain to students that they can think about their learning in each unit of the book. In this way they can monitor how much progress they make and the areas in which they think they need to do better. Students will thus have greater control over what they learn and will be able to give better feedback to the teacher about what is difficult and what is easy for them. Encourage students to fill in their charts and provide feedback about how they think they are doing.

Presentation

1. Have students fill in their charts individually.

2. Explain that they can look up the pages where they worked on a specific skill or structure. The page references are provided in the second column of the chart.

3. Circulate among the students and answer any questions they may have.

4. Encourage students to add extra details in the bottom row of the chart. If they do not wish to comment on something else they have learned, they can make comments about what they would like to do.

5. Encourage students to share their feedback with you. Make it clear to them that they will not be graded on this self-assessment.

Workbook

Workbook pages 5 and 6 can be assigned after students have completed Student Book page 10.

ANSWERS TO PROGRESS CHECKS

Progress Check A

Speak or Write

1. Rita's brothers are in Mexico.

2. Rita's mother is from Mexico.

3. Rita's father is from Texas.

Listen

Kim Ho is from Korea. Her family is in the United States now. She has 4 brothers and 2 sisters. Kim's parents are retired in Seattle. Kim's brothers and sisters live in California. Kim is married and lives in Philadelphia.

1. yes   2. no   3. no   4. yes   5. yes   6. no

Progress Check B

Language Structures

1. she   2. she   3. he   4. they   5. they   6. she   7. he   8. it

Content

1. a. g   2. b   3. a
   b. h
   c. e
   d. f

ANSWERS TO ACTIVITY MASTERS

Activity Master 1-1

Answers will vary.

Activity Master 1-2

Answers will vary.

REPRODUCIBLE MASTER
UNIT 1

WORKBOOK ANSWERS

Practice 1
1. She   2. He   3. They   4. They

Practice 2
1. b   2. e   3. a   4. d   5. c

Practice 3
1. She   2. She   3. She   4. I   5. They   6. I   7. He   8. They

Practice 4
1. she   2. they   3. they   4. he   5. she   6. it   7. it

Practice 5
Answers will vary.

Practice 6
1. is   2. is   3. are   4. are   5. is   6. are

Practice 7
1. is, She's 2. are, They're   3. are, They're   4. are, They're

Practice 8
1. are   2. am   3. are   4. is   5. is   6. is

7. are   8. is   9. is   10. is   11. is   12. is

REPRODUCIBLE MASTER
Unit 1

WORKBOOK ANSWERS

Practice 9

Joel	car mechanic	21	married
Ana	teacher	58	married
Pedro	machine operator	58	married
Laura	waitress	19	married

Practice 10

1. false   2. true   3. true   4. true   5. true

Practice 11

1. I am not a mechanic. I'm not a mechanic.

2. My son is not 2 years old. My son isn't 2 years old. My son's not 2 years old.

3. Chan and Ana are not students. Chan and Ana aren't students.

4. You are not a waitress. You aren't a waitress. You're not a waitress.

5. You are not machine operators. You aren't machine operators. You're not machine operators.

Practice 12

1. 'm not   2. 're not/aren't   3. 's not/isn't

4. 'm not   5. 's not/isn't   6. 're not/aren't

Name _____ Date _____

SPEAK OR WRITE

Look at the pictures from Unit 1. Tell or write the answers to the questions about the pictures.

Questions

1. Who is in Mexico?

2. Where is Rita's mother from?

3. Where is Rita's father from?

LISTEN

Listen and check (✓) yes or no.

	yes	no
1. Kim is from Korea.	_____	_____
2. Her family is in Korea now.	_____	_____
3. She has 2 brothers and 4 sisters.	_____	_____
4. Her brothers and sisters live in California.	_____	_____
5. Kim's parents live in Seattle.	_____	_____
6. Kim is married and lives in California.	_____	_____

PROGRESS CHECK B

LANGUAGE STRUCTURES

Read the story. Check (✓) the correct subject pronoun on the line.

Ann is from the United States. Her brother lives in New York. Ann's mother and father are from New York. They're retired. Rita is from Mexico. She has brothers in Mexico. Rita's parents are teachers.

	he	she	it	they
1. Ann	_____	_____	_____	_____
2. Rita	_____	_____	_____	_____
3. brother	_____	_____	_____	_____
4. brothers	_____	_____	_____	_____
5. parents	_____	_____	_____	_____
6. mother	_____	_____	_____	_____
7. father	_____	_____	_____	_____
8. Mexico	_____	_____	_____	_____

CONTENT

1. Match Column A with Column B.

Column A		Column B
a. retired	_____	e. having a wife or husband who died
b. divorced	_____	f. not married
c. widowed	_____	g. not working
d. single	_____	h. married before, but not now

2. Read the sentence. Circle *a, b,* or *c.*

Many retired American parents don't live with their adult children.

a. They don't like their children.

b. Their children work in a different city.

c. The children don't like their parents.

Mike isn't married. Mike's wife isn't married.

Mike and his wife live in different homes.

a. Mike is divorced

b. Mike's wife is widowed.

c. Mike is widowed.

Name _____ Date _____

ACTIVITY MASTER 1-1

INTERVIEW

Interview 3 students. Write the names in the boxes. Ask the questions. Write the answers in the boxes.

	Name	Name	Name
Where are you from?			
Are you married, single, divorced, or widowed?			
Do you have children? How many?			

Name _____ Date _____

ACTIVITY MASTER I-2

MAKING A PIE GRAPH

Work in groups of 3. Make a pie graph.
Compare your graph to another group's graph.

How many students are single? _____

married? _____

widowed? _____

divorced? _____

OVERVIEW

Objectives

Skills and Structures

Read a mini-résumé

Talk about workplace supervisors

Read a "Top Five" list

Make a group chart

Use present of *be* in yes/no questions and short answers

Use singular and plural nouns

Use demonstrative pronouns

SCANS Competencies

Understand systems: Student Book, Culture Corner, page 16

Organize and maintain information: Student Book, Reading for Real, page 15

Realia

A simple job application form

A 3"x 5" index card, typed or hand-printed

New pencils, sharpened

Photos of hotel employees, including clerks, cashiers, housekeepers, groundskeepers, laundry workers, maintenance people, and hotel managers

ACTIVITY NOTES

Page 11

Scene 1

Refer to the general instructions on page xii in the Introduction.

Preparation

1. Explain the meaning of the title of this unit by showing pictures or drawings of people at work. For example, show factory workers, restaurant workers, hotel workers, and workers in typical entry-level jobs in your area. Point to the words to teach *people* and *workplace*.

2. Encourage students to talk about their own workplaces, either by answering direct questions—such as "Do you work? Where?"—or, if your students are advanced enough, by responding to open-ended questions such as "Tell us about your workplace."

Sound Bites

Exercise 1

Refer to the general instructions on page xiii in the Introduction.

Preparation

Ask questions to help students make sure they understand the differences between the pictures. Here are some examples:

- (Number 1) Is he in a hotel or a restaurant?
- (Number 2) Is she at the front desk?
- (Number 3) Is he at a desk?
- (Number 4) Is she at work?

Listening Script

1. He's looking for the manager in a hotel.
2. I'm the cashier.
3. I'm not the manager.
4. Excuse me. I need a job application.

Answers to Exercise 1

1. a   2. b   3. a   4. b

Your Turn

Refer to the general instructions on page xiv in the Introduction.

Presentation

1. During the activity read or play the tape of the conversation between Hoa and the cashier from Scene 1 again. Have students read it silently as they listen to and then copy the conversation in their notebooks. Read or replay the Sound Bites.
2. Ask students to circle the sentences they hear in the Sound Bites and then to work with a partner to compare answers.

Extension

1. Make strip stories for individuals or partners to reconstruct. Write out the conversation, with one sentence to a line. Make the number of copies you want, including one on an overhead transparency if you have an overhead projector. Cut up each copy and keep whole sentences together, but mix up the sentence order. Keep the sentence strips for each story together with a paper clip.
2. Have students work alone or in pairs, as you see fit. Give a strip story to each student or pair.

Option: In a multilevel class you may wish to pair weaker students with stronger students. If there are not enough students to pair up effectively, try creating groups of three students of different proficiency levels.

3. Demonstrate on the overhead projector. Model moving the strips into the correct order. If you don't have an overhead projector, use tape and sentences written on long strips of large paper. Move around as students work. Offer help, especially to low-literacy students.

4. When students finish, have them check their work by referring to the Student Book or by comparing with other students.

Spotlight on Present of *Be* in Yes/No Questions and Short Answers

Refer to the general instructions on page xv in the Introduction.

Preparation

1. Ask students about their countries. Ask, for example, "Maria, are you from Mexico?" Then write the question on the board.

2. Ask one of the stronger students to ask another, similar question of a third student. Then write that question on the board.

Presentation

1. Have students look at the Spotlight box and show them the difference in word order between statements and questions. Point to the questions you have written on the board.

2. Read the questions and short answers in the Spotlight box and have students repeat them after you. Make sure to model the difference in intonation between the statements and the questions. Having students do choral repetition will help them with this difference.

Extension

1. Before class write out the words in the Spotlight box examples with a broad marker on cards or paper.

2. While presenting the Spotlight box, put masking tape on the back of the papers or cards and stick them to the wall or the board. Show students that the order of the subject and verb is reversed when forming questions by moving the word cards and repositioning them in the question formation. Use a separate card for a question mark.

Answers to Exercise 2

1. Are they   2. Is she   3. Is she   4. Is he

Answers to Exercise 3

1. Are they clerks? No, they aren't.

2. Is she a cashier? No, she isn't.

3. Is she the manager? Yes, she is.

4. Is he a groundskeeper? No, he isn't.

Workbook

Workbook pages 7 and 8 may be assigned after students have completed page 13.

Spotlight on Singular and Plural Nouns

Refer to the general instructions on page xv in the Introduction.

Extension

1. Add special emphasis to the final *-s* as you pronounce the examples from the Spotlight box. Write more examples on the board and highlight the final *-s* by underlining.

2. Create a quick listening exercise. Have students number from one to eight in their notebooks. Then ask students to write *S* or *P* in their notebooks to identify whether they hear a singular or a plural form, as you say the following numbered items:

   1. mother   2. fathers   3. friends   4. parent
   5. sister   6. brothers   7. daughters 8. son

3. Relate the formation of plurals to students' lives by creating a T-chart, as shown below, with students' names written on the left side and the number of brothers and sisters on the right side. You or a student may ask, "How many brothers and sisters do you have?" and fill in the T-chart with the responses, or you can have students come to the board and fill in the chart with their own information. Your T-chart might look something like the following:

Name	Number of Brothers and Sisters
Kim	2 brothers and 2 sisters
Juan	3 brothers and 1 sister

Answers to Exercise 4

1. a manager, he isn't   2. housekeepers, they are   3. cashiers, they aren't
4. a groundskeeper, he is   5. a busy hotel, it is

Your Turn

Refer to the general instructions on page xiv in the Introduction.

Extension

1. Prepare by dictating the following vocabulary list: *manager, housekeeper, cashier, groundskeeper, clerk, student.*

2. Have students write the list in their notebooks as they listen and then have them check their spelling as you write the list on the board.

3. Ask students to stand in two long lines, those in one line facing those in the other.

4. Each student in the first line should use his or her vocabulary list to form questions for a student in line two.

   Are you a manager?   Are you a housekeeper?

   Are you a cashier?   Are you a groundskeeper?

   Are you a clerk?   Are you a student?

5. Have students in the second line listen; answer the questions with either "Yes, I am" or "No, I'm not, I'm a _____," and give their actual job title or say *homemaker* or *student.*

6. You or someone you assign to be the activity leader should blow a whistle, clap hands, or give another audio signal after each round of questions and answers. At the signal, each student asking the questions should move down the line one place and face a different person. Then they ask their new partner a question with a different vocabulary word so that the questions will continually be different. Continue for five or six rounds.

7. Switch tasks for students in each line. Have the students asking questions become the ones who answer and those answering become the ones who ask questions. Continue for five or six rounds more.

Workbook

Workbook pages 9 and 10 can be assigned after students have completed page 14.

Page 15

Reading for Real

Refer to the general instructions on page xvii in the Introduction.

Preparation

1. Prepare students by asking them to look at the character's picture and silently read the card with her personal information.

2. Hand out red and green index cards to each student. Demonstrate that holding up the green card in response to your question means yes and holding up the red card means no.

3. See how much information students have been able to read on their own by asking these questions:

   - Is her name Marie?
   - Is she a manager? Is she a cashier?
   - Is her office phone number 555-1278?
   - Is her home phone number 555-1278?
   - Is Marie a cashier? Is Marie good with people?
   - Does Marie have seven years or eight years of experience?

Presentation

1. Have students read the short text again silently. Then read it aloud to them.

2. To check comprehension, ask, "Does Marie work? What does Marie want? What is this? (point to the card) Who does Marie give her mini-résumé to?"

Exercise 5

Refer to the general instructions on page xvi in the Introduction.

Answers to Exercise 5

1. no   2. yes   3. yes   4. no   5. no

Activity Masters

Activity Master 2-1 can be completed after page 15.

Preparation

1. Read the instructions to the students. Read the mini-résumé for Marie Frank to students.

2. Before continuing, ask the following comprehension questions:

   What's Marie's phone number?

   Can Marie work nights?

   What job does Marie want?

3. Ask students to make their own mini-résumé in the box provided. When students are finished, talk about where students can use the mini-résumé.

Page 16

Culture Corner

Refer to the general instructions on page xviii in the Introduction.

Preparation

1. Prepare the students for the reading by having them look at the organizational chart. Ask them to point to various jobs represented there. as you say the words *clerks, housekeepers, waiters, groundskeepers,* and *cashiers.*

2. Explain the meaning of the diagram showing the general manager at the top, middle management at the next level down, and non-supervisory positions at the bottom, with connecting lines that indicate the different work areas of the hotel.

3. Ask the question that appears above the diagram, "Who are the supervisors at the Hillsun Hotel?" Encourage all students to answer in some way.

Answers to Exercise 6

1. Yes, the restaurant manager is a supervisor.

2. No, the cashiers aren't supervisors.

3. No, the housekeepers aren't supervisors.

Your Turn

Refer to the general instructions on page xiv in the Introduction.

Presentation

1. Read the directions aloud and model them by using a couple of students in the class as your partners. Ask the following questions as you fill out the chart on the overhead projector or the board:

   • What's your name?

   • What job can you do in the hotel?

   • Do you have experience?

2. Assign small groups to fill in their charts. Provide a large piece of paper and a marker for each group. Have a recorder from each group copy the chart onto the paper for members of the group to fill in. Note that lower-level students do not need to ask the questions in order to complete the chart. Each one may simply write his or her own information on the chart. However, encourage as much questioning as possible.

Extension

1. Collect the charts from each group.

2. Create an organizational chart on the board with the names and job titles the students have used on their charts. Model your chart after the one in the Student Book. Alternatively, write part of the chart on the board and have students voluntarily come to the board and fill in other parts. For example, students can write the names of specific types of jobs, or the names of students, in boxes you have drawn.

3. Use the chart for oral questions such as the following:

   • Who are the housekeepers?

   • How many cashiers work here?

In Your Experience

Refer to the general instructions on page xiv in the Introduction.

Presentation

1. Read the directions aloud and model the activity.

2. Provide a large piece of chart paper and a marker for each student or, if supplies are limited, have students share.

3. Circulate around the room to help students with vocabulary and spelling. Write requested words on the board for everyone to refer to.

4. Post the organizational chart of each student as he or she shares it with the class.

Page 17

Scene 2

Refer to the general instructions on page xviii in the Introduction.

Preparation

1. Point to the sign in the background of the first frame of the comic strip. Elicit from students the fact that these are jobs that the hotel has available, or open.

2. Point out that the man in the frames is Hoa, from the beginning of the unit. He is looking for a job.

3. Ask students if they ever fill out job applications.

4. Have students point to the following things and people in the pictures: Hoa, the application, the manager, the sign, the desk, the telephone.

Page 18

Spotlight on Demonstrative Pronouns

Refer to the general instructions on page xv in the Introduction.

Preparation

1. Hold up a book and say, "This is a book." Point to a chair at a greater distance and say, "That is a chair."

2. Have students hold up their own books and repeat the first sentence after you. Then point to a chair that is away from both you and the students and have students repeat the second sentence after you.

Presentation

Have students silently read the sentences in the Spotlight box. Then use several notebooks to focus their attention on the meaning of *this, that, these,* and *those.* Demonstrate that distance from the speaker determines which demonstrative pronoun to use.

Exercise 7

Refer to the general instructions on page xvi in the Introduction.

Extension

1. Create a quick listening exercise. Have students number from one to eight in their notebooks.

2. Ask students to write *this* or *that* to identify whether they see you pointing to something in the classroom that is close or something that is distant from you. Then name eight items around you in the room as you point. (Note that students do not need to know the vocabulary in order to answer.)

3. On the board write the correct answers for students to check.

Answers to Exercise 7

1. This is a book.
2. That's a notebook.
3. These are pencils.
4. Those are chairs.

Person to Person

Refer to the general instructions on page xvi in the Introduction.

Presentation

Use realia to demonstrate the word *pencils.*

Your Turn

Refer to the general instructions on page xiv in the Introduction.

Preparation

Read the directions aloud and model the activity on the board.

Presentation

1. Circulate among the students to help them with vocabulary and spelling.

2. Have students present their conversations to the class. In a multilevel class you may wish to choose from among the following options:

Option 1: In a class with significantly different proficiency levels, have students volunteer to perform their conversation in front of the class.

Option 2: Have students make an audio- or videocassette to play for the class. Pair stronger students with weaker students.

Option 3: Collect the notebooks and photocopy the conversations. Then put all the conversation copies into a box. Ask student pairs to draw out at random and perform a conversation from the box.

Get Graphic

Refer to the general instructions on page xviii in the Introduction.

Presentation

1. Introduce the concept of a "top five list" by making a list of the top five countries represented by students in the class. First, ask how many people are from each of the countries you know your students are from. Write the country names and numbers on the board.

2. Next, on another area of the board, arrange the country names and numbers of students in descending order, starting with the country represented by the most students in the class as number 1, and so on through 5.

Exercise 8

Refer to the general instructions on page xvi in the Introduction.

Answers to Exercise 8

1. 178,700   2. places to eat and drink   3. 106,441   4. clothes and shoes

In Your Experience

Refer to the general instructions on page xiv in the Introduction.

Preparation

Read the directions aloud and use pictures of typical or familiar workplaces to help make sure the meaning is clear. Ask students for a few examples of stores, restaurants, and other places to work in your area.

Presentation

In a multilevel class you may wish to choose from among the following options:

 Option 1: In a large group lead the students in listing which workplaces employ larger numbers of people.

Option 2: In small groups chosen by the students or assigned by you, circulate to help students communicate and agree on the ranking. Then post the Top Five lists on a classroom wall so students can look at the ideas each group had. If you assign students to groups, you may want to pair stronger students with weaker students if there are significant differences of levels in your class.

Activity Masters

Activity Master 2-2, Making a T-Chart, can be completed after page 19.

Preparation

1. Write these names of places where people buy things on the board. Leave space under each item.

   places to eat and drink   clothes stores

   places to buy cars and services   furniture stores

   food stores   shoe stores

2. Ask students, "Where do you buy things?" Then, ask them to check their number one place—the place where they buy things most often. Demonstrate by checking your number one place.

3. Count the number of checks under each category.

4. Ask students to work in pairs to fill in the T-chart. The completed chart will show the top five places to buy things according to the class and will give the number for each place.

Page 20

Wrap-Up

Refer to the general instructions on page xix in the Introduction.

Preparation

Read the directions aloud and model the activity with three students in the class as your examples. Show the grid on an overhead projector or copy it onto the board so that students can see how to fill out the chart as they ask the questions.

Presentation

Move among the groups to help where needed. When the charts are complete, have each group share their chart with another one.

Extension

1. Have a team of students compile the information to find out the number of restaurant workers, factory workers, hotel workers, and store clerks in the class. First, have students compile a list of names of people in the class.

2. Then give students the grids the students filled out and have them tabulate all of the information on a T-chart. As a model, give them a T-chart that might look something like this.

Job	Number of Workers in This Class
restaurant worker	3
factory worker	7
hotel worker	2
store clerk	2

3. Next, have the students add the job titles of any class members whose titles do not already appear on the chart. Then also add the number of class members who are not working now. Have students ask each other, "Do you work?" and "What's your job?" The additions may look something like the following:

Job	Number of Workers in This Class
construction worker	1
greenhouse worker	1
not working now	3

4. Provide the compiled information in a handout or on a wall chart or overhead transparency so that all the students can see the results.

Workbook

Workbook pages 11 and 12 can be assigned after students have completed page 20.

ANSWERS TO PROGRESS CHECKS

Progress Check A

Speak or Write

1. yes   2. a job application   3. two groundskeepers

Listen

Carlos Ramirez is from Mexico. His wife, Maria, is from Texas.
Maria's parents are Mexican. Maria is American. Carlos is a
laundry worker. Maria is a clerk in a store.

1. yes   2. no   3. no

4. yes   5. yes   6. no

Progress Check B

Language Structures

1. These   those
2. That   clerk
3. This   those
4. That   this

Content

1. check: name, phone number, experience, job
2. hotel: waitress, waiter, front desk manager, groundskeeper, cashier,
               housekeeper, clerk, manager, laundry worker;

   restaurant: waitress, waiter, cashier, manager;

   food store: cashier, clerk, manager

ANSWERS TO ACTIVITY MASTERS

Activity Master 2-1

Answers will vary.

Activity Master 2-2

Answers will vary.

REPRODUCIBLE MASTER
Unit 2

WORKBOOK ANSWERS

Practice 1
Answers will vary.

Practice 2
1. Is Carlos from Puerto Rico?   4. Is Maria American?
2. Is Maria from Texas?   5. Is Maria a student?
3. Are Maria's parents Cuban?

Practice 3
1. she isn't   2. she is   3. we aren't   4. it is

Practice 4
1. They are students.   4. He is a postal worker.
2. They are electricians.   5. He is a police officer.
3. They are doctors.   6. She is an engineer.

Practice 5
1. clerks   4. waitresses
2. a cashier   5. groundskeepers
3. a manager   6. laundry workers

Practice 6
single: 2 clerks, 3 cashiers   widowed: 1 clerk
married: 1 manager, 3 clerks   divorced: 1 clerk

Practice 7
1. This is a job application.   4. These are pencils.
2. This is a book.   5. Those are chairs.
3. Those are photos.   6. That is a notebook.

Practice 8
1. Those   4. this
2. that   5. these
3. these   6. These

REPRODUCIBLE MASTER
UNIT 2

PROGRESS CHECK A

SPEAK OR WRITE

Look at the pictures from Unit 2. Tell or write answers to
the questions.

Questions

1. Is she the cashier?

2. What does Hoa need?

3. What does the hotel need?

LISTEN

Listen and check (✓) *yes* or *no*.

	yes	no
1. Carlos is from Mexico.	_____	_____
2. His wife is from Mexico too.	_____	_____
3. Maria's parents are American.	_____	_____
4. Maria is American.	_____	_____
5. Carlos is a laundry worker.	_____	_____
6. Maria is a clerk in a hotel.	_____	_____

REPRODUCIBLE MASTER
UNIT 2   PROGRESS CHECK B

LANGUAGE STRUCTURES

Read the sentences. Circle the correct words.

1. (*This / These*) books are for (*that / those*) students.

2. (*That / Those*) computer is for that (*clerk / clerks*).

3. (*This / These*) application is for (*that / those*) jobs.

4. (*That / Those*) clerk uses (*this / these*) computer.

CONTENT

1. **Check (✓) the information on a mini-résumé.**

   _____ name   _____ experience

   _____ married   _____ divorced

   _____ phone number   _____ car

   _____ clothes   _____ job wanted

2. **Who works here?**

   Copy the words under the correct work places in the chart.

   waitress   groundskeeper   laundry worker
   waiter   cashier   clerk
   front desk manager   housekeeper   manager

hotel	restaurant	food store

Name ______________________ Date ______________

REPRODUCIBLE MASTER

UNIT 2

ACTIVITY MASTER 2-1

MAKING A MINI-RÉSUMÉ

Read Marie Frank's mini-résumé.

MARIE FRANK

Home: (303) 555-1278

Job: Hotel Cashier

- 7 years experience
- Uses computers
- Good with people
- Can work day or night

Make your mini-résumé.

Name _____ Date _____

ACTIVITY MASTER 2-2

MAKING A T-CHART

Where do you buy things?

places to eat and drink	places to buy cars and services
food stores	clothes stores
furniture stores	shoe stores

Check your number one place on the board. Count the checks for the class. Work with a partner to fill in the chart. Make a list of the top five places for the class.

Top Five Places to Buy Things	Number in Class
1. _____	_____
2. _____	_____
3. _____	_____
4. _____	_____
5. _____	_____

Unit 3   Helpers in the Community

OVERVIEW

Objectives

Skills and Structures

Read a schedule

Make a chart

Read a bar graph

Read and talk about problems

Use possessive adjectives

Use prepositions of place

SCANS Competencies

Teach others: Student Book, Issues and Answers, page 30

Allocate human resources: Student Book, Culture Corner, page 26

Realia

Photos or drawings of teachers, doctors, and firefighters

Classroom objects, such as books, notebooks, and pencils

A towel and several fruits or vegetables, such as an apple, an orange, a tomato, and a lemon

ACTIVITY NOTES

Page 21

Scene 1

Preparation

1. Explain the meaning of the unit title before students talk about the pictures. Show pictures of people in helping professions. Show teachers, doctors, fire fighters, and police officers. Point to and teach the word *community*.

2. Encourage students to talk about community workers they know about in your area, either by answering direct questions—such as "Is there a Fire Department in Denver? Where?"—or, if your students are advanced enough, by responding to open-ended questions such as "Tell us about the helpers in Denver."

Sound Bites

Exercise 1

Preparation

Ask questions about the pictures to prepare students for listening. Students can point to the pictures or answer yes or no, as appropriate. Here are some examples:

- (Number 1) Who is talking? Who is reading?
- (Number 2) Is she happy?
- (Number 3) Is she reading?
- (Number 4) Who is a police officer? Who is a school principal?

Listening Script

1. They're talking about drugs in schools.
2. I'm worried about my son.
3. I read about drugs in our schools.
4. Talk to the principal.

Answers to Sound Bites

1. a   2. b   3. a   4. b

Your Turn

Presentation

During the activity read or play the Scene 1 tape of the conversation between Carla and Sue again. Have students read it silently as they listen. Read or replay Sound Bites. Ask the students to circle the sentences they hear in Sound Bites, then have them compare answers with a partner.

Extension

Ask students to make a T-chart. On one column write the heading *People;* on the other write the heading *Things*. Working alone or with a partner, students make this chart by copying words from the conversation.

People	*Things*
Carla	drugs
Sue	schools
son	
principal	

Spotlight on Possessive Adjectives

Preparation

1. Introduce this structure by picking up or pointing to one of the students' books. (Choose one of the more advanced students.) Ask, "Is this your book?" Elicit the answer yes. Then pick up your own book and ask, "Is this your book?" Elicit the answer no. Then say, "It's not your book. It's my book." Write these sentences on the board.

2. Demonstrate how possessive adjectives are used in comparison with subject pronouns. Provide additional examples, such as the following:
   - I am a teacher. My name is Pam Jones.
   - He is a student. His name is Javier Perez.

Exercise 2

Extension

1. For students who need more practice, use materials you have prepared before class. Make large words cards from paper or tag board. Make seven cards and write a subject pronoun on each one (*I*, *you*, *he*, *she*, *it*, *we*, and *they*). Make seven more cards and write a possessive adjective on each one (*my*, *your*, *his*, *her*, *its*, *our*, and *their*).
2. Use the cards as flash cards. For example, when you (or a student volunteer) hold up the card with the subject pronoun *they*, students should say or write *their*, and so on.

Answers to Exercise 2

1. Her   2. My   3. Our   4. Their   5. His

Your Turn

Presentation

1. Read the directions aloud and model the activity with a fictitious adult school, teacher, and class on the board or overhead transparency. For example, write sentences like these.

   Luc: I need more English for my job. Tell me about your school for adults.

   Dan: Lincoln School is a busy place. My Beginning English class is good. My teacher, Judy, helps me. I like my class.

2. Note where you made changes in the conversation to personalize it.

Extension

Ask pairs to perform their conversation for the class, either live or on an audio- or videocassette.

In Your Experience

Presentation

1. Read the directions aloud and model the activity. For example, say, "My friend is Donna. Her husband is Dick. His job is in Pasadena. Their children are Sandra and Allen."
2. Assign groups or have students choose their own groups of three.
3. As students talk, circulate among the groups to help those who need prompting.

Workbook

Workbook pages 13 and 14 can be assigned after students have completed page 23.

Spotlight on Prepositions of Place

Preparation

Demonstrate the prepositions in the Spotlight box by using some items from the classroom. For example, use a book, a notebook, and a pencil. Hold or place these items in various arrangements and say something like the following:

- The pencil is between the book and the notebook.
- The pencil in under the notebook, and the book is next to the notebook.

Exericse 3

Extension

Extend the practice by giving pairs of students some simple items from around the classroom. Encourage them to arrange and rearrange the items; then use prepositions of place to talk about the arrangements. Move around the room and listen in on the pairs to model correct answers, if necessary.

Answers to Exercise 3

1. on	5. next to (or beside)	9. between	13. in
2. on top of	6. in front of	10. next to (or beside)	
3. next to (or beside)	7. between	11. over	
4. under	8. behind	12. under	

Workbook

Workbook pages 15 and 16 may be assigned after students have completed page 24.

Activity Masters

Activity Master 3-1 can be completed after page 24.

Preparation

1. Read the instructions to the students. Show that item 1 has been completed. (Note that students use the clue provided to fill in item 1 down. There is no need to identify *across* and *down* items in this puzzle.)
2. Have students complete the exercise individually.

Reading for Real

Preparation

Prepare students by asking them to look at the format of the meeting schedule. Point out the title at the top and the dates running down the left side. Point out that the dates are all in September. Tell students the names and job titles beside each date. Explain that the job titles indicate helpers in the community.

Presentation

1. Have students read the meeting schedule silently. Then read it aloud to them.

2. Ask if students have questions and clarify anything that is unclear.

3. Check students' understanding before they begin the comprehension exercise. For example, ask the following questions:
   - When does Officer Ortega talk to the parents?
   - Where does he work?
   - What does he talk about?

Extension

Extend the activity by encouraging students to elaborate, when possible, by asking, "What kind of drugs are a problem in our community?"

Answers to Exercise 4

1. no   2. no   3. yes   4. yes   5. no

Activity Masters

Activity Master 3-2 can be completed after page 25.

Preparation

1. Read the instructions to the students.

2. Read the notice about classes for parents to students as shown. Ask them to read it silently and then check *yes* or *no*.

3. Students can complete the exercise individually.

Page 26

Culture Corner

Preparation

Show the difference between a factory or service worker and a community helper. Write the two category titles on the board and ask students what their jobs are. Write their job titles under the correct heading. (Most entry-level jobs fall under the factory or service job category.) Point out that your job, as teacher, falls under the community helper head. Cite more examples that students may be aware of in your school or community.

Your Turn

Extension

When students have finished, on the board write the two categories from the chart. Ask a volunteer from the class to write an answer on the board. Continue with more volunteers until the lists are complete. When errors occur, have students from the class explain the error. Then let the student who made the error correct it on the board.

Answers to Your Turn

Factory or service workers: groundskeeper, video store cashier, hotel manager, office clerk, factory worker, waitress

Community helpers: teacher, school principal, volunteer, police officer, drug counselor, doctor

In Your Experience

Preparation

Read the directions and then model the activity by talking about the jobs on the list that interest you. Make a chart on the board and check the jobs that you like.

Presentation

1. Have students work individually to complete the activity. Ask students to write their lists in their notebooks or on overhead transparencies.

2. When students finish making their lists, have them share them in one of these ways:

Option 1: Assign students to groups of three or four. Ask students to show the lists in their notebooks to the other people in their group.

Option 2: Show the lists on overhead transparencies to the class, allowing time for them to read each one carefully.

Option 3: Follow up by making a tally together and asking students to summarize the information about the people in the class. For example, ask, "How many want to be community workers? How many want to be factory/service workers?"

Page 27

Scene 2

Preparation

1. Point to the door in the background. Ask students whose office this is.

2. Have students identify Carla and the principal in the frames. Ask, "Which one is Carla?" and "Which one is the principal?" Less advanced students can point to the pictures. Circulate among the students to check which people they are pointing to.

3. Review the word *principal.* Ask a volunteer to explain what a principal does.

4. With the class make a list of words that students associate with school and principals. On the board put the words in an idea map proceeding from a center circle in which you have written the word *principal* or *school* or both. See how many words the class can generate on this topic. Have volunteers explain any words that are unfamiliar to other students in the class.

Spotlight on *A* and *An*

Preparation

1. The following tactile activity will help to prepare for teaching *a* and *an*. Bring in several fruits or vegetables along with a towel to cover them up. An apple, an orange, a tomato, and a lemon will work well, but bring in only one of each. Show the items to the class and give the name for each one. On the board write that name with the corresponding article.

2. Put all of the fruit and vegetables under the towel and ask students to come up to the desk in separate pairs or groups and guess what each item is by feeling it through the towel. If you wish, you can ask the question "What is it?" when a student touches a specific item through the towel. Students should answer, "It's an (orange)" or "This is a (tomato)," for example. If you spread the fruit and vegetables out far enough under the towel and if the towel is large enough, several students can do the activity at the same time.

3. When a student guesses, you can pull the item out and confirm the student's guess, if this is convenient. If too many students are doing the activity at the same time, you probably will not be able to do this, however.

Answers to Exercise 5

1. a school
2. a computer
3. a pencil
4. an auditorium
5. an application
6. a hotel

Get Graphic

Preparation

1. Prepare students for the reading by introducing items containing the problem substances *alcohol*, *nicotine*, and *caffeine* in pictures or drawings. For example, use pictures of beer or wine, coffee and cola drinks, and cigarettes and cigars. Teach the words *alcohol*, *nicotine*, and *caffeine*, and ask students to repeat them several times. Then write the words on the board.

2. Ask students to tell you more products containing each of the three problem substances, in addition to the ones you have shown.

3. Ask for a show of hands to answer yes and no to the question "Are alcohol, nicotine, and caffeine a problem in the United States?" Encourage students to answer yes or no according to their own opinions. Then ask if the same products are a problem in their home countries.

Answers to Exercise 6

1. 11   2. 130   3. 61   4. 1

In Your Experience

Presentation

1. Read the directions aloud. Show pictures of typical situations in which people are using alcohol, nicotine, and caffeine. Present pictures reflecting both positive and negative images of these substances to help students generate an opinion about the their use. For example, show a picture of a wedding reception or other formal celebration where the use of alcohol might be considered socially acceptable by some. Then show a picture of an auto accident obviously caused by a drunk driver, and so forth.

2. Complete the activity in either of these ways:

Option 1: Ask the students to indicate their opinion by moving to a part of the classroom designated for those who think the substances are acceptable for people or unacceptable for people. Have students vote their opinions on alcohol, nicotine, and caffeine. They can move or raise their hands to indicate each of their votes.

Option 2: Assign small groups and appoint a recorder in each group to tabulate the opinions. Then bring the class together again as a large group and combine all the opinions reported by the recorders.

3. Ask some individuals *why* or *why not?* as they give their opinions. Encourage them to express whatever they can and allow them to point to your pictures of negative and positive situations as part of their explanation.

Page 30

Issues and Answers

Extension

Tabulate the answers on the board so that students can see the count. Add an interesting twist by tabulating men's and women's answers separately. Or separately tabulate the opinions given by students over 30 years old from those given by students under 30 years old, for example.

Workbook

Workbook pages 17 and 18 may be assigned after students have completed page 30.

ANSWERS TO PROGRESS CHECKS

Progress Check A

Speak or Write

1. Yes, he's OK.
2. Sue reads about drugs in schools.
3. The principal knows about drugs in schools.
4. The classes are on Monday nights.

Listen

Isam Al-Ani is from Egypt. He lives in Dallas now. He and his wife have 3 children. Isam works for a large company. The pay is good. He likes the job. He has many friends at work.

1. yes   2. no   3. yes   4. no   5. yes   6. yes

Progress Check B

Language Structures

1. on
2. in
3. behind
4. in
5. next to
6. beside
7. between

Content

1. b, c, d, f, h

2. a. yes
   b. yes
   c. no
   d. yes

3. a. teachers
   b. counselors
   c. school principals

ANSWERS TO ACTIVITY MASTERS

Activity Master 3-1

1. between   2. under   3. next to   4. over   5. on

Activity Master 3-2

1. yes
2. no
3. no
4. no
5. yes
6. Answers will vary.

REPRODUCIBLE MASTER
Unit 3

WORKBOOK ANSWERS

Practice 1
1. their   2. his   3. her   4. its

Practice 2
1. your   2. their   3. his   4. her   5. their   6. their

Practice 3
1. his   2. their   3. his   4. his   5. his   6. its

Practice 4
1. your   2. my   3. Our   4. our   5. your   6. my   7. her   8. your

Practice 5
1. in   2. behind   3. on   4. on   5. between
6. over   7. behind   8. beside   9. in   10. in front of
11. in   12. beside

Practice 6
1. on   2. behind   3. over   4. next to   5. on   6. in front of
7. on   8. next to   9. next to   10. on   11. in front of   12. next to

Practice 7
1. A, a   2. A, a   3. an, a   4. A, a   5. A, an
6. an   7. A   8. A, a   9. a   10. an

Practice 8
1. a, an   2. an   3. a, a   4. a, a   5. a, a   6. a, an

REPRODUCIBLE MASTER
UNIT 3   PROGRESS CHECK A

SPEAK OR WRITE

Look at the pictures from Unit 3. Tell or write answers to
the questions.

Questions

1. Is Sue's son OK?

2. What does Sue read about?

3. What does the principal know about?

4. When are the classes?

LISTEN

Listen and check (✓) *yes* or *no*.

	yes	no
1. Isam is from Egypt.	_____	_____
2. His home is in Egypt now.	_____	_____
3. Isam and his wife have 3 children.	_____	_____
4. His wife works for a large company.	_____	_____
5. He likes his job.	_____	_____
6. The company pays its employees well.	_____	_____

Name _____ Date _____

UNIT 3   PROGRESS CHECK B

LANGUAGE STRUCTURES

Read the sentences. Circle the correct word.

1. The teacher has a book (*in / on*) the desk.

2. The cook is (*in / on*) the cafeteria.

3. The principal works (*behind / on top of*) his desk.

4. Read about drugs (*over / in*) school.

5. The gym is (*next to / over*) the cafeteria.

6. Sit down (*on / beside*) the principal.

7. The office is (*on / between*) the gym and the cafeteria.

CONTENT

1. Check (✓) community helpers.

a. _____ waitress   e. _____ groundskeeper

b. _____ doctor   f. _____ police officer

c. _____ counselor   g. _____ factory worker

d. _____ teacher   h. _____ school principal

2. Check (✓) *yes* or *no*.

	yes	no
a. Counselors can help communities.	_____	_____
b. Nicotine in cigarettes is a drug.	_____	_____
c. Caffeine in coffee is not a drug.	_____	_____
d. Children don't use drugs in school.	_____	_____

3. Who can parents talk to about children and drugs?

a. _____   b. _____   c. _____

REPRODUCIBLE MASTER
UNIT 3

ACTIVITY MASTER 3-1

PUZZLE

Fill in the boxes. Use prepositions of place.

Example:

The baby is N E X T   T O the book.

1. The child is ☐ ☐ ☐ ☐ ☐ ☐ ☐ the boxes.

2. The child is ☐ ☐ ☐ ☐ ☐ the box.

3. The child is ☐ ☐ ☐ ☐   ☐ ☐ the box.

4. The child is ☐ ☐ ☐ ☐ the box.

5. The child is ☐ ☐ the box.

REPRODUCIBLE MASTER

UNIT 3

ACTIVITY MASTER 3-2

READING SCHEDULES

Read the school meeting schedule. Answer the questions.

Classes for Parents
Thursdays in October   7:00–9:00 P.M.
Lincoln School Cafeteria
Oct. 1   Talk with Your Child Mr. Bob Hanes, school principal
Oct. 8   Good Food at Home Dr. Sam Ortega, children's doctor
Oct. 15   Help Your Child Read Ms. Susan Brown, teacher
Oct. 22   School Dinner for Parents and Children

Check (✓) yes or no.

	yes	no
1. The classes for parents are at the Lincoln School.	_____	_____
2. The classes are on Fridays in October.	_____	_____
3. Dr. Ortega talks about reading to your child.	_____	_____
4. Ms. Susan Brown is a doctor.	_____	_____
5. The school dinner is on October 22.	_____	_____
6. For Parents:	_____	_____

Check (✓) the class you want.

_____ My Child and Drugs   _____ Read with Your Child

_____ My Child and Crime   _____ Talking with Teachers

_____ Good Food at Home   _____ Talking with Counselors

Unit 4 Neighbors Helping Neighbors

OVERVIEW

Objectives

Skills and Structures

Read a fee chart

Talk about neighbors' services

Read a co-op work schedule

Make a work or study schedule

Make a yes/no chart

Use present continuous statements (affirmative)

Use present continuous statements (negative)

Use present continuous yes/no questions and short answers

SCANS Competencies

Allocate time: Student Book, Your Turn, page 39

Negotiate: Student Book, Your Turn, page 36

Realia

Photos of people involved in the following activities: babysitting, studying, checking the mail, and taking care of pets

A newspaper, some mail, and a telephone

ACTIVITY NOTES

Page 31

Scene 1

Preparation

1. Explain the meaning of the unit title before students talk about the pictures. Show pictures that convey the concept of neighbors. For example, show people in adjacent housing situations such as apartments and duplexes. Then show people in houses lined up on the same block. Point to and teach the word *neighbors*.

2. Encourage students to talk about their own neighbors, either by answering direct questions—such as "Do you have neighbors? Who are they? Do you talk with them?" or, if your students are advanced enough, by responding to open-ended questions such as "Tell us about your neighbors."

3. Lead a discussion about what neighbors do for one another in the countries represented by the students in your class. For example, ask, "Does a person in Mexico help a neighbor? How?" In many cultures it is only family members who help each other. Bring out this contrast by asking, "Does a person in Mexico help his family? How?"

Extension

Have pairs of students role-play the Scene for the class in one of several ways. Bring in props or costumes to make the activity more interesting.

Option 1: Students can perform the lines as written. You can assign pairs or let students choose their own partners.

Option 2: Students can make a simple substitution in some lines (by inserting the name of their own school, for example).

Option 3: More advanced students can ad-lib a conversation on the topic treated in the Scene or imagine they are in the conversation with the characters in the Scene.

Page 32

Sound Bites

Exercise 1

Preparation

1. Ask questions about the pictures in Sound Bites to prepare students for listening. Here are some examples:
   - (Number 1) Is he talking, or is he reading?
   - (Number 2) Is she in bed?
   - (Number 3) Is he in bed, or is he in his car?
   - (Number 4) Where is he? Where is she?
2. Read or play the tape from Scene 1 of the conversation between Mark and Rosa again.

Presentation

Read or replay the Sound Bites. Ask students to circle the sentences they hear. Then have them work with a partner to compare answers.

Listening Script

1. He's asking a neighbor for help.
2. My babysitter is sick!

3. I'm going to work.
4. She's on vacation.

Answers to Exercise 1

1. a   2. a   3. b   4. b

Your Turn

Extension

1. Divide the class into two groups. One group should say Mark's part of the conversation, the other should say Rosa's part.
2. Ask a volunteer from each of the groups to perform the conversation for the class. Encourage expressive performances and reward the best pair, who can be chosen by the class. You can reward individuals with a new pencil or some other small item or privilege.
3. Extend the reading practice further by dividing the class into three teams. Provide each team with a fly swatter (or rolled-up newspaper). Write the sentences from the conversation on the board or post them around the room on large pieces of paper. Place one member of each team behind a starting line. As you (or a student) read a sentence from the conversation, the team members should try to be the first to swat the sentence. That is, the team members should go to the sentence posted on the wall and touch it with their fly swatter. The first person to swat the sentence gets a point for their team.
4. Provide a reward for the team with the most points.

Spotlight on Present Continuous Affirmative Statements

Preparation

1. Review the conjugation of *be*.

I am	we are
you are	you are
he is	
she is	they are
it is	

2. Give examples of how the present continuous is used to talk about actions happening at the present moment or in the near future, such as the following:

   • *Talk:* I am talking to you.

   • *Write:* I am writing now.

Presentation

1. Have students look at the examples in the Spotlight box.

2. Show students that the present continuous requires two elements: a form of *be* first and a verb ending with *-ing* second.

Extension

1. Give additional examples of how *-ing* is added to words with and without a final *e*. Here are some examples:

   • talk: talking

   • write: writing

   • work: working

2. Ask students to put the two elements together. Tell them to finish sentences with the correct forms of the verbs you've given. Model one for them. For example, write the following sentences:

   • I <u>am</u> work<u>ing</u> now.

   • He _____ write_____ now.

   • They _____ talk_____ now.

Exercise 2

Presentation

Encourage students to work together as they write the sentences about Kamal in their notebooks.

Answers to Exercises 2 and 3

1. He's watching TV.

2. He's talking to a friend.

3. He drinking coffee.

4. He's looking at photos.

5. He's reading the newspaper.

6. He's calling a neighbor.

Workbook

Workbook pages 19 and 20 may be assigned after students have completed page 33.

Page 34

Spotlight on Present Continuous Negative Statements

Preparation

1. Demonstrate how present continuous negatives are used to talk about actions that are not happening at the present moment or in the near future by giving the following examples or similar ones:

   - *talk*—I am not talking to the principal.

   - *write*—I am not writing now.

2. Show students that the present continuous in the negative requires three elements: a *be* verb first, the word *not* second, and another verb ending with *-ing* third. Review the conjugation of *be* in the negative.

I'm not	we're not
you're not	you're not
he's not	
she's not	they 're not
it's not	

3. Ask students to put the three elements together. Tell them to finish sentences with the correct forms of the verbs you give. Model one for them, as shown here:

   - I'm not working now.

   - He _____ _____ write _____ now.

   - They _____ _____ talk _____ now.

Answers to Exercise 4

1. Glen isn't working today. He isn't (He's not) using a computer.

2. Sandy isn't working at the desk. She isn't (She's not) opening mail.

3. Glen and Sandy aren't going to a meeting.

4. They're not (They aren't) taking care of people. They're not (They aren't) talking.

Answers to Exercise 5

1. He's not watching TV now.

2. He's not talking to a friend now.

3. He's not drinking coffee now.

4. He's not looking at photos now.

5. He's not reading the newspaper now.

6. He's not calling a neighbor now.

Presentation

Encourage students to work together as they write negative sentences about Kamal in their notebooks. Provide the answers on the board or overhead projector so that students can check their work.

Your Turn

Preparation

1. Read the directions aloud and model the activity by using your own information on the board or overhead transparency, as shown here:

    A: I'm not going home now.

    B: What are you doing?

    A: I'm working at a school. I'm not reading books. I'm teaching English.

2. Note where you made changes in the conversation to personalize it.

3. Assign partners or have students choose a partner. Then, as they work on the activity, check their progress and help those who need it, especially those unsure about vocabulary or correct spelling.

Extension

Ask pairs to perform their conversation for the class, either live or on audio- or videocassette.

Workbook

Workbook pages 21 and 22 may be assigned after students have completed page 34.

Page 35

Reading for Real

Preparation

1. Prepare students for the reading by asking them to look at the format of the chart. Point out that the chart has lines going from side to side and columns going from top to bottom. Note that to find information, you look at the place where the lines and columns intersect. Note the title and the headings. Note the names of cities running down the left side of the chart. Have students locate these cities on the U.S. map. Help them, if necessary.

2. Have students read the short text and the chart silently. Then read both aloud to them. Invite questions and clarify any words or phrases whose meaning is not clear to students.

Exercise 6

Check understanding before students begin Exercise 6. For example, ask questions such as the following:

- How much does child care in Boston cost for a three-year-old child?
- How much does it cost for a six-year-old child?

Answers to Exercise 6

1. yes   2. Answers will vary.   3. no   4. no   5. yes

Talk About It

Presentation

Ask the Talk About It questions in a large group or assign small groups to answer them. Encourage students to elaborate, when possible, by asking, "How much does child care cost here in (your city or town)?"

Culture Corner

Preparation

1. Prepare students for the reading by asking questions about their housing and their travel habits. For example, ask the following questions:

   • Do you have a house or an apartment?

   • Do you go on vacation?

   • For how long?

2. Use realia to review the vocabulary of things that might need to be taken care of when a person is on vacation. Show a newspaper, some mail, and a telephone. Although students may not have the vocabulary to answer in detail, ask the following questions:

   • Do you get a newspaper at home?

   • Do you get mail at home?

   • Do you have a telephone at home?

   • What happens when you're on vacation?

   • Do you know your neighbors?

3. Provide drawings of a mailbox overflowing with mail and a telephone ringing. Draw a picture of newspapers piling up in front of an apartment door and a person bringing the newspapers inside. Students can point to the scenes they feel express their situation. Then point to the woman bringing in the newspapers and say, "neighbor."

Presentation

Have students read the short text silently. Then read it aloud to them. Invite questions and clarify as needed.

Your Turn

Preparation

Read the directions aloud and model the activity.

Presentation

1. Tell students to complete the activity individually. Circulate to help students who have questions or low literacy skills.

2. Assign partners or allow students to choose a partner. Ask, "How many answers are different?"

In Your Experience

Preparation

1. Read the directions aloud and model the activity. Tell students they can use the list from the Your Turn activity to help them express things (if any) neighbors do for each other in their countries of origin.

2. Talk about the cultural differences between the United States and the students' home countries. In many countries only family members do the things listed in Your Turn.

Extension

1. Bring the class back together in a large group and write the names of some students' home countries on the board. Under each country name, write some of the things neighbors do for other neighbors as students volunteer their ideas.

2. You may also wish to have students transfer the ideas on the board to individual index cards and pin the index cards onto a map in the classroom.

Page 37

Scene 2

Preparation

1. Point to the dryers in the background of each of the two frames of the comic strip. Ask students if they can identify the machines. Elicit the word and write it on the board. Then ask students if they know where Mark, Jenny, and Rosa are. Elicit the phrase *at the laundromat* or say it for the class and write it on the board.

2. Tell students that Mark, Jenny, and Rosa are three neighbors. Ask students what neighbors help each other with in their native countries.

3. Introduce the topic of child care. Ask students how working parents take care of children in the students' native countries. Ask whether neighbors help each other with children.

Extension

Have pairs of students role-play the Scene for the class in one of several ways. Bring in props or costumes to make the activity more interesting.

Option 1: Students can perform the lines as written. You can assign pairs or let students choose their own partners.

Option 2: Students can make a simple substitution in some lines (by inserting the name of their own school, for example).

Option 3: More advanced students can ad-lib a conversation on the topic treated in the Scene or imagine they are in the conversation with the characters in the Scene.

Activity Masters

Activity Master 4-1 can be completed after page 37.

Presentation

1. Read the instructions to the students. Show them that they'll need to cut on the lines to make sentence strips. Have students read the strips then put them in the correct order. When finished, students can read the dialogue with a partner.

2. Read the instructions for item 2 to students. Show them that they'll need to cut on the lines to make sentence strips. Have students read the strips and then put them in the correct order.

Spotlight on Present Continuous *Yes/No* Questions and Short Answers

Preparation

Demonstrate the reversed position of the subject and the *be* verb in question formation. Note that the short answer contains only the *be* verb, not the simple verb + *-ing.*

Presentation

1. As you read the examples in the Spotlight box aloud, emphasize the different intonations for the questions and the short answers. Have students repeat them with you. Practice a few questions aloud with the class. For example, ask the following:

   • Are you reading English now?

   • Are you watching TV now?

2. Let students use the short answers in response to your questions. Then encourage students to use the present continuous to ask you questions. If they need a hint, write the words *work* and *teach* on the board.

Answers to Exercise 7

1. Is Lee working? she is
2. Are her children studying? they are
3. Are they going on vacation? they're not
4. Is Lee's sister babysitting? she is
5. Is she watching TV? she is

Your Turn

Preparation

Model the activity by choosing a student from the class and asking that student a question with one of the verbs on the list. Have the student give an appropriate answer.

Presentation

Ask students to try to write six questions individually, but allow them to work together if they have questions or difficulty. Circulate to help students form their questions correctly. When students have finished writing their questions, assign partners or permit students to choose a partner. Have students ask their questions and answer with short answers.

Option: In a multilevel class of significantly different literacy levels, you may wish to pair students up to write the questions and have the more literate students help the less literate students write questions and answers and then practice them. Students can first think of questions and answers together, and the more advanced students can help the less literate students write the sentences.

Extension

Have a few students ask their questions of two students in front of the class. They must answer, "Yes, we are," or "No, we're not."

Get Graphic

Preparation

1. Prepare the students for the reading by reviewing the days of the week. Remind the class that the American calendar starts with Sunday, not Monday, as in many other countries.

2. Ask students how many of them have children. Ask the following:

   • Do your children need a babysitter?

   • When?

3. Point to the title and read it aloud. Note the days of the week in columns and the characters' names on the lines. Show that the check marks indicate the day that person babysits.

Presentation

Have students read the text and the work schedule silently first. Then read them aloud to students. Answer any questions that students may have about vocabulary.

Answers to Exercise 8

1. 1   2. 2   3. 6   4. 3

Your Turn

Answers to Your Turn

Students should show the following information with check marks on a chart like the one at the beginning of Get Graphic:

   Mark—Friday and Saturday

   Rosa—Monday and Thursday

   Jenny—Tuesday and Wednesday

   (No babysitting is necessary on Sunday.)

In Your Experience

Presentation

1. Read the directions aloud and model the activity.

2. Assign groups of three, or let students choose their groups. Supply each group with a large piece of chart paper or newsprint and a marker.

3. Encourage students to model their charts on the one for the babysitters in the book, but remind them that instead of check marks, they will write the letters *w* and *s* for the days they work and attend school.

4. When groups are finished, post the charts on the walls around the classroom.

Activity Masters

Activity Master 4-2 can be completed after page 39.

Presentation

Read the beginning paragraph describing Jenny's and Sam's family. Before continuing with the activity, ask comprehension questions such as the following:

- How many children does Jenny have?
- Who are the children?
- Are they busy?

Have students look at the schedule, read the statements, and check *yes* or *no*.

Page 40

Wrap-Up

Presentation

1. Read the directions aloud and model the activity on the board or an overhead transparency. Ask some volunteers from the class the questions.

2. Assign groups of three, or let students choose their own work groups. Encourage them to form questions and short answers and write *yes* or *no* on the chart.

3. Have groups show other groups the results on their charts.

Workbook

Workbook pages 23 and 24 can be assigned after students have completed page 40.

ANSWERS TO PROGRESS CHECKS

Progress Check A

Speak or Write

1. Rosa is going to work.

2. No, she can't.

3. Yes, they're looking for a babysitter.

Listen

Jenny is on vacation. The neighbors are taking care of her house. Annie is taking care of the pets and checking the mail. Mark and Rosa are getting the newspaper. Rosa is watching the house.

1. yes   2. yes   3. no   4. yes   5. no   6. no

Progress Check B

Language Structures

1. Is Rosa watching TV? , she is.

2. Are the neighbors on vacation? , they are.

3. Is Annie watching the house? , she isn't.

4. Is Mark going to work? , he is.

5. Are Annie and Mark looking for a babysitter? , they are.

Content

1. b, e, f   2. c

ANSWERS TO ACTIVITY MASTERS

Activity Master 4-1

1. Help, Rosa! My babysitter is sick.

   What are you doing?

   Sorry, Mark. I'm going to work.

   Ask Jenny. She's not working today.

   She's on vacation!

2. Mark, Rosa and Jenny are doing laundry.

   They are talking about child care.

   Rosa is reading about a child care co-op.

   Mark is asking about a child care co-op.

   Jenny is telling him about a child care co-op.

Activity Master 4-2

1. yes   2. no   3. yes   4. no   5. no   6. yes

WORKBOOK ANSWERS

Practice 1

1. The clerks are using a computer behind the desk.

2. The manager is sitting inside his office.

3. The cashier is helping people.

4. The groundskeepers are working in front of the hotel.

5. The housekeeper is calling the maintenance manager.

6. The workers are making something good in the restaurant.

Practice 2

1. 'm making   2. 'm looking   3. are working

4. is filling out   5. 'm doing the laundry.

Practice 3

1. Jenny   2. Rosa, Annie, Mark   3. Annie

4. Rosa   5. Mark, Rosa

Practice 4

1. Yvonne is not calling her mother. She is watching TV.

2. Mike isn't talking to his friends. He's reading a book.

3. Monica isn't playing with the pets. She's listening to the stereo.

4. Jack isn't sleeping. He's doing laundry.

Practice 5

1. clerks: yes   5. cashier: yes   8. waiters: no

2. cashier: no   6. housekeepers: yes   9. waiters: yes

3. housekeepers: no   7. manager: no   10. clerks: no

4. manager: yes

WORKBOOK ANSWERS

Practice 6

1. Are the housekeepers watching TV?, they are

2. Is the cashier helping people?, she's not

3. Are the waiters smoking cigarettes?, they are

4. Are the clerks working at the front desk?, they're not

5. Are the clerks drinking beer?, they are

6. Is the manager sleeping on the sofa?, he is

Practice 7

1. Are 75 people working at Hi-Tec?

2. Is Ron talking with new employees?

3. Is Ron making products?

4. Are the clerks taking care of things?

5. Are the factory workers making products?

Name _____ Date _____

PROGRESS CHECK A

SPEAK OR WRITE

Look at the pictures from Unit 4. Tell or write answers to the questions.

Questions

1. What is Rosa doing?
2. Can Rosa help Mark?
3. Are they looking for a babysitter?

LISTEN

Listen and check (✓) *yes* or *no*.

	yes	no
1. Jenny is on vacation.	_____	_____
2. The neighbors are taking care of the house.	_____	_____
3. Mark is checking the mail.	_____	_____
4. Rosa is getting the newspaper.	_____	_____
5. Rosa is taking care of the pets.	_____	_____
6. Rosa is watching TV.	_____	_____

REPRODUCIBLE MASTER
UNIT 4   PROGRESS CHECK B

LANGUAGE STRUCTURES

Write the question. Complete the short answer.

1. Rosa is watching TV.

   _____

   Yes, _____.

2. The neighbors are on vacation.

   _____

   No, _____.

3. Annie is watching the house. _____

   _____

   No, _____.

4. Mark is going to work. _____

   _____

   Yes, _____.

5. Annie and Mark are looking for a babysitter. _____

   _____

   Yes, _____

CONTENT

1. **Check (✓) how neighbors can help neighbors on vacation.**

   a. _____ going to work   d. _____ opening the mail

   b. _____ checking the mail   e. _____ watching the house

   c. _____ watching TV.   f. _____ getting the newspaper

2. **What is a child care co-op? Circle *a, b,* or *c.***

   a. Two or three neighbors take turns going to work.

   b. Two or three neighbors take turns watching houses.

   c. Two or three neighbors take turns caring for children.

Name _____ Date _____

ACTIVITY MASTER 4-1

PUT IT IN ORDER

1. Look at the pictures from Unit 4. What are they saying?
   Cut out the lines. Put them in order.

✂

She's on vacation.
Sorry, Mark. I'm going to work.
Help, Rosa! My babysitter is sick. What are you doing?
Ask Jenny. She's not working today.

2. Look at the picture from Unit 4. Read the lines. Tell what is
   happening. Cut out the lines. Put them in order.

✂

Jenny is telling him about a child care co-op.
Rosa is reading about a child care co-op.
Mark, Rosa and Jenny are doing laundry.
Mark is asking about a child care co-op.
They are talking about child care.

REPRODUCIBLE MASTER
UNIT 4

ACTIVITY MASTER 4-2

READING SCHEDULES

Jenny and Sam have 4 children, 2 boys and 2 girls.
They are Tod, Beth, Kate, and Matt. They are a busy family.

Look at their schedule for the week.

Sunday	Monday	Tuesday	Wednesday	Thursday	Friday	Saturday
Neighborhood Family Dinner 5:00	Matt, basketball 7:00	Kate, babysit 6:00

Jenny, check Mark's mail | Beth and Tod study at school.

Jenny, parent class 7:00 | Tod drives Matt to school | Sam on vacation

Sam works late. | Beth checks Mark's mail

Kate does laundry. |

Check (✓) yes or no.

	yes	no
1. There's a neighborhood dinner on Sunday.	_____	_____
2. Matt has baseball at 8:00 on Monday.	_____	_____
3. Kate babysits at 6:00 on Tuesday.	_____	_____
4. Jenny has parents class on Friday.	_____	_____
5. Sam works on Friday.	_____	_____
6. On Saturday Kate does the laundry.	_____	_____

EATING HEALTHY FOOD

OVERVIEW

Objectives

Skills and Structures

Read the food pyramid

Talk about fast food

Read a height and weight chart

Plan healthy food for one day

Use simple present in affirmative statements

Use simple present in negative statements

Use simple present in yes/no questions and short answers

SCANS Competencies

Improve and design systems: Student Book, Reading for Real, page 45; Student Book, Get Graphic, page 49

Participate as a member of a team: Student Book; In Your Experience, page 48; Student Book, Get Graphic, page 49

Realia

Photos or drawings of foods such as chicken, beef, rice, bread, milk, cheese, and various fruits and vegetables

Photos or drawings of cookies, butter, ice cream, candy, and potato chips.

Packaged food from each of the food groups

A diet scale (for weighing food in grams)

Photos of people who are thin and photos of people who are overweight

A wooden lath marked with feet and inches for measuring height (an inexpensive piece of wood lath from a lumber yard.)

A bathroom scale (for measuring weight)

ACTIVITY NOTES

Page 41

Scene 1

Preparation

1. Explain the meaning of the unit title before students talk about the pictures. Show pictures of foods high in fat and sugar, such as french fries, candy bars, soft drinks, and doughnuts. Then show pictures of foods that are high in nutrients— fresh vegetables and fruits, dried beans, meats, and dairy products. Point to and review (or have students review) the names of specific foods. Then distinguish which are healthy.

2. Encourage students to use the food vocabulary that they know and to name the foods they eat, either by answering direct questions—"Do you eat meat?"—or by responding in an open-ended way—"Tell about your food"—depending on the abilities of your students.

Extension

Have pairs of students practice the Scene dialogue for the class in one of several ways. Bring in props or costumes to make the activity more interesting.

Option 1: Students can perform the lines as written. You can assign pairs or let students choose their own partners.

Option 2: Students can make a simple substitution in some lines (by inserting dishes from their native countries, for example).

Option 3: More advanced students can ad-lib a conversation on the topic treated in the Scene or imagine they are in the conversation with the characters in the Scene.

Page 42

Sound Bites

Exercise I

Preparation

Ask questions about the pictures in Sound Bites to prepare students for listening. Here are some examples:

- (Number 1) Are they in a restaurant or a movie theater?
- (Number 2) Is he in a store or a restaurant? Where is she?
- (Number 3) Which picture shows fruits and vegetables?
- (Number 4) Is she eating in *a?* Is she eating in *b?*

Presentation

1. Read or replay the Sound Bites. Ask students to circle the sentences they hear in the Sound Bites.
2. Then have them work with a partner and compare answers.

Listening Script

1. They are in a restaurant.
2. Are you ready to order?
3. I like fish and chicken and beef.
4. I don't like fish.

Answers to Exercise I

1. a   2. b   3. b   4. b

Your Turn

Preparation

Read or play the tape of the conversation among Ted, Ava, and the waitress from Scene 1 again. If you have asked students to copy the conversation, have students read their handwritten copy silently as they listen. Otherwise, they can read the conversation in the comic strip on page 41.

Extension

1. Divide the class into three groups with equal numbers of students for dialogue practice. Have one group say Ted's lines, another say Ava's lines, and the third group say the waitress's lines.

2. After practicing in large groups, have students form threesomes for another practice, each threesome with one member from each of the larger groups. (If the large groups are uneven, have the extra students take turns with someone in the threesome.)

Page 43

Spotlight on Simple Present in Affirmative Statements

Preparation

Review the subject pronouns. Group singular and plural pronouns in separate categories.

Presentation

1. Demonstrate the addition of -s or -es in the third person plural form of *eat* and several additional regular verbs. (Use verbs the students have already learned, such as *work, like, buy,* and *miss*.)

2. Demonstrate the changes to form the third person plural in some irregular verbs (*have / has, do / does,* and *try / tries*).

Exercise 2

Extension

1. For students who need additional practice, play a game. Make some large flash cards with the simple form of one of the following previously learned verbs on each one: *buy, babysit, come, check, call, drink, do, fill out, give, get, go, know, live, like, listen, look, miss, open, order, phone, play, read, repeat, see, sit down, sleep, teach, take care of, take turns, try, use, watch out, watch, work.*

2. Sit in a circle. Start by showing a flash card, such as *live,* and saying aloud a subject pronoun, such as *you.*

3. Have the next person in the circle supply the correct form of the verb to match the pronoun you gave, in this case, *you live.* Then have that person supply another pronoun, such as *he.* Then the next person should say *he lives,* and so on, until everyone in the circle has participated.

4. Next, show another verb flash card and continue around the circle again. (Optional competitive version: Set a time limit for play and eliminate from the circle any players who answer incorrectly. When you reach the time limit for play, reward the students who answered correctly and stayed in the circle.)

Answers to Exercise 2

1. works	3. eats	5. tries
2. knows	4. likes	

Exercise 3

Extension

Extend Exercise 3 in one or more of these ways:

 Option 1: Invite some volunteers from the class to write one or two of their sentences on the board.

Option 2: Have your students remove their sentences from their notebooks and hang the papers on a bulletin board for others to read during break or after class.

Option 3: Have students tear the page with their sentences from their notebooks, exchange papers with a partner, read their partner's information, and then use the information to introduce the partner to the class and give personal information about him or her.

Your Turn

Preparation

1. Read the directions aloud. Model the activity by presenting a conversation about different but previously learned foods and drink. For example, write the following on the board or on an overhead transparency:

   Waitress: Are you ready to order?

   Teacher: Yes. I want the **chicken with corn and potatoes.** And I want **tea,** please.

2. Note where you make changes in the conversation to personalize it.

Presentation

1. Assign partners or have students choose a partner.
2. As students work on the activity, check their progress and help those who need it, especially those who need help with spelling.

Extension

Ask pairs to perform their conversation for the class, either live or on an audio- or videocassette tape. (If possible, have people from the class run the video camera, record the performances, and play back the tapes.)

In Your Experience

Presentation

1. Read the directions aloud and model the activity by first using the example given in the directions and then providing another one. For example, say, "I buy beef, potatoes, lettuce, and tomatoes. What do you buy?"
2. Assign groups or have students choose their own groups of three or four.
3. As students talk, circulate among the groups to help those who need prompting.

Workbook

Workbook pages 25 and 26 may be assigned after students have completed page 43.

Spotlight on Simple Present in Negative Statements

Preparation

1. Review the verb *do* and write the conjugation on flipchart paper or on a section of the board you can save.

2. Post the flipchart page for reference or refer students to the board throughout the activities that follow.

Presentation

1. Demonstrate the formation of the negative with other previously learned verbs, such as *buy, like, know,* and *cook.*

2. Emphasize the need to use both the correct form of *do* and *not* in the formation of present tense negatives. For some quick practice, ask students to write the negatives in their notebooks for the following sentences, which you write on the board:

You write:	Students write:
I like fish.	*I do not like fish.*
He cooks beef.	*He does not cook beef.*
They buy bananas.	*They do not buy bananas.*

3. After each example, supply the correct answer for the students to check their work.

4. Continue with additional examples, but ask students to write contractions this time, as shown below.

You write:	*Students write:*
She eats fruit.	She doesn't eat fruit.
You order coffee.	You don't order coffee.
We get vegetables.	We don't get vegetables.

Exercise 5

Extension

Follow up Exercise 5 in one or more of these ways:

Option 1: Invite some volunteers from the class to write one or two of their sentences on the board.

Option 2: Have your students tear their sentences from their notebook and hang the papers on a bulletin board for others to read during break or after class.

Option 3: Have students remove the page with their sentences from their notebooks, exchange papers with a partner, read their partner's information, and then use the information to introduce the partner to the class and give personal information about him or her.

Answers to Exercise 5

Lucy doesn't eat beef. She doesn't like fish. Lucy doesn't order fruit in restaurants. She doesn't cook well, and she doesn't buy good food.

Answers to Exercise 6

Lucy and Bob <u>don't eat</u> beef. They <u>don't like</u> fish. Lucy and Bob <u>don't order</u> fruit in restaurants. They <u>don't cook</u> well, and they <u>don't buy</u> good food.

Answers to Exercise 8

Ray and Pam <u>go</u> to restaurants. They <u>don't like</u> to eat at home. Pam <u>doesn't cook</u> well, but Ray <u>wants</u> to eat good food. In restaurants Ray <u>orders</u> beef, fish, or chicken. He <u>doesn't drink</u> milk. Pam <u>eats</u> fruit or vegetables.

Workbook

Workbook Pages 27 and 28 can be assigned after students have completed page 44.

Page 45

Reading for Real

Preparation

1. Prepare students by asking them to look at the format of the Food Guide Pyramid. Point out the title and explain that the shape is a pyramid.

2. Tell students that the small spaces within the pyramid indicate fewer servings and the large spaces indicate more servings.

3. Point out the names of the food groups and review the food items pictured in each. Have students offer additional vocabulary for foods in each food group.

4. Note that the Food Guide Pyramid shows servings for one person for one day.

Presentation

1. Have students read about Tom and review the Food Guide Pyramid silently. Then read Tom's story aloud to them.

2. Invite questions and clarify meaning as needed.

3. Check understanding before students begin the comprehension exercise by asking questions such as the following:

   • How many servings of beef, chicken, and fish can Tom eat in one day?

   • How many servings of vegetables can he eat?

   • How many servings of fruit can he eat?

Answers to Exercise 9

1. yes   2. no   3. yes   4. yes   5. no

Talk About It

Presentation

Ask the Talk About It questions in large groups or assign small groups to answer them. To encourage students to elaborate, when possible, ask, "How many servings from each group do you eat?"

Activity Masters

Activity Master 5-1 may be completed after page 45.

Presentation

1. Present this information gap after students read the food guide pyramid. Have students work with a partner to ask and answer questions and fill in the charts.

2. Read the instructions to the students. Show how to do the information gap activity by taking the role of partner A and asking a volunteer or student to take the role of partner B. Demonstrate the example.

3. Ask students to find a partner or assign partners. While partners complete the activity, circulate among the students and provide any help necessary.

Culture Corner

Preparation

Show students a real food scale or draw one on the board. Show that a gram is a small measure of weight. Using a diet scale and some shortening or butter, show students the look of approximately 9 grams of fat, 17 grams of fat, and 27 grams of fat.

Presentation

Have students to read the text and the comparison chart silently. Then read it aloud to them. Invite questions and clarify, as needed.

Your Turn

Extension

1. Write the food lists from the two fast food restaurants on the board.

2. By a show of hands, have students vote on whether each food is healthy or unhealthy while you count the votes and write the number beside each food on the list.

3. If the number of votes is close for any given food, ask why, and encourage students to give reasons for their votes. Then take a recount to see if some have changed their minds.

Answers to Your Turn

0–9 grams of fat: Beef Hamburger, Chicken Salad, Broccoli Soup

10–17 grams of fat: Cheeseburger, Chicken Nuggets, Apple Pie

18–27 grams of fat: Large French Fries, Beef Sandwich, Fish Sandwich

Check the healthy foods: Answers will vary.

Scene 2

Preparation

1. Introduce the words *thin* and *overweight*. (The word *overweight* comes up later in the Vocabulary Prompts box on page 49, but it can be taught at this point. When you reach the Vocabulary Prompts, refer students to page 47 again.) You may wish to show photos of people who are thin and people who are overweight.

2. Ask students if they know people who are thin or overweight. Ask students what those people eat.

3. Ask students to think of foods that can make people overweight. Have students think of as many as possible and put the names of those foods on the board.

Presentation

Have students look at the comic strip. Ask questions such as the following:

- Which man is thin?
- Which man is overweight?
- What is Sam eating?
- (In the second picture) does Ted (the other man) look happy or worried?

Activity Masters

Activity Master 5-2 can be completed after page 47.

Part 1

Presentation

1. Read the instructions to the students. Use the example provided to show how to complete the activity.

2. Have students complete the activity individually.

Part 2

Presentation

1. Read the instructions to the students. Use the example provided to show how to complete the activity.

2. Have students complete the activity individually.

3. When students have finished the activity, have them find a partner to practice the conversation with.

Page 48

Spotlight on Simple Present Yes/No Questions and Short Answers

Preparation

Review the present tense of *do* and post the conjugation in a prominent place so students can refer to it during the activities.

Presentation

1. Have students look at the Spotlight box. Demonstrate the forms and position of *do* to make questions.

2. Emphasize the position of the subject pronoun between the conjugated form of *do* and the main verb. Then point out that the main verb is never used with *do* and *don't* in short answers.

3. Practice by asking a few questions with verbs familiar to students and encourage short answers. For example, ask the following questions:

- Do you like cookies?
- Do you buy candy?
- Do you eat potato chips?
- Do you use butter?

4. First practice the questions as a class and then have students ask a partner. Provide prompting as necessary. After students know how their partners answered, refer to the partners and ask the following questions:

- Does he like cookies?
- Does she buy candy?
- Does he eat potato chips?
- Does she use butter?

Encourage a few students to try the same procedure and talk about their partners.

Answers to Exercise 10

1. Do you like beef?
2. Does Sam eat cookies?
3. Do your friends buy too much candy?
4. Does your family cook healthy food?
5. Do you drink milk?

Your Turn

Preparation

1. Model the activity by presenting a conversation about different but previously learned foods. For example, write the following on the board or on an overhead projector:

   Student 1: Do you eat bananas?

   Student 2: Yes, I do.

   Student 1: Do you like candy?

   Student 2: No, I don't. I don't like it.

2. Note where you make changes in the conversation to personalize it.

In Your Experience

Presentation

1. Read the directions aloud and model the activity on the board or overhead projector. Show that the activity is a two-step process of making a list first and then checking the foods with too much fat.

   _____ cola

   ___✓___ potato chips

   ___✓___ french fries

2. Students need to decide within their groups what *too much fat* means to them.

3. Assign students to groups of three or four according to your preference or allow students to choose their groups.

4. Have students use their own paper and pencils or you may wish to provide large pieces of chart paper and markers for them to use.

5. Ask each group to report their opinions and then post their lists around the room for people to see and compare during break or after class.

Get Graphic

Preparation

1. Prepare students for the reading by introducing a bathroom scale for measuring weight and a piece of wooden lath on which you have previously marked feet and inches up to seven feet. Show how these are used to determine pounds, feet, and inches. Also explain that in the United States some people prefer not to tell others their height and weight. Avoid asking students to publicly weigh and measure themselves, but make the scale and lath available in a private area of the building in case students would like to use them during break or after class.

2. Point out that the chart shows three important facts: (1) a person's height, (2) a person's weight, and (3) whether the range is currently considered healthy or overweight. Point out that other charts give different information with respect to healthy weights and that opinions change as doctors learn more.

Answers to Exercise 11

1. overweight   2. healthy   3. Ted and Ava   4. unhealthy

In Your Experience

Preparation

1. Model the activity by making a simple chart on the board or an overhead transparency.

2. Refer students to the Food Guide Pyramid on page 45 for a review of healthy daily food planning.

Presentation

1. Assign groups of three or four students or allow students to choose their own groups.

2. Provide each group with a piece of flipchart paper and a marker.

3. As groups create their plans for Sam, circulate among them, offer help, and give special attention to groups that need help with vocabulary and spelling.

4. Have a representative from each group show their plan to the class and post it on the wall for the class to see and compare with other plans.

Extension

1. Have the class vote for the plan they consider best for Sam. Number the posted plans and have students write the number of the plan each likes best on paper ballots.

2. Ask a committee of three students to count the ballots and identify the preferred food plan.

3. Reward the group that produced the winning plan. Give a healthy food as the reward. For example, give apples, carrots, celery sticks stuffed with peanut butter, or trail mix of dried fruit and nuts.

Page 50

Issues and Answers

Presentation

After students have read the letters, lead a large group discussion to help with reading comprehension. Ask questions such as the following:
- Who has a problem?
- What is the problem?
- What does Anita answer?

Extension

Ask students for their opinions about Anita's answer. Have someone tally the responses on the board where the class can see the count. Add interest by tallying the responses of certain groups separately, such as men versus women, or those under 40 years old versus those over 40, and so forth.

Workbook

Workbook pages 29 and 30 can be assigned after students have completed Student Book page 50.

ANSWERS TO PROGRESS CHECKS

Progress Check A

Speak or Write

1. Ted likes chicken, fish, and beef.
2. Sam needs potato chips, ice cream, butter, and candy.
3. No, Sam doesn't eat healthy foods.

Listen

Alex wants a new job. He fills out an application. He talks to the manager. He has many questions about the job. He wants to know about the pay, the work schedule, the sick days and the vacation days!

1. yes   2. yes   3. no   4. no   5. no   6. yes

Progress Check B

Language Structures

1. Do Ted and Ava go to a restaurant?   Yes, they do.
2. Are they ready to order?   No, they aren't.
3. Does Ted like chicken?   Yes, he does.
4. Does Ava like fish?   No, she doesn't.
5. Do they eat healthy food?   Yes, they do.

Content

1. a. h   b. g   c. e   d. f

2. pasta, vegetables, bread, rice, milk, fruits, potatoes

3. Answers will vary. Some possible answers are hamburger, salads, soups, chicken sandwiches.

ANSWERS TO ACTIVITY MASTERS

Activity Master 5-1

Partner A	Partner B
2. 2–3 servings	1. don't eat many
4. 3–5 servings	3. 2–3 servings
6. 6—11 servings	5. 3–5 servings

Activity Master 5-2

1. beef	4. broccoli
2. milk	5. bread
3. candy	6. fish

Ted: Do you like fish, Ava?

Ava: No, I don't like fish.

Ted: Do you like hamburger?

Ava: No, I like fruits and vegetables.

Ted: You can order the pasta and vegetables.

UNIT 5

WORKBOOK ANSWERS

Practice 1

1. takes   2. babysits   3. likes   4. like   5. reads

6. helps   7. cooks   8. gives   9. want   10. eat

Practice 2

1. work   2. cooks   3. take   4. make   5. eat

6. has   7. go   8. watch   9. answer   10. help

Practice 3

1. doesn't   2. doesn't   3. doesn't   4. don't   5. doesn't   6. don't

Practice 4

1. Isabel doesn't like her job.

2. The company doesn't pay employees much.

3. The manager doesn't give the employees good work schedules.

4. Many employees don't want to work on Sundays, but the manager doesn't listen.

5. Please don't tell the manager, but she's looking for a different job!

Practice 5

1. Nancy   2. Nora   3. People   4. People   5. Nancy

Practice 6

1. Do   2. do   3. Do   4. don't   5. Do   6. do, Does   7. doesn't

Practice 7

1. Does, pay

2. Do, work

3. Do, need

4. Does, give

5. Do, get

REPRODUCIBLE MASTER
UNIT 5

PROGRESS CHECK A

SPEAK OR WRITE

Look at the pictures from Unit 5. Tell or write answers to the questions.

Questions

1. What does Ted like?

2. What does Sam need?

3. Does Sam eat healthy foods?

LISTEN

Listen and check (✓) *yes* or *no*.

	yes	no
1. Alex wants a new job.	_____	_____
2. He has a job application.	_____	_____
3. Alex talks to the workers.	_____	_____
4. He has one question.	_____	_____
5. He wants to know about the food.	_____	_____
6. He wants to know about the pay.	_____	_____

Name _____ Date _____

PROGRESS CHECK B

LANGUAGE STRUCTURES

Write the question. Complete the short answer.

1. Ted and Ava go to a restaurant.

   <u>Do Ted and Ava go to a restaurant?</u> _____

   Yes, <u>they do.</u> _____

2. They are ready to order.

   _____

   No, _____

3. Ted likes chicken.

   _____

   Yes, _____

4. Ava likes fish.

   _____

   No, _____

5. They like healthy food.

   _____

   Yes, _____

CONTENT

1. **Match column A with column B.**

   Column A   **Column B**

   a. beef   _____   e. corn, carrots

   b. sweets   _____   f. apples, oranges

   c. vegetables   _____   g. candy

   d. fruits   _____   h. hamburger

2. **Check (✓) the healthy foods.**

   candy   rice   potato chips   pasta   cookies   milk

   vegetables   French fries   fruits   bread   butter   potatoes

3. **Write three healthy foods to order in a restaurant.**

   a. _____   b. _____   c. _____

HEALTHY FOOD INFORMATION GAP

Healthy eating is planning what to eat every day. Ask a partner about the number of servings for each food. Write the number of servings on the line.

Example: **A:** How many servings of milk and cheese?
            B: Two to three servings.

Partner A

Foods	Servings
sweets, fats	Don't eat many.
milk and cheese	_____
beef, fish, chicken	2–3 servings
vegetables	_____
fruits	3–5 servings
bread, rice, and pasta	_____

✂ -

Healthy eating is planning what to eat every day. Ask a partner about the number of servings for each food. Write the number of servings on the line.

Example: **B:** How many servings of sweets and fats?
            A: Don't eat many.

Partner B

Foods	Servings
sweets, fats	_____
milk and cheese	2–3 servings
beef, fish, chicken	_____
vegetables	3–5 servings
fruits	_____
bread, rice, and pasta	6–11 servings

UNIT 5   ACTIVITY MASTER 5-2

WORKING WITH WORDS

Cross out the word that does not belong.

1. apples	bananas	~~beef~~	fruit
2. peas	vegetables	carrots	milk
3. cheese	candy	milk	ice cream
4. broccoli	fish	beef	chicken
5. cookies	candy	butter	bread
6. pasta	rice	fish	spaghetti

Unscramble the sentences. Write the conversation on the lines.

Ted: fish/Ava?/Do/like/you

_____

Ava: I/No/fish/like/don't

_____

Ted: hamburger?/Do/like/you

_____

Ava: No/vegetables/I/like/fruits/and

_____

Ted: pasta/You/can/the/order/vegetables/and

_____

Practice the conversation with a partner.

TRAVELING BY CAR

OVERVIEW

Objectives

Skills and Structures

Read a map

Make a "top five" list with percentages

Read pie chart with percentages

List car maintenance needs

Make an idea map

Make information questions with *be*

Use introductory *It*

Make information questions with simple present

SCANS Competencies

Allocate money: Student Book, Get Graphic, page 59

Interpret and communicate information: Student Book, Reading for Real, page 55; Student Book, Culture Corner, page 56

Realia

A clock, a calendar, a large U.S. map, and a ruler

Magazines with lots of pictures to be cut out

A road atlas

A color wheel showing basic colors, including black, white, red, green, blue, yellow, and brown

ACTIVITY NOTES

Page 51

Scene 1

Preparation

1. Explain the meaning of the unit title before students talk about the pictures. Show pictures of different kinds of vehicles for car travel—cars, trucks, vans, campers, sport-utility vehicles. Then show pictures of places associated with travel, such as hotels, motels, and campgrounds.

2. Encourage students to use the vocabulary that they know and to name the things that are familiar to them, either by answering direct questions—"Do you stay in hotels?"—or, if your students are advanced enough, by responding to open-ended questions such as "Tell us about your car."

Extension

Have pairs of students practice the Scene conversation for the class in one of several ways. Bring in props or costumes to make the activity more interesting.

Option 1: Students can perform the lines as written. You can assign pairs or let students choose their own partners.

Option 2: Students can make a simple substitution in some lines (by inserting places or roads in their community, for example).

Option 3: More advanced students can ad-lib a conversation on the topic treated in the Scene or imagine they are in the conversation with the characters in the Scene.

Page 52

Sound Bites

Exercise 1

Preparation

Ask questions about the pictures in Sound Bites to prepare students for listening. Here are some examples:

- (Number 1) Are they in a car or on a plane?
- (Number 2) What's the number on the sign?
- (Number 3) Is she happy or angry?
- (Number 4) Is he hot or cold?

Listening Script

1. They're traveling by car.
2. The hotel is on Exit 150
3. The map is hard to read.
4. It's snowing!

Answers to Exercise 1

1. a   2. a   3. a   4. b

Your Turn

Presentation

During the activity read or play the tape of the conversation among Bob, Fran, and their children from Scene 1 again. Have listeners read their hand-written copy silently as they listen. If you have asked students to copy the conversation, have students read their handwritten copy silently as they listen. Otherwise, they can read the conversation in the comic strip on page 52. Read or replay Sound Bites. Ask students to circle the sentences they hear in the Sound Bites and then practice them with a partner.

Extension

1. Divide the class into groups with equal numbers of students for dialogue practice. Have one group say Bob's lines, another group say Fran's lines, a third group say the girl's lines, and a fourth group say the boy's lines. Practice a few times.

2. Rotate parts and practice again. Continue so that each group says each character's lines a few times.

3. Write the conversation on the board. Invite students to change any of the vocabulary but to keep the same meaning. For example, the class could change *hard* to *difficult*. They could also change *read* to *see*.

4. Write the changes in the conversation on the board. When the class has no more changes to suggest, have students copy the new conversation in their notebooks.

5. Invite a few volunteers from the class to use the new conversation to act out the scene.

6. In a multilevel class you may wish to choose from among the following options instead of working with the entire class to make changes to the conversation:

Option 1: In a highly divided class with significant differences in proficiency levels among students, you may wish to group the stronger students separately from the weaker students. The weaker students can simply copy the conversation and then repeat it in groups. You may need to provide extra help with the vocabulary. Use of photographs and realia will be very important. More advanced students can work in a separate group to suggest changes to the conversation.

Option 2: In a class with a high proportion of students who know very little English and a few students who are significantly more advanced, you may wish to have the more advanced students either work in groups with the less advanced students or circulate among the groups as peer tutors.

Page 53

Spotlight on Information Questions with *Be*

Preparation

1. Demonstrate the meaning of each wh- question by using realia and gestures.

2. Use a clock to indicate *hour,* a calendar to for *date/day,* a large U.S. map for *place,* and a ruler for *distance* between points on the map. Use gestures and objects in your classroom to indicate *person, thing,* and *quantity.* Use simple verbal examples such as the following to indicate reason:

   • Hoa is worried. Why is Hoa worried? Because he needs a job.

   • Rita is sleeping today. Why is Rita sleeping today? Because she is sick.

3. Read the examples in the Spotlight box to the students. Ask the following questions as additional examples:

   • (pointing to a picture of yourself) Who is it? It's (your name).

   • (pointing to a picture of an apple) What is it? It's an apple.

   • (pointing to the clock in the classroom) What time is it? It's 2:00 P.M.

   • (pointing to a date on the calendar) When is it? It's Tuesday, February 7.

   • (pointing to a nearby city on the map) Where is it? It's Houston, Texas.

   • (indicating distance between cities with your finger) How far is it? It's 50 miles.

   • (pointing to a tag on an item of clothing) How much is it? It's $25.00.

   • (pointing to a picture of a sick child) She isn't in school. Why? Because she's sick.

4. Show students that forming a wh-question with *be* requires that the question word *be* placed at the front of the construction for a yes/no question. You can convey this idea by using words cards with wh- question words printed on them. Using tape, attach them to the beginning of some yes/no questions you've written on the board. (You may want to review the formation of yes/no questions with *be* at this point.)

Answers to Exercise 2

1. What time is it?
2. Where is it?
3. When is it?
4. Who are they?

Your Turn

Preparation

Make magazines and scissors available for students to cut out pictures to illustrate the questions they write.

Presentation

1. Encourage students to make a drawing if they do not find an appropriate magazine picture to accompany a question.

2. Join pairs to create foursomes. Have them show their pictures or drawings and ask their questions.

Workbook

Workbook pages 31 and 32 may be assigned after students have completed Student Book page 53.

Page 54

Spotlight on Introductory *It*

Preparation

1. Ask students, "Is it cold today?" or "Is it hot today?" Elicit the appropriate answer and write it on the board. Underline *It's.* Then ask, "What day is it today?" Again, elicit the answer and write it on the board. Underline *It's.* Repeat the procedure with the question "What time is it?" (Put a clock on the board and help students with the correct answer if they have trouble.)

2. Give the class further examples, such as the following:
   - It's October 1. (or the real date)
   - It's 46°. (or the real temperature)

3. Review the contraction *it's* if this seems necessary.

Answers to Exercise 3

1. It's Sunday. It's April 12. It's raining.
2. It's Wednesday. It's March 15. It's windy.
3. It's Friday. It's October 2. It's cloudy.
4. It's Tuesday. It's December 22. It's cold.
5. It's Thursday. It's August 4. It's hot.
6. It's Saturday. It's February 28. It's snowing.

In Your Experience

Presentation

1. Read the directions aloud and model the activity.

2. Follow up during class periods over next week.

3. On the same day of the following week, assign groups of three or four to share notes about the weather. Have students decide how the groups' notes are the same and how they are different.

Extension

Collect the notebook pages, trim the margins, and post them beside a calendar of the current month for students to compare during break or before and after class.

Workbook

Workbook pages 33 and 34 may be assigned after students have completed Student Book page 54.

Page 55

Reading for Real

Preparation

1. Prepare students for the reading by introducing the format of the map, with *North* at the top, *East* on the right, *West* on the left, and *South* at the bottom.

2. Point to Highway 61, running north–south, and show the highway exits and the streets of the city, which run east–west.

Presentation

1. Have students read the text and the map silently. Then read them aloud.

2. Check understanding before students begin the written comprehension exercise. For example, ask, "Where is the Dory Motor Inn? What street is Exit 105 on?" and other similar questions.

Answers to Exercise 4

1. yes   2. yes   3. no   4. no   5. no

Extension

1. Write the names of major streets or highways in your area on the board.

2. Assign students to groups of three. Provide each group with pieces of flipchart paper and a marker.

3. Have students draw a simple map of your local area with major streets and highways represented correctly. Tell them to represent correctly *north, south, east,* and *west* on their maps.

4. If possible, have students indicate the school on their maps.

5. Hang the maps for students to compare during break or after class.

Culture Corner

Preparation

1. Review the names of colors on the color wheel you made or brought in. If possible, show light and dark versions of each color. Say the names as you point to the colors.

2. Review the meaning of *percent* by showing that 100 percent means all, 50 percent means half, and 25 percent means a quarter. Have the class stand and group themselves all together for 100 percent. Then have them form two groups equal in number to show that each group represents 50 percent. Then have each of the two groups split again so that each group represents 25 percent.

3. Using a pattern of dots on a piece of flipchart paper, show that 10 percent means 10 of every 100, for example.

4. Ask students about their cars and refer to the color wheel as they answer. Ask questions such as the following:

   • Do you have a car?

   • What color is it?

   • What color car do you like?

Answers to Exercise 5

1. white   2. dark green   3. medium red   4. black   5. light brown

Extension

Have students use the information in the list to find out what percentage of cars in the United States are colors other than the favorites listed. Reward the first student who volunteers the correct answer. Demonstrate the arithmetic used to solve the problem.

Example:

$9 + 15 + 8 + 10 + 18 = 60$

$100 - 60 = 40$

Forty percent of the cars in the United States are colors other than the favorite colors listed in the Top Five list.

In Your Experience

Presentation

1. Tally the favorite car colors of class members. Invite one or more students to volunteer to ask the questions. Have them ask each person in the class.

2. Have each student listen to the oral responses and keep a tally on paper while you keep one on your own paper. Tell students they do not have to own a car in order to contribute their favorite car color.

3. When everyone has answered, invite students to volunteer their tallies, as you record them on the board. Where there is disagreement, have students vote on the correct number or refer to your own tally.

4. Once the tallies are complete, have students tell you how to rank them to show the top five favorite car colors of the students in the class. Post results for the class to review during break or after class.

Scene 2

Extension

To extend the activity, invite volunteers from the class to role play a similar situation between a car mechanic and a customer with a truck that needs new tires. Encourage students to use vocabulary they know, but remind them that it's not important to repeat the dialogue word for word.

Activity Masters

Activity Master 6-1 can be completed after page 57.

Presentation

1. Read the instructions and provide an example by writing this question on the board:

   How far away is the hotel?

2. Cross out the words *how, far, is, the,* and *hotel* in the box. Have students use as many of the words in the box as they can.

3. When you have finished, have students practice asking and answering their questions with a partner.

Spotlight on Simple Present in Information Questions

Preparation

You may wish to use realia and gestures to review the meaning of each type of wh-question. Use a clock to indicate the hour, a calendar for the date and the day, a large map for the place, and a ruler to indicate the distance between points on the map. Use gestures and objects in your classroom to indicate person, thing, and quantity. To indicate reasons, use simple verbal examples such as the following:

- Hoa fills out an application. Why does Hoa fill out an application? Because he needs a job.

- Rita misses her brothers. Why does Rita miss her brothers? Because they live in Mexico.

- Carla worries about her son. Why does Carla worry about her son? Because she reads about drugs in the schools.

Presentation

1. Read the examples in the Spotlight box aloud and give additional examples, if needed.

2. Using word cards, show students that forming a wh- question with simple present requires that the question word be placed at the front of the construction for a yes/no question. Review the formation of yes/no questions with simple present, if needed.

Answers to Exercise 6

1. What does the car need?
2. How much does a new battery cost?
3. When does the mechanic work?
4. Why does the car need a battery?

Your Turn

Presentation

1. Have students volunteer to write their questions for Bob to ask on the board. Have students help the writers correct any errors they have made.
2. Have student pairs voluntarily role-play a mechanic and a customer in front of the class. Customers should use the questions they have written. Mechanics should invent answers.
3. Reward students who perform their role play with a piece of candy, a new pencil or eraser, or a special privilege.

Your Turn

Extension

Have students form pairs with new partners. Each student dictates the conversation he or she wrote in Your Turn as the partner listens and writes it in a notebook. Have partners compare written conversations to make needed corrections. and then have them practice their conversations.

Page 59

Get Graphic

Presentation

1. Review percentages and show that 100 percent means all, 50 percent means half, and so forth.
2. Ask students how many of them have cars, trucks, vans, or sport utility vehicles. Ask what expenses students have. Try to elicit the answers *gas* and *insurance,* among other expenses.
3. Point to the pie graph. Note that all of the percentages add up to 100 percent and that each relates to the dollar amount shown in the legend.

Answers to Exercise 7

1. 1,600.00   2. 400.00   3. 25   4. 20

In Your Experience

Extension

To extend the activity, have a few students volunteer to compile the lists. Have them take care not to duplicate any items. Post the complete list for students to read during break or after class.

Activity Masters

Activity Master 6-2 can be completed after page 59.

Presentation

1. Assign partners or let students choose a partner to practice talking about the weather. Have partners ask and answer questions to fill in the charts.

2. Read the instructions to the students. Show them how to do the information gap activity by taking the role of Partner A and asking a volunteer or student to take the role of Partner B. Demonstrate the example given.

3. Monitor student pairs while they complete the activity.

Page 60

Wrap-Up

Extension

To extend the activity, ask pairs to write and perform a role-playing activity between a customer and a car salesperson. Students can use the questions created in the Wrap Up and add more if they choose. Ask students to include invented answers to the questions in their role play.

Workbook

Workbook pages 35 and 36 can be assigned after students have completed page 60.

ANSWERS TO PROGRESS CHECKS

Progress Check A

Speak or Write

1. The motel is off exit 105.
2. It's hard to read.
3. It needs a new battery.
4. It's only a year old

Listen

The Garcia family goes on vacation. They travel by car. On Monday they stay at the Dory Motor Inn. It's five miles from the highway. The Garcias eat at the motel restaurant. It's a good restaurant. They check out on Tuesday.

1. yes   2. no   3. no   4. yes   5. yes   6. no

Progress Check B

Language Structures

1. Who goes to Denver?
2. When do they go to Denver?
3. Why do they do to Denver?
4. Where does their daughter live? OR Where are they going?
5. How far is the hotel?

Content

1. a. g   b. e   c. f   d. h
2. oil, gas, mechanic, tires, battery, insurance, map
3. Answers will vary. Possible answers include: map, gas, motel/hotel, food, tires, oil, etc.

ANSWERS TO ACTIVITY MASTERS

Activity Master 6-1

Answers will vary.

Activity Master 6-2

Partner A	Partner B
1. 3:00 P.M.	1. 4:00 P.M.
2. 1:00 P.M.	2. 2:00 P.M.
3. 50°	3. 42°
4. 60°	4. 85°

REPRODUCIBLE MASTER
UNIT 6

WORKBOOK ANSWERS

Practice 1
1. What is it?   3. How much is it?

2. How far is it?   4. What time is it?

Practice 3
1. What   2. Where   3. How far   4. Wh

5. When   6. How much   7. How many   8. Why

Practice 5
1. It's 72°.   3. It's raining.   5. It's 5:00 P.M.

2. It's November 12.   4. It's cold.   6. It's Friday.

Practice 6
1. It's Monday.   4. It's 42°.

2. It's March 14.   5. It's windy.

3. It's 9:00 A.M.

Practice 8
1. What time is it in Denver?

2. What's the weather like in San Diego?

3. What's the temperature in Chicago?

4. What's the weather like in Denver?

Practice 9
1. Where does Albert live?

2. How far is it from here?

3. Where does Albert work?

4. What time does Albert work?

UNIT 6

PROGRESS CHECK A

SPEAK OR WRITE

Look at the pictures from Unit 6. Tell or write answers to the questions.

Questions

1. Where's the motel?

2. What's the problem with the map?

3. What's the problem with the car?

4. How old is the battery?

LISTEN

Listen and check (✓) *yes* or *no*.

	yes	no
1. The Garcia family goes on vacation in a car.	_____	_____
2. They stay at the Dory Motor Inn on Tuesday.	_____	_____
3. It's four miles from the highway.	_____	_____
4. The Garcias eat at the motel restaurant.	_____	_____
5. They like the food.	_____	_____
6. They check out on Monday.	_____	_____

Name _____ Date _____

PROGRESS CHECK B

LANGUAGE STRUCTURES

Read about the Garcias. Write questions for each answer.

In June the Garcias go to Denver to visit their daughter.
They stay at a hotel off the highway.

1. Question: _____

   Answer: The Garcias

2. Question: _____

   Answer: In June

3. Question: _____

   Answer: To visit their daughter

4. Question: _____

   Answer: In Denver

5. Question: _____

   Answer: Six miles from the highway

CONTENT

1. **Match Column A with Column B.**

   Column A   **Column B**

   a. It's cold.   _____   e. It's 10:00.

   b. It's 10 o'clock. _____   f. It's 9 P.M.

   c. It's 9 at night. _____   g. It's snowing.

   d. It's hot.   _____   h. It's 90°.

2. **Check (✓) the car expenses.**

   oil   mechanic   battery

   gas   east   north

   south   tires   insurance

   van   west   map

3. **Write three things you need when you travel by car.**

   a. _____ b. _____ c. _____

REPRODUCIBLE MASTER
UNIT 6
ACTIVITY MASTER 6-1

USING QUESTION WORDS

Write 6 questions to ask when you travel by car.

who	motel	how much
stays	the	van
goes	what	car	when
has	is	truck
how far	why	what time
highway	mechanic	oil	eat
tires	battery	cost	a

1. _____

2. _____

3. _____

4. _____

5. _____

6. _____

Ask and answer the questions with a partner.

ACTIVITY MASTER 6-2

WEATHER INFORMATION GAP

**Look at the map. Read the weather chart.
Ask a partner about the time, temperature, and
weather in different cities.**

Example: **A:** What time is it in Chicago?
             B: It's 3:00 P.M.

Partner A
Friday,

October 19	Boston	Chicago	Denver	San Diego
Time	4:00 P.M.	1. 3:00 P.M.	2:00 P.M.	2. _____
Temperature	3. _____	42°	4. _____	85°
Weather	5. _____	windy	6. _____	hot

✂ -

**Look at the map. Read the weather chart.
Ask a partner about the time, temperature and
weather in different cities.**

Example: **A:** What time is it in Boston?
             B: It's 4:00 P.M.

Partner B
Friday,

October 19	Boston	Chicago	Denver	San Diego
Time	1. 4:00 P.M.	3:00 P.M.	2. _____	1:00 P.M.
Temperature	50°	3. _____	60°	4. _____
Weather	cloudy	5. _____	raining	6. _____

OVERVIEW

Objectives

Skills and Structures

Read "How to Ask for a Raise"

Talk about the minimum wage

Read a skills chart

Talk about the skills you want to learn

Tell what you think

Make an idea map

Use *can* statements

Use *can* in yes/no questions and short answers

Use prepositions of time

SCANS Competencies

Allocate human resources: Student Book, Get Graphic, page 69

Exercise leadership: Student Book, Issues and Answers, page 70

Realia

A photo of a fax machine

Several window envelopes with invoices inside

A computer keyboard and a picture of a computer system

A phone

A calculator

An office memo

Several file folders in a file box

ACTIVITY NOTES

Page 61

Scene 1

Preparation

1. Explain the meaning of the unit title before students talk about the pictures. Show pictures or drawings of workers receiving paychecks. Show a drawing of a paycheck made out to a fictitious person. Then show a picture or drawing of a paycheck dated two weeks later, made out to the same person, and for a bigger dollar amount. Explain that the worker did not work more hours—he got a raise.

2. Explain that many Americans do not like to tell others the amount of their paychecks. Without discussing the amount of money students make on the job, encourage them to talk about when they get a raise at work., either by answering direct questions—"Do you get a raise after one year?"—or, if your students are advanced enough, by responding to open-ended questions such as "Tell us about your raises at work."

Sound Bites

Preparation

To prepare students for listening, ask questions such as the following:

- (Number 1) In which picture are the husband and wife talking?
- (Number 2) Are they eating, or are they working?
- (Number 3) Which person is a clerk, and which person is a mechanic?
- (Number 4) How many months are there?

Listening Script

1. They're talking about bills.
2. Bills, bills, and more bills. How can we pay them?
3. You're a good office clerk.
4. I can't ask for a raise after just 6 months on the job.

Answers to Exercise 1

1. a   2. a   3. b   4. b.

Your Turn

Extension

1. Divide the class into groups of men and women for dialogue practice.
2. Have the men say Carl's lines and the women say Molly's lines.
3. Provide props (some bills in envelopes) and ask for two volunteers (one man and one woman) to act out the conversation for the class.
4. Trade roles. Have the men read Molly's lines and the women read Carl's lines several times, as if Molly were the office clerk who needs a raise.

   Molly: Bills, bills, and more bills! How can we pay them all, Carl?

   Carl: Well, you're a good office clerk. Can you ask for a raise?

   Molly: No, I can't ask for a raise after just 6 months on the job!

   Carl: Why not?

5. Have students work in pairs to write a conversation in which they substitute other words they know for some of the vocabulary in the original. For example, a pair may write the following:

   - Expenses, expenses, expenses! What can we do Molly?
   - I can't ask for a raise after just 6 weeks at the hotel.

6. Have volunteers from the class perform their new conversations for the class. Reward the performers with a small bag of popcorn, a pocket folder, or another inexpensive item of your choosing.

Spotlight on *Can* in Affirmative and Negative Statements

Presentation

1. Point that, in sentences with *can*, the third-person singular form of the simple verb does not add *-s* or *-es*.

2. Create some quick oral practice by asking students some of the questions below and eliciting the answer "Yes, I can" or "No, I can't."

   • Can you cook? Can you plan healthy food for a week?

   • Can you take care of a car? Can you plan car expenses for a year?

   • Can you babysit? Can you take care of children and play with them?

   • Can you work in a factory? Can you make a product for people to buy?

3. Have students write one question using *can*.

4. Have the class listen as volunteers from the class ask their question to another class member.

Answers to Exercise 3

1. can   2. can   3. can   4. can't   6. can't

Your Turn

To extend the practice, have students write six complete sentences in their notebooks about what Roy can and can't do, then check with a partner to correct.

Workbook

Workbook pages 37 and 38 may be assigned after students have completed page 63.

Spotlight on *Can* in Yes/No Questions and Short Answers

Presentation

1. Show the reversed position of the subject pronoun and *can* in questions. Use word cards taped to the board and reverse their position to show the formation of the questions in the Spotlight box.

2. Give additional examples of question formation, such as these two:

   • Wanda can help customers. Can Wanda help customers?

   • Richard and Judy can fax. Can Richard and Judy fax?

Answers to Exercise 5

1. Can, she can   2. Can, she can
3. Can, she can   4. Can, she can't

Your Turn

Extension

1. Have each pair write their names on the conversation they write and then put 2 copies of it into a box. Have each person in the class draw out one of the copies and find a new partner who has the same conversation.

2. Have each new pair practice the conversation they drew from the box and present it to another pair of students. Credit the authors of the conversations as they are performed.

Workbook

Workbook pages 39 and 40 may be assigned after students have completed page 64.

Reading for Real

Preparation

1. Prepare students for the reading by calling for a show of hands on (1) the number of students who have asked for a raise at work and (2) those who actually got the raise. Encourage them to tell the class how they asked for a raise.

2. Show the format of a "how to" list by pointing out the bullets and explaining that they begin each new piece of information. Read the title aloud.

Presentation

1. Have students read the short text and the *How to* list silently. Then read these sections to students.

2. Invite questions, and clarify as needed.

3. Check comprehension before students begin the written exercise. For example, ask questions such as the following:

   • Who can you talk to about a raise?

   • When can you ask for a raise?

   • What can you say?

4. Ask the Talk About It questions in large groups or assign small groups to answer them. Encourage students to elaborate, when possible, by asking, "How long do you need to work at a job to ask for a raise?"

Answers to Exercise 6

1. no   2. no   3. yes   4. no   5. yes

Talk About It

Extension

1. Assign students to groups of three or four classmates or allow students to choose their own groups.

2. Have each group write one more item for the How to Ask for a Raise list. Members might write something like either of the following:
   - Ask after a year of experience at your job.
   - Talk about your good work for the company.

3. Have representatives from each group write their additional item to a list on the board or an overhead transparency.

4. Have students copy the extended list in their notebooks.

Page 66

Culture Corner

Preparation

Explain that the President gives Congress the idea for a new minimum wage. (In your explanation use the name of the current President.) Congress votes. Then Congress tells businesses how much to pay workers. The businesses pay the workers. When the workers want more money again, they ask the President for a raise.

Extension

Have students circle the years in which the largest increase in the minimum wage occurred. Then have them circle the years when the smallest increases occurred.

Answers to Exercise 7

1. $.50   2. $.50   3. $.85   4. $1.00   5. $2.05

In Your Experience

Presentation

1. Assign groups of three or more, or allow students to choose a group.

2. Ask each group to choose a recorder to write down the group's answers and a reporter to tell them to the class.

3. Read the directions aloud and model the activity.

4. Circulate among the groups to offer help, as needed.

5. In three areas of the board, write the responses of each group as given by the reporters. One area is for *minimum wage now,* another for *why the minimum wage is or isn't good pay,* and the third for the *amount the minimum wage needs to be.*

Scene 2

Preparation

1. Ask working students at what moments they talk to their supervisor in the United States. Ask if they feel that they can go into their supervisor's office and talk about issues that are important to them. Explain that Americans often talk to their direct supervisors. (Of course, in many blue-collar jobs such communication may be more difficult.)

2. Survey students to see if they find differences between the situation in their native countries and the situation in the United States. Have students talk about the topics they can discuss with supervisors in the United States and in their native countries. Put the topics on the board and discuss any cultural differences that arise.

Activity Masters

Activity Master 7-1 can be completed after page 67.

Part I

Presentation

1. Read the directions to the students. Then explain how the example is completed. In this exercise, the verbs are listed in the first box in each item. Have students read the three words in the other boxes and cross out the one that does not make sense after a particular verb.

2. Have students complete the exercise individually.

Part 2

Presentation

1. Read the instructions to students. Provide an example of a sentence about an office skill that a person may want to learn, such as *I want to learn to write memos.*

2. Have students complete the activity individually. Then read sentences to a partner as follow up.

Spotlight on Prepositions of Time

Presentation

1. Provide plenty of pronunciation practice to help students hear and say *on* and *in* clearly and distinctly.

2. Provide oral practice by asking the following questions and encouraging answers that use prepositions of time.

3. When do you come to school?

4. When does your (husband, wife, brother, etc.) work?

5. When is the next school vacation?

6. When do you watch TV?

7. When do you go to work?

Answers to Exercise 8

1. On   2. at   3. at   4. in   5. in   6. in   7. in

Your Turn

Extension

1. Ask each partner about the date of his or her partner's birthday. For example, ask, "When is Alma's birthday?"

2. As students answer, write their names and birthdays on a list. Provide each member of the class with a photocopy of the list.

3. Each month, assign a pair or threesome to make birthday cards for class members who have birthdays that month.

Page 69

Get Graphic

Preparation

1. Be sure the vocabulary is clear to students by presenting realia whenever possible. Show a computer keyboard and a picture of a computer system, a phone, a calculator, and so forth. If your school has a copy machine and a fax, take the students to their locations and demonstrate how to use them.

2. Show the format of a checklist by reading the headings aloud and pointing to the skills that are listed along the left side.

Answers to Exercise 10

1. calculator

2. copy machine, memos

3. computer, supplies

4. skills

In Your Experience

Extension

On the board make another chart. Head the chart columns *Skills to learn* and *Places to learn.* Under each heading write the skills and the places to learn more skills in the community, as students complete that portion of the activity.

Activity Masters

Activity Master 7-2 can be completed after page 69.

Presentation

1. The purpose of this activity is to practice asking and answering questions using Yes/No short answers. Students focus on listening skills and grammar by working in pairs.

2. Cut the page on the dotted line. Ask students to work with a partner. One gets the Partner A half and the other gets the Partner B half.

3. Read the instructions to students. Model the example given with a volunteer or student. Note that Partner A says, "Number 1. Can you work on weekends?" Partner B writes *1* on the line next to *No, on weekdays.* Then, Partner A checks *No.* To ensure that students understand the activity, have students repeat the example in the first item.

Issues and Answers

Presentation

Be sure each student has ample opportunity in his or her group to really tell give an opinion of Abdul's answer. Ask, "Can you use Abdul's ideas where you work?"

Workbook

Workbook pages 41 and 42 can be assigned after students have completed page 70.

ANSWERS TO PROGRESS CHECKS

Progress Check A

Speak or Write

1. He has bills, bills, and more bills.

2. He's an office clerk.

3. No, he doesn't.

4. Classes are on the weekends.

Listen

Andrew works in a drug store now. He likes the job, but it pays only minimum wage. He needs a raise to pay his bills. Andrew asks the store manager for a raise. Andrew is looking for another job. He wants to work in a doctor's office. The office needs a clerk. Andrew doesn't have office experience, but he is learning some new skills at college.

1. yes   2. yes   3. no   4. no   5. yes   6. no

Progress Check B

Language Structures

1. on   2. at, in   3. at   4. At   5. on, in   6. in

Content

1. a. f *or* e   b. h   c. g   d. e

2. use a computer, write memos, order supplies, use a calculator, answer phones

3. Possible answers:

   Talk to your supervisor.

   Ask in the right place.

   Ask at the right time.

   Talk about your job skills.

ANSWERS TO ACTIVITY MASTERS

Activity Master 7-1

Part 1

1. keyboard
2. copy machine
3. computers
4. customer
5. manager
6. memo
7. managers

Part 2

Answers may vary.

Activity Master 7-2

Answers for Student A may vary. Possible answers include:

Student A	Student B
1. No	5
2. Yes	3
3. No	1
4. Yes	6
5. Yes	4
6. Yes	2

REPRODUCIBLE MASTER
UNIT 7

WORKBOOK ANSWERS

Practice 2
1. can   2. can   3. can't   4. can

5. can   6. can't   7. can   8. can't

Practice 3
1. can   2. can   3. can   4. can't   5. can't

Practice 4
Type: *can*   Use computer programs: *can*

Answer phones: *can*   Fax: *can*

Write memos: *can't*   Order supplies: *can't*

File: *can*

Practice 5
1. Can Kathy type?, she can

2. Can she file?, she can

3. Can she write memos?, she can't

4. Can she use computer programs?, she can

5. Can Kathy order supplies?, she can't

Practice 8
1. Can you type?

2. Can you use any computer programs?

3. Can you fax?

4. Can you use a copy machine?

Practice 9
1. c   2. b.   3. d   4. a

Practice 10
1. on   2. on   3. at   4. at   5. at   6. At   7. on   8. at   9. at

Practice 13
1. We cook at 10:00 in the morning.

2. We eat a big dinner at 2:00 in the afternoon.

3. We watch TV at 7:00 in the evening.

4. We drive home at 10:00 at night.

Name _____ Date _____

REPRODUCIBLE MASTER
UNIT 7

PROGRESS CHECK A

SPEAK OR WRITE

Look at the pictures from Unit 7. Tell or write answers to the questions.

Questions

1. What is Carl's problem?

2. What is Carl's job?

3. Does Carl have computer skills?

4. When are classes at North Community College?

LISTEN

Listen and check (✓) *yes* or *no*.

	yes	no
1. Andrew works in a drugstore.	_____	_____
2. He needs a raise to pay bills.	_____	_____
3. Andrew doesn't ask for a raise.	_____	_____
4. Andrew has office experience.	_____	_____
5. The office needs a clerk.	_____	_____
6. Andrew can't learn new skills.	_____	_____

PROGRESS CHECK B

LANGUAGE STRUCTURES

Complete the sentences with *on*, *in*, and *at*.

1. Andrew works _____ Saturdays.

2. He goes to work _____ 8:00 _____ the morning.

3. He has lunch _____ noon.

4. _____ 5:00 he goes home.

5. Working _____ weekends is difficult _____ July.

6. Andrew's friends take vacations _____ July.

CONTENT

1. Match Column A with Column B.

Column A	Column B
a. sort the _____	e. memos
b. talk to _____	f. mail
c. use the _____	g. computer
d. write the _____	h. customers

2. Check (✓) the office jobs.

use a computer	use a calculator
order food	fix cars
write memos	write menus
clean rooms	answer phones
order supplies	visit friends

3. What do you do when you ask for a raise? Write three things.

a. _____

b. _____

c. _____

UNIT 7   ACTIVITY MASTER 7-1

WORKING WITH WORDS

Part 1

Cross out one word that doesn't belong.

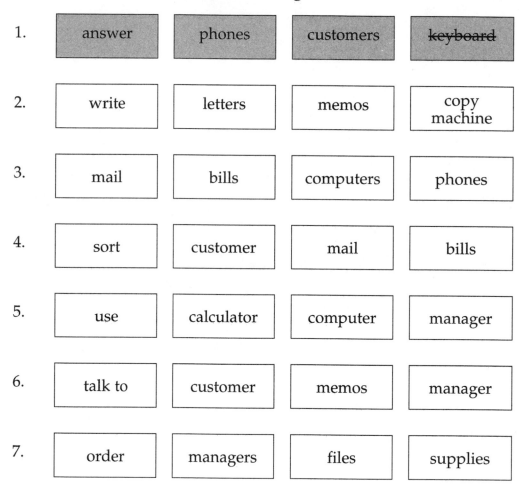

1. answer	phones	customers	~~keyboard~~
2. write	letters	memos	copy machine
3. mail	bills	computers	phones
4. sort	customer	mail	bills
5. use	calculator	computer	manager
6. talk to	customer	memos	manager
7. order	managers	files	supplies

Part 2

Use the words above to write four sentences about office skills you want to learn.

1. _____

2. _____

3. _____

4. _____

REPRODUCIBLE MASTER
UNIT 7   ACTIVITY MASTER 7-2

QUESTIONS AND ANSWERS

Ask your partner the questions. Listen and check (✓) *yes* or *no*.

Example: **A:** Number 1. Can you work on weekends?
                  B: No, on weekdays.
                  A: yes   no
                  _____   ____✓____

                                                          yes   **no**

1. Can you work on weekends?   _____   _____

2. Can Carl use a calculator?   _____   _____

3. Does he use a computer?   _____   _____

4. Does he file and fax?   _____   _____

5. Does the college have weekend classes?   _____   _____

6. Does Carl work nights?   _____   _____

✂ -

Listen to the question. Give an answer from the list.
Write the number of the question on the line.

Example: **A:** Number 1. Can you work on weekends?
                  B: _____ No, on weekdays.

_____   Yes, it does.

_____   No, he doesn't.

_____   No, on weekdays.

_____   No, days.

_____   Yes, he does.

_____   Yes, he can.

WATCHING TV

OVERVIEW

Objectives

Skills and Structures

Read a TV program guide

Make a Top Three List of favorite cable channels

Read chart of averages

Write the number of hours a week I watch TV

Make an idea map

Use past tense of *be* in affirmative statements

Use past tense of *be* in negative statements

Use past tense of *be* in yes/no questions and short answers

SCANS Competencies

Acquire and evaluate information: Student Book, Reading for Real, page 75; Student Book, Get Graphic, page 79

Realia

Pictures or drawings of baseball, basketball, football, hockey, and soccer games and players

A football

A *TV Guide* or program guide from a local Sunday newspaper

ACTIVITY NOTES

Page 71

Scene 1

Preparation

1. Explain the meaning of the unit title before students talk about the pictures. Show pictures or drawings of people watching television. Include pictures or drawings of TV screens with different types of programming—sports, cartoons, news, dramas, and so on. Show a football and explain that football is the number one sport on TV in the United States.

2. Explain that conversations about TV programs and sports are common among co-workers in the United States. Encourage students to talk about their experiences with TV in this country, either by answering direct questions—"Do you watch TV on Sunday evening?"—or, if your students are advanced enough, by responding to open-ended questions, such as "Tell us about watching TV in the United States."

Extension

1. Provide each pair of students with a copy of the conversation cut as a strip story. To make the strip story, hand print or type the conversation, with each sentence of the conversation on a separate line but in scrambled order. Make one copy for each pair of students. Have students cut their copy of the conversation into strips, one line of dialogue on each strip. Make a strip story on an overhead transparency or large strips of chart paper so that you can model the activity easily. Using an overhead projector or chart paper with tape, model the process of putting the lines of dialogue in the correct order. Then tell pairs to recreate the conversation with their copies of the strip story.

2. You may also wish to have pairs of students role-play the Scene for the class in one of several ways. Bring in props or costumes to make the activity more interesting.

Option 1: Students can perform the lines as written. You can assign pairs or let students choose their own partners.

Option 2: Students can make a simple substitution in some lines (by inserting the name of their own school, for example).

Option 3: More advanced students can ad-lib a conversation about sports or imagine they are in the conversation with the characters in the Scene.

Page 72

Sound Bites

Exercise 1

Preparation

Ask questions about the pictures in Sound Bites to prepare students for listening. Here are some examples:

- (Number 1) Is the nurse working or resting?
- (Number 2) What is on TV?
- (Number 3) Are they at home or in a movie theater?
- (Number 4) Is she happy or angry?

Listening Script

1. They are on break at work.
2. The football game was on yesterday.
3. We weren't home.
4. My wife doesn't like football.

Answers to Exercise 1

1. b   2. a   3. a   4. a

Activity Masters

Activity Master 8-1 can be completed after page 72.

Preparation

Show students the model for a Venn diagram on the board. Tell students that they will compare sports in their countries with sports in the United States.

Presentation

1. Read the instructions to students. Give an example for Mexico on the board. Draw two circles that overlap. Title the circles as shown on the master.

2. Write the word *football* in the first circle, *soccer* in the middle, overlapping area, and *jai alai* in the second circle. When the example is complete, point to each part of the circles and show that you are listing sports in the United States, in both countries, and in students' native countries.

3. Have students complete the activity individually or in small groups of two to four students from the same cultural background. When they have completed their work, students can compare Venn diagrams with those of another small group.

Page 73

Spotlight on Past of *Be* in Affirmative Statements

Preparation

1. On the board write the words *home, school,* and *work,* in a horizontal row. Just to the left of these words, in a vertical column running down the side of the board, write *yesterday, last week,* and a day of the week of your choice.

2. Point to the word *yesterday.* Ask individual students where they were. Were they home, at school, or at work? Or all three? Accept even one-word answers. Point out that *be* has two different forms in the past tense, *was* and *were.*

3. Create a quick listening exercise. Give each student one red and one green index card. Tell students to show the green index card when they hear past tense and the red card when they hear present tense. Demonstrate with sentence 1 from the story below. Then read the remaining sentences at normal tone and speed, with one repetition:

   - It was July.
   - It is Saturday.
   - The weather is hot.
   - My sister is home.
   - Her children were home too.
   - The baseball game was on TV.
   - The game was on for three hours.
   - The San Diego team is in Denver.
   - It was a good game.
   - The score was 12–10.

4. Dictate the sentences to the class as they write them in their notebooks. Then write the sentences on the board so they can check their work.

5. Have students change the present verbs to past by crossing them out and writing in the correct forms.

Answers to Exercise 2

1. were   2. was   3. was   4. was   5. was   6. were

Answers to Exercise 3

1. It *was* Saturday.
2. Amir, Fatima, and their children *were* at home.
3. Amir *was* in the garage.
4. He *was* busy with the car.
5. Fatima *was* in the house.
6. She *was* busy in her home office.
7. The children *were* in front of the TV.
8. They *were* happy to watch a soccer game.

Your Turn

Extension

1. Have each pair record its new conversation on an audiotape. You can use the same tape for all the conversations. Have the pairs record one after another at a tape recorder set up in a corner of the room or in the hallway.

2. Play the entire tape for the class. As they listen, have them write as much information as they can on a sheet of their own paper. Suggest the following chart format:

	City	Temperature	Weather	Sport
pair 1				
pair 2				
pair 3				

3. Reward the person with the most correct information. Give the student a blank picture postcard of your area to send to someone back home.

In Your Experience

Preparation

Model the activity by answering the questions in the directions. For example, say the following:

"Yesterday, I was at home. It was 5:08. It was windy. I was very busy. It was a good day for me."

Presentation

1. Assign groups or have students choose their own groups of three or four.
2. As students talk, circulate among the groups to help those who need prompting.

Workbook

Workbook pages 45 and 46 may be assigned after students have completed page 73.

Spotlight on Past of *Be* in Negative Statements

Preparation

1. Create a quick listening exercise. Read the following story to the class at normal tone and speed. Repeat it as many times as students want.

   Jose wasn't home yesterday. He was in Chicago. It was windy in Chicago, but it wasn't cold. José wasn't in Chicago for a vacation. He was there to work for his team, the Florida Marlins. The Marlins were in Chicago to play baseball. They were ready for a hard game. It was a good day for them. The score was Florida 8, Chicago 5.

2. Hand out a red and green index card to each student. Tell them to show the green card for *yes* and the red card for *no*, to show their agreement or disagreement with the following statements:

   - José was home yesterday.
   - He wasn't in Florida.
   - He was in Chicago for a vacation.
   - He was part of the Florida team.
   - Chicago was windy and cold.
   - The Marlins weren't ready for the game.
   - It was a good day for them.
   - They were happy with the score.

3. Write the story on the board for students to copy in their notebooks.

Answers to Exercise 4

1. weren't   2. wasn't   3. wasn't   4. wasn't   5. wasn't   6. weren't

Answers to Exercise 5

1. It <u>wasn't</u> a good day for Alex yesterday.
2. It <u>wasn't</u> sunny.
3. He <u>wasn't</u> happy about the weather.
4. At work, the manager <u>wasn't</u> happy because the waiters <u>weren't</u> ready to take food orders at 12:00 noon.
5. And the customers <u>weren't</u> happy because the service <u>wasn't</u> fast and the food <u>wasn't</u> good!

Reading for Real

Preparation

1. Prepare students for the reading by showing a TV Guide or a program guide from your local Sunday newspaper. Ask for a show of hands of people who have used a program guide to choose a TV program. If any have used one, encourage them to tell the class about the experience and what information they got from the program guide.

2. Show the format of a prime time grid by pointing out the channel numbers on the left and the length of each program according to the times across the top.

Presentation

1. Have students read the short text and the program guide silently. Then read these sections aloud to students.

2. Invite questions and clarify as needed.

3. Check understanding before students begin the written comprehension exercise. For example, ask questions such as the following:
   - What's on Channel 2 at 9:00?
   - What channel teaches English on TV?
   - What time is NBC News?

Extension

1. Assign groups of three or four, or allow students to choose a group.

2. Have groups work together to write a list of TV programs they watch. Then have the group choose a program from their list to find in the program guide.

3. Have representatives from each group use the program guide to find the TV listing they chose. If possible, photocopy the page to show the group.

Answers to Exercise 6

1. no   2. no   3. no   4. no   5. yes

Page 76

Culture Corner

Preparation

Bring a TV set connected with cable into the room or show a video tape you've made at home or at a friend's house with a sampling of the program offerings on ESPN, CNN, and TBS. Ask students to name the type of shows (e.g., *sports, news, movies*) they see on each of these channels as you tune to it.

Extension

Have students stand and silently find all others in the room with the same Top Three list as theirs. In order to do this, they will have to show their lists and read to compare. When all students have grouped themselves, ask a representative from each group—in descending order with the largest group first—announce their Top Three list to the other class members.

In Your Experience

Presentation

1. Lead the class in the activity at the overhead projector or board. Read the directions aloud and use the example question in the text to model the activity. Ask the question and encourage students to answer with a show of hands. Write the number of responses in the *Answer* column.

2. Encourage students to write the remaining questions privately on their own paper and then read to them aloud so that you can write them on the overhead.

3. Have a person from the class ask the questions aloud. Have another student count the show of hands for each one and tally the responses on the board or overhead transparency.

Page 77

Scene 2

Preparation

1. Begin by asking questions such as the following:
   - Do you like sports?
   - Do you have cable TV at home?
   - Do you talk about sports with your co-workers, classmates, or friends?
   - Do you discuss movies with your co-workers, classmates, or friends?
   - What do people like to watch on TV in your native country?
2. Review the words *cable* and *score*.

Activity Masters

Activity Master 8-2 can be completed after page 77.

Preparation

1. Read the instructions for the first step to the students. In a natural tone and speed, dictate each of the following items twice:

   baseball   5:00 P.M.   TV   football   soccer   hockey   basketball   5:00 A.M.   score

2. After you say each word, have students choose a square and write the word inside that square. In order to ensure that students choose squares at random, you may need to show how Student A chose one square and Student B chose a different square for the same vocabulary item. At the completion of the dictation, each student will have a different bingo card.

3. Read directions for step 2. Write the words on the board in a list. Students should find the words on their cards and correct the spelling if needed.

4. Read the directions for step three. Provide students with markers such as paper clips, buttons, or pennies. Then present each of the items below by using a picture, realia, or a verbal clue. If you use a picture, don't say the word. Students mark the items as they are presented. When one student has marked three squares in a row, he or she says, "Bingo!"

Teacher Cue	Vocabulary Item
5:00 in the morning	5:00 A.M.
picture or baseball realia	baseball
picture or basketball realia	basketball
six to one	score
picture or football realia	football
picture or soccer realia	soccer
5:00 in the afternoon	5:00 P.M.
picture or TV realia	TV

5. Because students have different bingo cards, this game can be played more than once with the same student-created cards.

Spotlight on Past of *Be* in Yes/No Questions and Short Answers

Preparation

Choose a student from the class and ask whether he or she was at school (or at home) yesterday afternoon. Emphasize *yesterday afternoon* and accept a plain yes or no answer. Repeat the student's answer and ask the same question of a second student. Then write the questions and the answers on the board with complete short answers. Have other students answer the same question.

Answers to Exercise 8

1. Was, was   2. Were, were   3. Was, wasn't   4. Was, was

Your Turn

Presentation

1. Read the directions aloud and model the first item on a chart you have created on an overhead projector or board.

2. Assign partners, or have students choose a partner and work together to complete the chart. When students are finished, have them share their chart with another pair.

Get Graphic

Preparation

Prepare the students for the reading by clarifying the meaning of *Weekday evenings before 10:00 P.M.* and *Weekend evenings before 10:00 P.M.* Review both A.M. and P.M.

Presentation

1. During the activity, have students first read the short text and chart silently. Then read them aloud. Invite questions about vocabulary and clarify as needed. Model item 1 in the matching exercise.

2. After students complete item 2, have them check for the correct answer. Provide the answer or have students check with a partner.

Answers to Exercise 10

1. 1½ hours   2. 2 hours   3. 5 hours   4. 5½ hours

In Your Experience

Extension

1. Write the following sentence stems on the overhead projector or board:

   - On weekdays I watch . . .
   - On weekends, I watch . . .
   - To practice English, I watch . . .

2. Have each student begin with a half sheet of lined paper. Tell students to complete the sentences with their own information. Circulate among them to provide help as needed.

3. Have class members form groups of three and read their statements aloud to one another.

4. Collect the papers and post them on the wall or bulletin board for all to read during a break or after class.

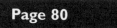

Wrap-Up

Extension

1. Ask students to keep a chart for one week of TV programs they watch. Provide this T-chart format.

Good Programs	So-so Programs

2. At the end of the week, have students check (✓) the programs that were in English.

3. Collect the charts and post them for all to see during a break or after class.

Workbook

Workbook pages 47 and 48 may be assigned after students have completed page 80.

ANSWERS FOR PROGRESS CHECKS

Progress Check A

Speak or Write

1. Yes, it was. 2. No, he wasn't. 3. He watched two great movies.

Listen

Bart was at work yesterday in the video store. It was a hard day. The store was busy. Many of the movies were out. Some customers weren't happy. Their favorite movies were in the homes of other customers. It wasn't a happy day for the customers or for Bart!
1. yes 2. no 3. no 4. yes 5. yes 6. no

Progress Check B

Language Structures

1. was, Was, wasn't

2. Were, were, were

3. Was, was, was

Content

1. a. h   b. e   c. g   d. f
2. baseball, basketball, soccer, hockey, football
3. Answers vary.

   time or hour, channel, day, program

ANSWERS FOR ACTIVITY MASTERS

Activity Master 8-1

Answers will vary.

Activity Master 8-2

Answers will vary.

REPRODUCIBLE MASTER
UNIT 8

WORKBOOK ANSWERS

Practice 1
1. was   2. was   3. was   4. was   5. was   6. were

7. Were   8. was   9. were   10. were   11. was

Practice 2
1. no   2. no   3. yes   4. no   5. no

Practice 4
It was June. Cheryl was on vacation with her friend Julie. They were in Mexico. Their hotel was big, with beautiful grounds and a nice restaurant. But it wasn't expensive. The weather was sunny. It was 84°. They were at a soccer game. The team was their favorite. This was a good place for their vacation!

Practice 6
1. I wasn't home last night.

2. The hockey game wasn't on TV.

3. My favorite team wasn't in the game.

4. It wasn't a good game.

Practice 7
1. was   2. weren't   3. were   4. was   5. wasn't

Practice 10
It was November in Boston. It was cloudy and rainy. Driving was difficult. Mirella was in her car. She was on the highway. She was going to her brother's new office, but she wasn't at the right exit. Her map was hard to read, and her car was behind a big truck!

Practice 11
1. Was Mirella in Boston?

2. Was it sunny?

3. Was it rainy?

4. Was she at the right exit?

5. Was the map hard to read?

6. Was the car behind a big truck?

UNIT 8

PROGRESS CHECK A

SPEAK OR WRITE

Look at the pictures from Unit 8. Tell or write answers to the questions.

Questions

1. Was the game on TV yesterday?

2. Was José at the game yesterday?

3. What did José watch on TV?

LISTEN

Listen and check (✓) *yes* or *no*.

	yes	no
1. Bart was at work yesterday.	_____	_____
2. He works in a movie theater.	_____	_____
3. It was an easy day.	_____	_____
4. Some customers were upset.	_____	_____
5. Many of the movies were out.	_____	_____
6. It was a happy day.	_____	_____

UNIT 8   PROGRESS CHECK B

LANGUAGE STRUCTURES

Complete the sentences with *was, wasn't, were,* **and** *weren't.*

1. The clerk _____ in the office yesterday.

   _____ he happy to be at work? No, he _____.

2. _____ the students at school on Saturday?

   Yes, they _____. They _____ at a football game.

3. _____ Susan at home last night?

   Yes, she _____. She _____ sick in bed.

CONTENT

1. Match Column A with Column B.

Column A	Column B
a. soap	e. show
b. talk	f. guide
c. cable	g. TV
d. program	h. opera

2. Check (✓) the names of team sports.

cartoon	talk show	hockey
baseball	comedy	drama
basketball	soccer	football

3. Name three things you can find in a program guide.

   a. _____

   b. _____

   c. _____

REPRODUCIBLE MASTER
UNIT 8

ACTIVITY MASTER 8-1

SPORTS HERE AND THERE

Compare U.S. sports with sports in your home country. In one circle
list U.S. sports. In the other circle list sports in your native country.
In the middle, list sports in the United States and in your country.

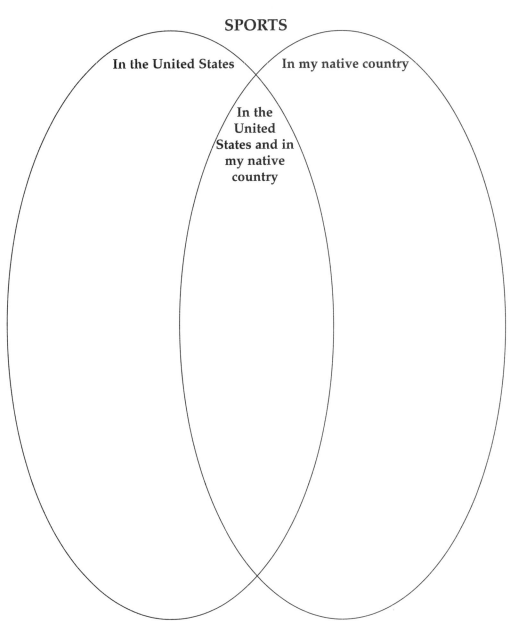

SPORTS

In the United States

In my native country

In the
United
States and in
my native
country

With a partner talk about how sports are different and how they are
the same.

REPRODUCIBLE MASTER
UNIT 8

ACTIVITY MASTER 8-2

CLASS BINGO

1. **Make the bingo card.**

   Listen to the teacher say a word.

   Write the word in any square.

2. **Check your words.**

3. **Play bingo.**

   The teacher reads a definition or shows a picture.

   Watch and listen. Mark the square.

   Bingo is five squares in a row.

WOMEN OF CHANGE

OVERVIEW

Objectives

Skills and Structures

Read a table of contents

Read about Mary Lyon

Read a time line

Make a time line

Tell what you think

Use simple past in affirmative statements

Use simple past in negative statements.

Use simple past in questions

SCANS Competencies

Organize and maintain information: Student Book, Get Graphic, page 89

Understand systems: Student Book, Reading for Real, page 85

Realia

Pictures or drawings of planes and pilots

Social studies textbooks (to show their tables of contents, for example)

Pictures of Mary Lyon, Susan B. Anthony, Amelia Earhart, and Maya Angelou (look in the women's history section of your library or on the Internet)

A brochure from your local League of Women Voters

Photographs of a GED diploma and a high school diploma or a real sample of each

ACTIVITY NOTES

Page 81

Scene 1

Preparation

1. Explain the meaning of the unit title before students talk about the pictures. Show pictures or drawings of women working at traditional and nontraditional jobs. Include pictures of women (You can find these at your local library in the women's history section: Lyon, Earhart, Anthony, and Angelou among others, such as Rosa Parks, Geraldine Ferraro, and Sally Ride) whose work has contributed to cultural change in the United States.

2. Using simple language, explain the difference between a GED and a high school diploma (and, if possible, show real samples or photographs of each). For example, say, "Many Americans go to high school. Some study very well. After high school they get a diploma from the school. Some students have problems and they don't finish. They can study at home and get a diploma from their state. A GED is a diploma from the state." Encourage the students to talk about their experiences with secondary school, either in the United States or a home country, by answering direct questions—such as "How many years did you go to school?"—or, if your students are advanced enough, by responding to open-ended questions such as "Tell about your experience with high school."

Extension

Have pairs of students practice the Scene conversation for the class in one of several ways. Bring in props or costumes to make the activity more interesting.

 Option 1: Students can perform the lines as written. You can assign pairs or let students choose their own partners.

Option 2: Students can make a simple substitution in some lines (by inserting places or roads in their community, for example).

Option 3: More advanced students can ad-lib a conversation on the topic treated in the Scene or imagine they are in the conversation with the characters in the Scene.

Option 4: With a mixed class with a significant number of more advanced students, put the phrase list below on the board or an overhead projector. Tell students to recreate (in their notebooks) the conversation from the phrase list below. Model the activity by choosing two listed phrases to create the first sentence—*Good news, Alicia*—on the board. Tell students they can work together if they like, and encourage the lower-level students to seek help from other students informally, without an assigned partner. Encourage the more advanced students to help the less advanced students. Have them check their books to correct their work when they finish.

Phrase List

and I didn't finish	my GED test	I wanted
I passed	is great	you're smart!
good news	great	Donna!
to study history	why not study	in college
yesterday!	your English	high school
but	Alicia	now?

Page 82

Sound Bites

Exercise 1

Preparation

Have students look at the pictures. Point to each picture and ask questions to elicit the differences between the pictures in each pair. Here are some examples:

- (Number 1) Are they working or relaxing?
- (Number 2) In which picture does she have her GED diploma?
- (Number 3) In which picture is she still studying?
- (Number 4) Is she happy or sad about her English?

Listening Script

1. They're talking about going to school.
2. Good news! I passed the GED test!
3. I didn't finish high school.
4. Your English is great, and you're smart.

Answers to Exercise 1

1. b   2. b   3. b   4. b

Your Turn

Extension

1. Write the conversation on the board. Underline the words in the conversation as shown below.

   <u>Good</u> news, Alicia. I passed my GED test yesterday!

   <u>Great</u>, Donna! I wanted to study <u>history</u> in college. But I didn't finish high school.

   Why not study now? Your English is <u>great</u>, and you're <u>smart</u>!

2. Lead the class in changing as many of the underlined words in the conversation as possible and encourage students to find alternative vocabulary that keeps the basic meaning of each sentence intact. Ask students to contribute ideas for interchangeable vocabulary words, such as *great* and *good*. Also, have them contribute any known vocabulary they have heard outside of class, maybe *wonderful* or *fine*. As students contribute, the new conversation might look something like the following:

   Great news, Alicia. I passed my GED test yesterday.

   Wonderful, Donna! I wanted to study the past in college, but I didn't finish high school.

   Why not study now? Your English is very good, and you're intelligent!

3. Tell students to copy the new version of the conversation in their notebooks. Then have them practice the new conversation twice with a partner of their choosing and trade roles after the first time through.

Page 83

Spotlight on Simple Past in Affirmative Statements

Presentation

1. Explain the difference between regular verbs (those that take *-ed* to form the past) and irregular verbs (those that do not add *-ed* to form the past).

2. Help students practice the correct pronunciation of the irregular verbs listed in the Spotlight box. Then, on the board write the following list of regular verbs—grouped according to the pronunciation of final *-ed* (/t/, /d/, or /id/)—and help students practice the correct pronunciation:

   asked   finished   helped   liked   passed   talked

   watched   worked   filled out   ordered   wanted   started

Answers to Exercise 2

1. wanted 2. talked 3. asked 4. helped 5. worked 6. passed 7. finished

Exercise 3

Extension

1. Play Pronunciation Baseball. Have the class form two teams with equal numbers of people. Decide on the location of the *bases, home plate,* and the *pitcher's mound* in your classroom.

2. Have each team prepare for the game by writing both regular and irregular verbs of their choosing on 4" x 12" cards. Each team should make at least 15 cards.

3. For this game, only the pitcher is on the field. Have each team choose a pitcher and give him the cards. Determine which team pitches first by the toss of a coin. Have the pitcher from the team that wins the coin toss get into position on the pitcher's mound. All other players line up with their teams on opposite sides of the room.

4. As a player from the opposite team comes to bat at home plate, the pitcher on the mound shows a word card. The batter must pronounce the word correctly in order to move to first base. Mispronounced words count as strikes. Three strikes and a player is out (moves to the back of the team's line). After three outs, the pitcher from the other team goes to the mound and play continues with the other team at bat. Teams score by moving around the bases and crossing home plate.

5. The teacher acts as both umpire and scorekeeper. Play continues for as many innings as the class wishes. The words cards are repeated often, and many students get a chance to try the same pronunciation.

6. Reward the winning team members with baseball cards, bubble gum, or something similar.

Answers to Exercise 3

1. wanted 2. asked 3. helped 4. talked 5. answered 6. started 7. liked

Your Turn

Extension

1. Have each pair perform its new conversation for the class while another student records and photographs them on a video camcorder, if available. If one is not available, use a cassette tape recorder.

2. Play the video tape for the class. If the class wants to see the tape again, make the tape and TV monitor available to those who come early to the next class period.

Workbook

Workbook pages 49 and 50 can be assigned after students have completed page 83.

Spotlight on Simple Past in Negative Statements

Presentation

Contrast the formation of negative statements with *be* and the simple past. Note that all verbs except *be* take *did* to form the negative past. Provide clear examples such as the following:

Past of *Be:*	I wasn't happy in school.
	They weren't ready for college.
Past of Other Verbs:	I didn't finish high school.
	They didn't go to college.

Answers to Exercise 4

1. didn't finish   2. didn't like   3. didn't want
4. didn't learn   5. didn't study   6. didn't pass

Answers to Exercise 5

1. didn't go   2. didn't have   3. didn't get   4. didn't eat   5. didn't go.

In Your Experience

Presentation

1. Model the activity by answering the questions in the directions. Here are some examples:

   • I didn't go to class because I was sick.

   • I didn't go to school because I didn't have a babysitter.

2. As students write their answers, circulate among them and pay close attention to those with low literacy skills. Provide help as needed.

3. Ask students to read their sentences aloud to the whole class or to groups of three or four students.

Workbook

Workbook pages 51 and 52 can be assigned after students have completed page 84.

Reading for Real

Preparation

1. Prepare students for the reading by having them open their books to the table of contents. Whether or not you have looked at this table of contents with students at the beginning of the course, tell students that you are going to study (or learn more about how to use) this one. First ask for a show of hands of people who already have used a table of contents to choose a reading selection or find a page. If some have, ask when they used it, and encourage them to tell the class what information they got from the table of contents.

2. Show the format of a table of contents by pointing out the chapter numbers, chapter titles, and page numbers in the table of contents of the Student Book, because most tables of contents are a variation of this one.

Presentation

1. Have students read the short text and the table of contents silently. Then read them aloud to students.

2. Invite questions and clarify as needed.

3. Check comprehension before students begin the written exercise. For example, ask questions such as the following:

   • Where can you read about Susan B. Anthony?

   • What is Maya Angelou's job?

   • When did Mary Lyon live?

Answers to Exercise 6

1. no   2. yes   3. yes   4. no   5. yes

Activity Masters

Activity Master 9-1 can be completed after page 85.

Presentation

1. Students design a table of contents for a book about great women. This activity allows for practice reading a table of contents and acts as an interest inventory. Students tell what subjects they would like to study that are related to the unit topic. Read the instructions to students. Demonstrate the instructions by doing one example on the board or making a transparency of Master 9-1. Write the chapter number, name and page. The number of pages students choose for each chapter should show how much interest they have in each area of study. Try to demonstrate this in your example.

2. Students may complete the activity with a partner or in groups of three. When the work is completed, students can share with another pair or group.

3. An extension of this activity can be to ask students to create a table of contents for other books. Here are a few suggestions:

   • A Great English as a Second Language Book

   • Great Men of the World

   • My Country

Page 86

Culture Corner

Preparation

Invite students to talk about great men and women in the histories of their home countries. Then show a picture of Mary Lyon, which you can obtain one from a women's history book or an encyclopedia. Copy it onto an overhead transparency or enlarge it, if necessary. Ask pre-reading questions that will help students make predictions about the reading. For example, using a picture of Lyon dressed in period clothing and in her office setting, you could ask the questions below. Students can guess the answers to the questions or tell what they think is true.

- When did Mary Lyon live?
- Where did Mary Lyon work?
- What was her job?

Extension

Have four students volunteer to write their answers on the board. Ask the class members to suggest any needed corrections (such as capitalization, spelling, and punctuation) in addition to details from the story. Allow the author of each sentence to make the corrections he or she believes are necessary.

Answers to Culture Corner

1. People wanted women to stay home with the children.
2. In 1800, women did not learn math and science.
3. In 1837 Mary Lyon started Mount Holyoke, a college for women.
4. Women studied English, math, history, and science at Mount Holyoke.

In Your Experience

Presentation

1. Assign partners or allow students to choose a partner.
2. Read the directions aloud and model the activity.
3. Circulate among the students and answer any questions they may have.
4. Ask a partner from each pair to contribute an answer for each question as you write them on the board or overhead projector.

Page 87

Activity Masters

Activity Master 9-2 can be completed after page 87.

Presentation

1. Read the instructions for item 1 to students. Point out the example with the word *law*.
2. Students should complete the word search independently. However, some students may benefit from working with a partner. The word search can be done as a timed activity or a race between two teams.
3. Read the directions for items 2 and 3. Ask students to name school subjects. Give an example of a sentence containing the subject *English*. Give an example of a question with *health* and *study*.
4. Have students complete the sentences independently. Check their progress. Offer assistance when needed. In these free writing exercises, there is no need to expect perfect spelling or grammar. Students need a chance to express themselves freely and try to write comprehensible sentences.
5. Students may read their sentences and questions aloud after completing the exercise.

Spotlight on Simple Past Yes/No Questions, Short Answers, and Information Questions

Answers to Exercise 7

1. Did you buy food today?

2. Did you study at home today?

3. Did you pay the bills?

4. Did you cook dinner?

Answers to Exercise 8

Where did David go yesterday?

What did David learn?

Why did he study verbs at home?

Who came home?

When did she come home?

What did they cook?

Who helped him study irregular verbs?

Get Graphic

Preparation

Prepare the students for the reading by showing a simple time line of classroom activities such as the following:

6:30	7:30	7:40	8:30
class starts	break starts	break finishes	students go home

Exercise 9

Presentation

1. Have students read the short text and the time line silently. Then read these sections aloud to students. Invite questions about vocabulary and clarify as needed.

2. Read the directions aloud and model the first item in the matching exercise.

3. After students complete the second item, have them check for the correct answer. You can provide the answer, or students can check with a partner.

Answers to Exercise 9

1. 1820   2. women   3. died   4. 1851

In Your Experience

Presentation

1. Provide large sheets of flipchart paper or rolled newsprint and markers for students. Provide yardsticks or meter sticks to use as straightedges.

2. Read the directions and model the activity for students by using your life events as an example. Post your time line on the wall or board so that students can use it as a reference.

3. Invite students to talk about their life activities and jobs as you write them on the board. Leave these for students to use as a reference.

4. Circulate among students as they work. Assist with spelling, vocabulary, or other problems as needed.

5. Have volunteers post their time lines on the wall with masking tape. Ask students to tell the class about their lives and use their time lines as visual references.

Issues and Answers

Presentation

1. Be sure all students have ample opportunity in their groups to tell what they really think of Anita's answer.

2. Lead the class in answering the second question. Ask, "What other things can 'Sorry' do now?" Students may offer answers such as the following:

   - Listen to the radio.
   - Read magazines.

3. Record their answers on the board or on an overhead transparency.

Workbook

Workbook pages 53 and 54 can be assigned after students have completed page 90.

ANSWERS TO PROGRESS CHECKS

Progress Check A

Speak or Write

1. No, Donna passed the GED test yesterday.

2. No, she didn't.

3. Donna studied today.

4. Donna didn't buy food today.

Listen

Gary had a job, but he didn't make much money. He asked the manager for a raise. She listened, but she didn't answer. And she didn't give Gary a raise! So Gary looked for another job.

1. yes   2. no   3. yes   4. no   5. no   6. yes

Progress Check B

Language Structures

1. Did Donna pass the GED test yesterday? , she did.

2. Did Donna and Alicia talk about school? , they did

3. Did Tom want to buy food today? , he didn't.

4. Did you want to study English? , I did.

Content

1. a. f   b. h   c. e   d. g

2. math, English, science, art, history

3. Here are some possible answers: worked for the vote, started schools, improved education, law, politics, health, business

ANSWERS TO ACTIVITY MASTERS

Activity Master 9-1

Answers will vary.

Activity Master 9-2

1.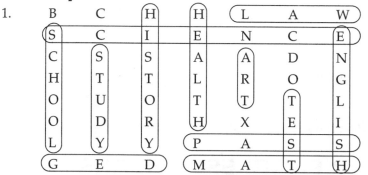

2. Students should write five sentences with the names of school subjects.

3. Students should write two sentences using the words listed.

WORKBOOK ANSWERS

Practice 1
1. was   2. wanted   3. called 4. asked   5. went   6. got   7. cooked
8. had   9. came   10. loved   11. talked   12. went

Practice 4
1. Susan B. Anthony
2. Mary Lyon
3. Susan B. Anthony
4. Susan B. Anthony
5. Mary Lyon
6. Susan B. Anthony

Practice 5
1. Susan B. Anthony was born in 1820.

2. Susan B. Anthony started a newspaper in 1868.

3. Susan B. Anthony died in 1906.

4. Mary Lyon died in 1849.

5. A new law allowed women to vote in 1920.

6. Mary Lyon was born in 1797.

7. Mary Lyon opened a college in 1837.

Practice 6
1. didn't go
2. didn't have
3. didn't have
4. didn't want
5. didn't like
6. didn't get
7. didn't take
8. didn't finish
9. didn't get

Practice 9
1. didn't see
2. didn't come
3. didn't want
4. didn't miss
5. didn't work
6. didn't have

Practice 10
1. didn't come
2. didn't open
3. didn't help
4. didn't talk
5. didn't write
6. didn't close

Practice 11
1. wanted   2. had   3. listened   4. didn't give

Unit 9

WORKBOOK ANSWERS

Practice 12

1. Did Gary have a job? , he did

2. Did Gary make much money? , he didn't

3. Did he ask for a raise? , he did

4. Did the manage listen to Gary? , she did

5. Did the manager give Gary a raise? , she didn't

Practice 13

1. did, want

2. did, help

3. did, go

4. did, study

5. did, finish

© NTC/Contemporary Publishing Group, Inc.

REPRODUCIBLE MASTER
UNIT 9

PROGRESS CHECK A

SPEAK OR WRITE

Look at the pictures from Unit 9. Tell or write answers to the questions.

Questions

1. Did Donna pass the GED test today?

2. Did Alicia finish high school?

3. What did Donna do today?

4. What didn't Donna do today?

LISTEN

Listen and check (✓) *yes* **or** *no*.

	yes	no
1. Gary didn't make much money.	_____	_____
2. Gary asked a co-worker for a raise.	_____	_____
3. The manager listened.	_____	_____
4. The manager answered.	_____	_____
5. Gary got a raise.	_____	_____
6. Gary looked for another job.	_____	_____

Name _____ Date _____

PROGRESS CHECK B

LANGUAGE STRUCTURES

Write the question. Complete the short answer.

1. Donna passed the GED test yesterday.

   _____

   Yes, _____.

2. Donna and Alicia talked about school.

   _____

   No, _____.

3. Tom wanted to buy food today. _____

   _____

   No, _____.

4. You wanted to study English.

   _____

   Yes, _____.

CONTENT

1. **Match Column A with Column B.**

   Column A   **Column B**

   a. Mary Lyon   _____   e. pilot

   b. Susan B. Anthony   _____   f. teacher

   c. Amelia Earhart   _____   g. poet

   d. Maya Angelou   _____   h. worker for the vote

2. **List two ways women changed history.**

   a. _____

   b. _____

ACTIVITY MASTER 9-1

MAKING A TABLE OF CONTENTS

A table of contents is in the front of a book. A table of contents tells chapters and page numbers. On a separate sheet of paper, make a table of contents for the book *Great Women of the World*.

1. What chapters do you want in the book?
   Use chapters from the box. Number the chapters.

2. How many pages do you want for the chapters?
   Write the page numbers.

Women in Education	Women in Business
Women in Law	Women in Health
Women in Politics	Women in Poetry

Example

Great Women of the World

Table of Contents

Women in Poetry	1
Women in Law	12
Women in Education	27
Women in Health	39
Women in Politics	52
Women in Business	73

UNIT 9

ACTIVITY MASTER 9-2

WORD SEARCH

1. **Find these words in the box below. Circle the words.**

history	health	test	study
science	math	pass	GED
English	art	law	school

B	C	H	H	(L	A	W)
S	C	I	E	N	C	E
C	S	S	A	A	D	N
H	T	T	L	R	O	G
O	U	O	T	T	T	L
O	D	R	H	X	E	I
L	Y	Y	P	A	S	S
G	E	D	M	A	T	H

2. **Write sentences with the school subjects from the box above.**

    a. _____

    b. _____

    c. _____

    d. _____

    e. _____

3. **Write two questions with these words:**

    school   study   pass   test

    _____

    _____

© NTC/Contemporary Publishing Group, Inc.

CARDS AND MACHINES

OVERVIEW

Objectives

Skills and Structures

Read steps for using a phone card

Read about smart cards

Read a bar graph

Ask about phone cards and make a T-chart

Make an idea map about computers

Use future with *going to* in statements

Use future with *going to* in questions

Use compound sentences

SCANS Competencies

Monitor and correct performance: Workbook, Spotlight on Future with *Going to* in Statements, page 55; Workbook, Future with *Going to* in Yes/No Questions, Short Answers, and Information Questions, page 57

Teach others: Student Book, Spotlight on Compound Sentences, page 98

Realia

Pictures or drawings of a rotary phone and a touch-tone phone

A pre-paid phone card from a local store

Photographs of computer chips and computerized scanners that read bar codes, magnetic strips, and other coded information

Various types of cards used for payment or delivery of coded information, such as major credit cards, a hotel key card, and a grocery discount card

Credit cards for local stores and credit card application forms

ACTIVITY NOTES

Page 91

Scene 1

Preparation

1. Explain the meaning of the unit title before students talk about the pictures. Show pictures or drawings of people using cards for payment. Include pictures of major credit cards, key cards, grocery discount cards, and encoded medical insurance cards.

2. Using simple language, explain how machines read the information from the magnetic strip on the card or from a bar code printed in the plastic. Encourage students to talk about their experiences with cards by answering direct questions—such as "Do you have a credit card?"—or, if your students are advanced enough, by responding to open-ended questions, such as "Tell us about your experience with cards."

Extension

Have pairs of students practice the Scene conversation for the class in one of several ways. Bring in props or costumes to make the activity more interesting.

Option 1: Students can perform the lines as written. You can assign pairs or let students choose their own partners.

Option 2: Students can make a simple substitution in some lines (by inserting places or roads in their community, for example).

Option 3: More advanced students can ad-lib a conversation on the topic treated in the Scene or imagine they are in the conversation with the characters in the Scene.

Page 92

Sound Bites

Exercise 1

Preparation

Ask questions about the pictures in Sound Bites to prepare students for listening. Here are some examples:

- (Number 1) Do you see a father and a daughter or a mother and a daughter?
- (Number 2) Does the father have a card, or does he have money?
- (Number 3) Is she with her friends, or is she talking on the phone?
- (Number 4) Is she talking to her mother, or is she talking to her father?

Listening Script

1. The father and his daughter are talking.
2. This is a phone card to use in Cancun.
3. I'm going to call my friends.
4. When are you going to call your father?

Answers to Exercise 1

1. a   2. a   3. b   4. b

Your Turn

Extension

1. Write the conversation on the board and turn it into a cloze passage by omitting every third word. Write a blank for each omitted word in the conversation, as shown here:

   Marisol, this _____ a long-_____ phone card _____ use in _____.

   Thanks, Dad! _____ going to _____ my friends _____ and in _____ City.

   And _____ are you _____ to call _____?

   Oh, I'm _____ going to _____ you, Dad.

2. Ask students to write the conversation on their own paper (with their books closed), filling in the blanks with the correct words. Model the activity by filling in the first blank (*is*). Tell them they can ask another person for help, if necessary. Allow them to freely request assistance from other students without formally assigning a partner.

3. Have students check their work by referring to the conversation in the textbook and making any necessary corrections.

Page 93

Spotlight on Future with *Going to* in Statements

Preparation

1. Have volunteers from the class come up and write the schedule for the next week's classes on the board. Have them begin by writing all of the days of the week on the board. Then ask students questions such as the following:

   - When is the next class?

   - Are we going to have class next (Tuesday)?

2. Have the volunteers mark the days that you are going to have class. On the board write the stem "We are going to have class _____." Then have a volunteer read the chart and say which days students are going to have class.

3. Write another stem in the negative: "We are not going to have class _____." Have another volunteer say which days you are not going to have class.

Presentation

1. Have students look at the Spotlight box. Guide them through the structures. Make sure that students understand that *going to* does not change. With more advanced students you may wish to introduce *gonna*, but less advanced students may find this confusing.

2. Have students look back at the comic strip conversation on page 91 and pick out all of the instances in which *going to* is used.

Answers to Exercise 3

1. is going to go	3. are going to see	5. isn't going to have
2. is going to stay	4. isn't going to study	

Your Turn

Extension

1. Invite students to volunteer, or choose students by lottery to perform their conversations for the other students in the class. (To choose by lottery, determine the number of pairs that will perform. Then write the numbers from one through your determined number on small pieces of paper and place them in a box. Have one student from each pair draw out a number from the box. Student pairs will perform in the order they drew.)

2. After all the pairs have performed their conversations, ask them to vote by show of hands for the conversation they liked best. Ask one of the winners to write that pair's conversation on the board for other students to copy into their notebooks.

3. Reward the winning pair with calendars, rulers, or other prizes of your choice.

4. In a multilevel class you may wish to choose from among the following options instead of working with the entire class to make changes to the conversation:

 **Option 1:** In a highly divided class with significant differences in proficiency levels among students, you may wish to group the stronger students separately from the weaker students. The weaker students can simply copy the conversation and then repeat it in groups. You may need to provide extra help with the vocabulary. Use of photographs and realia will be very important. More advanced students can work in a separate group to suggest changes to the conversation.

Option 2: In a class with a high proportion of students who know very little English and a few students who are significantly more advanced, you may wish to have the more advanced students either work in groups with the less advanced students or have them circulate among the groups as peer tutors.

Workbook

Workbook pages 55 and 56 can be assigned after students have completed page 93.

Page 94

Answers to Exercise 4

1. Is Marisol going to go to Mexico?
2. Is she going to stay with her sister?
3. Are they going to visit their friends?
4. Is she going to have a job?

Answers to Exercise 5

1. When is she going to go?
2. Where is she going to stay?
3. Who are they going to see?

Workbook

Workbook pages 57 and 58 can be assigned after students have completed page 94.

Page 95

Reading for Real

Preparation

1. Prepare students for the reading by showing a phone card and an enlarged copy or drawing of the instructions that appear on the back. Ask for a show of hands of people who have used a phone card to call long distance. If some have, ask when they used it and where they called. Encourage them to tell the class the steps involved in the process.

2. Ask students if anyone knows what a PIN number is. Have a volunteer explain to the class or tell students, if no one knows, that it is a personal number for the person who owns the card and that card users keep their PIN numbers secret so that no one else can use their cards.

3. Show the format of instructional steps by pointing out the sequential order on the left and the instructions on the right.

Presentation

1. Have students read the short text and the PhoneCard easy steps silently. Then read the steps aloud to them.

2. Invite questions and clarify as needed.

3. Check comprehension before students begin the written exercise. For example, ask questions such as the following:

   - What is the first step?
   - What number do you give in the second step?
   - When do you need an area code?

Answers to Exercise 6

1. yes   2. no   3. no   4. no   5. no

Page 96

Culture Corner

Preparation

Show the class a picture of a computer chip and talk about how chips work. You can obtain a picture from a magazine or download one from an Internet source. Copy it onto an overhead transparency or enlarge it, if necessary. Ask pre-reading questions to help students make predictions about the reading. For example, ask questions such as the following and have students make guesses about the answers:

- Where do people put computer chips?
- What information do computer chips have?
- What helps people get information from computer chips?

Extension

Have students tally their responses on the board. When you finish, ask the class to suggest why smart cards will or won't help or why people aren't sure, according to the majority of responses to each statement. Students will probably not be able to give complete reasons, but you can assist them in making simple statements about their reasoning. Students may offer ideas such as the following:

- Smart cards aren't going to help people get more jobs because computers do some jobs that people did before.
- Smart cards are going to help people who want fast service because computers give information fast.

Answers to Your Turn

1. Smart cards are going to help.
2. Smart cards aren't going to help.
3. Smart cards are going to help.
4. Smart cards are going to help.
5. Smart cards aren't going to help.

In Your Experience

Presentation

1. Assign groups of three or allow students to choose their own groups. Ask each group to choose a recorder.

2. Provide an overhead transparency prepared with the chart structure and a transparency marker to each recorder. If you don't have an overhead projector, you can use chart paper and markers.

3. Read the directions aloud and model the activity. Ask the recorders to write their group's responses on the transparency.

4. Circulate among the students to offer help, if needed, as they work.

5. Have a representative from each group show their chart on the overhead projector. Tell students to watch for and report on the differences between how men and women in the class use the cards.

6. After showing all the transparencies, ask the following questions:

   - Who uses cards and machines more—men or women?

   - Who wants to use cards and machines more in the future—men or women?

7. Have students give reasons for their answers and discuss them with the class.

Page 97

Scene 2

Preparation

1. Ask questions about banks. Here are some example:
   - How do you get money out of the bank?
   - Do you usually go into a bank?
   - Do you have any bank cards?

2. Have students talk about the difference between a credit card and an ATM (Automatic Teller Machine) card. (In Vocabulary Prompts there is a drawing of an ATM card and an ATM machine. You may wish to refer to this picture at this point.)

3. Ask students if they can buy things with an ATM card; explain that ATM cards are used only for taking money out of the bank. (However, students may also know about debit cards, which are special ATM cards that allow customers to pay directly from a checking or savings account; no bill is received.) Explain that credit cards allow customers to buy now and pay later and that a customer can spend up to a specific amount of money (the customer's *credit line*).

Activity Masters

Activity Master 10-1 can be completed after page 97.

Presentation

1. The purpose of this activity is to practice yes/no questions and short answers. Working in pairs, students focus on listening skills and grammar skills. Cut the page on the dotted line. Ask students to work with a partner. One gets the *Partner A* half and the other gets the *Partner B* half.

2. Read the instructions to students and use the example to show how to complete the activity. Take Part B and ask a student to take Part A for the example.

3. Partner A says, "Number 1. Are you going to study at school?" Partner B writes *1* on the line next to *Yes, I am.* Then Partner A checks *Yes.* To ensure understanding, have students repeat the example in the first item.

Page 98

Answers to Exercise 7

1. Daniel wants to go to Canada, and he plans to visit his family.
2. He can stay with his father, or he can stay with his sister.
3. He wants to drive his car, but the car needs new tires.
4. He can go to Canada, and he can buy new tires.

Page 99

Get Graphic

Preparation

Prepare the students for the reading by showing them a simple bar graph of student nationalities. For example, make a bar graph on the board that looks something like the following:

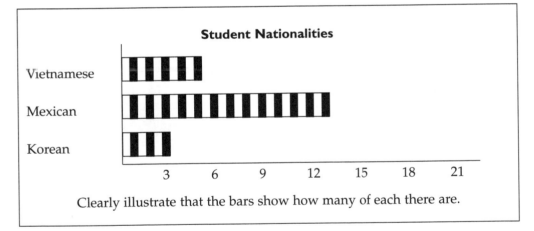

Clearly illustrate that the bars show how many of each there are.

Presentation

First have students read the short text and the bar graph silently. Then read them aloud. Invite questions about vocabulary and clarify as needed.

Exercise 8

Presentation

1. Read the directions aloud and model the first item in the matching exercise.
2. After students complete the second item, have them check for the correct answer. You can provide the answer or students can check with a partner.

Answers to Exercise 8

1. $1.25   2. $3.75   3. $1.50   4. $4.25

In Your Experience

Extension

1. Write the following sentence stems on the overhead projector or the board:

   I call _____ because _____.

   I talk for _____.

   I pay for the calls with _____.

2. Have students tear a half sheet of paper from their notebooks. Tell them to complete the sentences with the information they gave their group. Circulate among them to provide help as needed.

3. Collect the papers and post them on the wall or bulletin board for all to read during a break or after class.

Page 100

Wrap-Up

Extension

1. Provide half sheets of flipchart paper and a marker to each person.

2. Tell students to choose one idea from the idea map and make a drawing to show the future scene.

3. Have them write a sentence appropriate to their drawing under their picture. Model the activity. For example, the statement "Computers, not clerks, are going to help customers in some stores" is appropriate under a picture of a machine that is issuing a product to a customer (a simple drawing with stick figures).

4. Post the pictures on the walls or bulletin boards for all to see during a break or after class.

Workbook

Workbook pages 59 and 60 can be assigned after students have completed page 100.

Activity Masters

Activity Master 10-2 can be completed after page 100.

Presentation

1. Read the instructions to the students. Show how to complete the activity by asking the three questions of one student and recording his or her responses.

2. Check student progress during the pair work. Note that the focus in student interviews is on communication, not form or spelling.

ANSWERS TO PROGRESS CHECKS

Progress Check A

Speak or Write

1. He's giving her a phone card.
2. She's going to call from Cancún.
3. The other card is an ATM card.
3. No, she can't.

Listen

Sandra is going on vacation for a week. She's going by car to New York City with her husband, Ed. They aren't going to stay in hotels. They are going to stay with their daughter, Tracy. They are going to see the city and visit their friends. Sandra and Ed want to start their vacation tomorrow!

1. yes   2. no   3. no   4. yes   5. yes   6. no

Progress Check B

Language Structures

1. Marisol has a phone card, and she is getting an ATM card.
2. Marisol has an ATM card, but she doesn't know how to use it.
3. She's going to call her friends, and she's not going to forget her father.
4. She's going to use a rotary phone, or she's going to get a touch-tone phone.
5. They're going to Mexico, but they're not going with friends.

Content

1. a. h   b. e   c. f   d. g
2. Answers will vary. some possible answers are hotels, restaurants, hospitals, airports, etc.
3. Answers will vary. Some possible answers are grocery stores, clothing stores, drug stores, hotels, restaurants, etc.

ANSWERS TO ACTIVITY MASTERS

Activity Master 10-1

Partner A	Partner B
1. yes	2
2. yes	1
3. no	5
4. yes	3
5. no	6
6. no	4

Activity Master 10-2

Answers will vary.

REPRODUCIBLE MASTER
UNIT 10

WORKBOOK ANSWERS

Practice 1
1. is going to
2. isn't going to
3. isn't going to
4. Leo isn't going to
5. Leo isn't going to
6. Leo is going to
7. Leo is going to

Practice 2
1. Leo is going to work in Japan.

Leo is going to learn about Japanese food.

Leo is going to visit a computer company.

Leo is going to stay four or five days.

2. Leo isn't going to stay with friends.

Leo isn't going to stay four or five years.

Leo isn't going to see much of Japan.

Leo isn't going to eat American food.

Practice 6
1. Paul: Are you going to smoke cigarettes?

Robert: No, I'm not.

2. Paul: Are you going to get a phone card?

Robert: Yes, I am.

3. Paul: Are you going to forget family birthdays?

Robert: No, I'm not.

Practice 8
1. Where
2. Who
3. W.hat
4. When

Practice 9
1. Where are Sandra and Ed going to stay?
2. Who are they going to visit?
3. How long is Sandra going to stay?
4. What are they going to buy?

Practice 10
1. You're going to have a credit card, and you're going to use it to pay bills.
2. You're going to have a phone card, and you're going to use it in pay phones.
3. We're going to have smart cards, and they're going to have important information.

REPRODUCIBLE MASTER
UNIT 10

WORKBOOK ANSWERS

Practice 11

1. We're going to use pay phones, but we're not going to use coins.

2. You're going to get cash, but you're not going to go to a bank.

3. Marisol is going to buy gas for the car, but she isn't going to pay a clerk.

Practice 12

1. You're going to have a key, or you're going to use a key card.

2. We're going to talk to a clerk, or we're going to talk to a computer.

9. I'm going to buy expensive foods, or I'm going to use a grocery discount card.

REPRODUCIBLE MASTER
UNIT 10

PROGRESS CHECK A

SPEAK OR WRITE

Look at the pictures from Unit 10. Tell or write answers to the questions.

Questions

1. What is Marisol's father giving her?

2. Is Marisol going to call from Mexico City or from Cancún?

3. What is the other card?

4. Can Marisol make phone calls with the other card?

LISTEN

Listen and check (✓) *yes* **or** *no.*

	yes	no
1. Sandra is going on vacation with Ed.	_____	_____
2. Sandra is going by bus.	_____	_____
3. They are going to stay at hotels.	_____	_____
4. They are going to see the city.	_____	_____
5. Sandra and Ed have friends in New York City.	_____	_____
6. Sandra and Ed want to start their vacation on Friday.	_____	_____

© NTC/Contemporary Publishing Group, Inc.

REPRODUCIBLE MASTER
UNIT 10
PROGRESS CHECK B

LANGUAGE STRUCTURES

Write compound sentences using *or, and,* or *but.* Use the word in parentheses for each new sentence.

1. (*and*) Marisol has a phone card.
      She is getting an ATM card.

   _____

2. (*but*) Marisol has an ATM card.
      She doesn't know how to use it.

   _____

3. (*and*) She's going to call her friends.
      She's not going to forget her father.

   _____

4. (*or*) She's going to use a rotary phone.
      She's going to get a touch-tone phone.

   _____

5. (*but*) They're going to Mexico.
      They're not going with friends.

   _____

CONTENT

1. **Match Column A with Column B.**

   Column A   **Column B**

   a. ATM card   _____   e. hotel

   b. key card   _____   f. service station

   c. gas card   _____   g. grocery store

   d. grocery discount card _____   h. bank

2. **List three places people are going to use smart cards.**

   a. _____   b. _____   c. _____

3. **List three places people can use cards or money.**

   a. _____   b. _____   c. _____

Name _____ Date _____

QUESTIONS AND ANSWERS

Partner A

Ask a partner the questions. Listen and check (✓) *yes* or *no*.

Example: **A:** Number 1. Are you going to study at school?
                B: Yes, I am.
                A: yes _____ no _____

	yes	no
1. Are you going to study at school?	_____	_____
2. Is Marisol going to get an ATM card?	_____	_____
3. Is Marisol going to call her brother?	_____	_____
4. Are we going to learn English?	_____	_____
5. Is Marisol's father going with her?	_____	_____
6. Is Marisol going to visit China?	_____	_____

✂ -

Partner B

Listen to the question. Give an answer from the list.
Write the number of the question on the line.

Example: **A:** Number 1. Are you going to study at school?
                B: _____   Yes, I am.

_____   Yes, she is.

_____   Yes, I am.

_____   No, he isn't.

_____   No, she's going to call her father.

_____   No, she's going to visit Mexico.

_____   Yes, we are.

Name _____ Date _____

INTERVIEW

Ask three classmates three questions.

a. Are you going to use English tomorrow?

b. How are you going to practice English in the future?

c. When are you going to study English?

Name	Answers
1.	a.
	b.
	c.
2.	a.
	b.
	c.
3.	a.
	b.
	c.

Precision
Wedge and Bunker Shots

Precision Golf
SERIES

JIM FITZGERALD
Head Golf Professional Chevy Chase Club

with
Dave Gould

Human Kinetics

Library of Congress Cataloging-in-Publication Data

Fitzgerald, Jim, 1956-
    Precision wedge and bunker shots / by Jim Fitzgerald with Dave
Gould.
       p.   cm. -- (Precision golf series)
    ISBN 0-88011-727-3
    1. Wedge shot (Golf)   2. Bunkers (Golf)   I. Gould, Dave, 1957-
    II. Title. III. Series
    GV979.W43F58   1998
    796.352'34--dc21   97-49862
                                          CIP

ISBN: 0-88011-727-3

Acquisitions Editor: Martin Barnard; **Developmental Editors:** Syd Slobodnik and Kirby Mittelmeier; **Assistant Editors:** Katy Patterson, Cynthia McEntire, and Pam Johnson; **Copyeditor:** Bob Replinger; **Graphic Designer:** Keith Blomberg; **Graphic Artist:** Kathleen Boudreau-Fuoss; **Photo Manager:** Boyd LaFoon; **Cover Designer:** Jack Davis; **Photographer (cover):** © GolfStock/ Pete Marovich; **Photographer (interior):** © Charles Tack, unless noted otherwise; **Illustrator:** Keith Blomberg; **Printer:** United Graphics

Human Kinetics books are available at special discounts for bulk purchase. Special editions or book excerpts can also be created to specification. For details, contact the Special Sales Manager at Human Kinetics.

Printed in the United States of America   10 9 8 7 6 5 4 3 2 1

Human Kinetics
Web site: http://www.humankinetics.com/

United States: Human Kinetics, P.O. Box 5076, Champaign, IL 61825-5076
1-800-747-4457
e-mail: humank@hkusa.com

Canada: Human Kinetics, Box 24040, Windsor, ON N8Y 4Y9
1-800-465-7301 (in Canada only)
e-mail: humank@hkcanada.com

Europe: Human Kinetics, P.O. Box IW14, Leeds LS16 6TR, United Kingdom
(44) 1132 781708
e-mail: humank@hkeurope.com

Australia: Human Kinetics, 57A Price Avenue, Lower Mitcham, South Australia 5062
(088) 277 1555
e-mail: humank@hkaustralia.com

New Zealand: Human Kinetics, P.O. Box 105-231, Auckland 1
(09) 523 3462
e-mail: humank@hknewz.com

Contents

Acknowledgment

I would like to acknowledge and thank Dave Gould for asking me to be his partner in this venture.

I'd like to dedicate this book
to Bill Strausbaugh, Professional Emeritus
at Columbia Country Club.
Through his influence I've learned to appreciate
the responsibility and the privilege it is
to teach the game of golf.

Introduction

This book is for golfers who want to hit accurate shots from 120 yards and in. What you learn in these pages will allow you to turn predicaments into pars and basic short-game shots into birdie opportunities.

Every time you play a round of golf, you'll face a variety of short-game situations. This book can help you recognize and diagnose those situations, and then make your best possible shot. I'm talking about the chip or pitch shot that turns a 7 or 6 into a 5, or a 5 into a 4. At the end of the day, a 92 becomes an 84 that you can be proud of.

But this is possible only if you know the strategies and work on the techniques.

You need to know what club and swing to use if you're in a deep sand trap beside the green, or in a shallow trap 50 yards away. You may have to chip uphill over 15 feet of fairway, or hit a short, downhill pitch shot over a few feet of medium rough. On the 10th hole, you'll face a high flop shot over a bank. On the 11th hole, you'll have to hit a low, running punch shot to save par.

If you think the game is fun now, you'll be thrilled to learn how much better you can perform and how much lower you can score by mastering the gamut of golf's short-game scenarios. There's a bit of mystery to these short shots, but you can solve the puzzles if you have the right advice.

Once you have the expertise to know how much farther a chip shot will roll when you use a pitching wedge instead of a sand wedge, you'll be in control of your chips. You'll end up with a 2- or 3-foot putt, not a 10- or 12-footer. Getting to know how a ball will react when you hit it off moist sand versus dry sand will tell you just how hard to swing in each case. In systematic fashion, this book can teach you how the swing, the club, the lie, and the requirements of the shot all come together.

The book embraces all the short-game ideas and drills I've developed in my 20 years as a professional. Yes, we all love the feeling of powering a straight drive or rifling a long iron shot. But distance in golf is like the home run in baseball. It's such a thrill that it overshadows the subtle plays that are more likely to win or lose games.

The golf we play with our higher-lofted clubs gives us something sublime and intricate. It allows us to use our creativity and our sense of touch and finesse. Some golfers naturally love the challenge of playing short shots. For others, it's an acquired taste. I guarantee this: the lower a golfer's handicap, the more he or she enjoys and appreciates the beauty and creativity of short-game play.

Accomplished golfers love the art and skill of the short game because they know it's the part of golf that provides the best chance to shave strokes off their final score. I hope you like what you find in these pages. I know what's here will help you shoot lower scores and have more fun on the golf course.

Chapter 1

Understanding the Short Game

On par-4 and par-5 holes, after you have hit your drive and hit a second shot, you are either putting or trying to solve a short-game problem.

Shots from outside 125 yards are pretty basic: you select a club, aim, then hit the ball with a full swing. Shots from 125 yards and in are much more varied. When two balls are lying 200 yards from the hole and 10 yards apart, odds are good they will call for similar shots. If they vary from each other, it's usually only because one is in the fairway and one is in the rough—or, less likely so, in a bunker.

But two balls lying 10 yards apart and only 30 yards from the hole will probably require entirely different shot strategies and techniques. A shot from 200 yards will usually demand that the golfer make one or two decisions. But a shot from 20 yards or 50 yards is likely to require six or seven decisions. That's why, when they call golf a "thinking person's game" they're talking to a great degree about the short game.

That's also why the organizational format of this book is situation-by-situation—or, if you will, problem-by-problem. The small maps that accompany each drill or situation give the reader a pictorial table of contents for the strategies and drills in this book. As you look at them, I'm sure you'll quickly recognize the spots that give you the most trouble, as well as the spots from which you feel most comfortable and eager to play your shot.

Each of these maps corresponds to the situations and drills we have described in pictures and text. Use these maps to help visualize the instruction and strategy being provided. Throughout this book there are also instructions about which club best suits each shot—most often the recommended club is some type of wedge.

One particular point must be made about the very high-lofted wedges—clubs with as much as 57 or 60 degrees of loft angle. These wedges allow golfers to take a full swing from very close to the green.

The good news is that to hit a 70-yard pitch you don't have to throttle back or teach yourself the delicate art of a three-quarter-force swing. But be aware that it's tough for some people to take a full swing from such close range. When you get your first superlofted wedge, spend some time hitting it to specific targets. Otherwise you're liable to tell yourself to swing full as you stand over the shot, then quit on the swing halfway through. Somewhere in your brain you haven't accepted the idea that your shot won't fly 20 or 30 yards over the green.

As you prepare to use this book, keep the following principles in mind.

• The most important fundamental in the short game is this: your forward swing should match your backswing in length and speed, and the pace of your swing should never slow until after impact.

• Never swing hard with a short club. With rare exceptions, you should never swing the 8 iron, 9 iron, or wedges at full force. The short game is about scoring and control, not distance. If you need more distance, use a longer, less-lofted club.

• A good short-game player is a land surveyor. Hitting accurate shots from 125 yards and in requires that you understand slope, different types of grasses and sand textures, the effect of moisture on a short shot, and the type of bounce and roll you're likely to get on various landing areas.

• When you have a choice between lofting your shot high in the air or hitting a low, running shot along the ground, you should always hit the low runner. A high flop shot is definitely a second choice, to be used when the first choice isn't available (because of a hazard or other obstruction).

• When faced with a high, floating shot over a bunker, creek, or ridge, don't be cute by trying to hit it close to the pin. Hit it up on the green and settle for a 20-footer or even a 40-footer. Good short-game play is about strategies, skills, and percentages—not hitting miracle shots.

• Centered impact, which is difficult in the long-iron and driving games, is a bit easier in the short game. But you still have to concentrate on it. Everything we say in this book assumes solid, square contact unless otherwise specified.

• The shape of your swing will give you a mirror-image preview of the shot trajectory you desire. A steep and V-shaped swing tends to produce a high-arcing shot. A shallow and U-shaped swing tends to produce a lower, humpbacked shot.

• The essence of the short game is clubhead loft. As you will see later, the loft angle of a wedge or a short iron is an apparently simple variable with complex effects. We'll be talking about loft angle quite a bit in this book, but the key point to remember about it is this: when your high-lofted club isn't sending the ball high in the air, it's doing something else—it's softening the force of your swing (by turning launch force into spin) and installing a set of brakes on your shot, again through the phenomenon of spin.

High and Low: Two Ways to Go

We've said that low shots are preferable to high shots because they are easier to control. Here are some swing fundamentals that go with each type of trajectory.

Low, Running Shot: Ball back in stance; clubface square; hands ahead of clubhead; swing shallow and U-shaped; wrists firm and not hinging; clubhead doesn't release at impact; finish low and abbreviated (figure 1.1).

High, Floating Shot: Ball forward in stance; clubface open; hands even with clubhead; swing steep and V-shaped; wrists actively hinging; full release at impact; full finish (figure 1.2)

Figure 1.1

Figure 1.2

The Tools Are There in Your Bag

Before you start down the road to a new, improved short game, take a look at your equipment. If you understand how the 7 iron, 8 iron, 9 iron, and wedges are designed, you'll know better how to use them.

On shots that don't have to travel too far, we use clubs whose faces point upward. On these clubs, loft angles range from about 35 degrees (the 7 iron) to about 60 degrees, which is the most lofted wedge you're likely to find.

Here's the subtle part: we think of loft as a factor that shoots the ball on a high launch angle. On a full swing from a good lie, that's what loft does. But on short, greenside shots where we don't make a full swing, clubhead loft does something else: it spills a little energy out of the stroke. The effect is similar when a major-league hitter takes a big rip but contacts the ball on the lower half of his bat. The result is less distance and a softer landing for the baseball.

Loft on a clubhead functions like tapering on a baseball bat. Loft lets the golfer make a purposeful stroke and still send the ball off the clubface with limited velocity. Without having to make a tiny stroke that is more a tense flick than a swing, the golfer can keep the ball from darting forward far past the hole. Just as important, the golfer can continue with a downswing and ignore the urge to slow the clubhead before impact.

So use your 7, 8, and 9 irons for a low, running shot. The appropriate situation is when you are close to the green and the pin is away from the edge of the green. Use your pitching wedge, gap wedge (a club with a loft angle midway between the pitching wedge and sand wedge), and sand wedge for higher shots that want to run less after they land. Use these wedges when you're a little farther off the green and the pin is closer to the edge.

On pitch shots, you will usually want to take a sand wedge or a lob wedge. These high-lofted clubs will help you get the ball up higher or will impart extra backspin to stop the ball.

On bunker shots, you need a very high-lofted club, and a club with a good deal of bounce angle on the sole (see figures 1.3 and 1.4).

In this photo, note the relationship between a club's loft and the launch trajectory of the shot. This is the natural takeoff flight of any chip with a 7 iron (lower launch) and a 60-degree wedge. This an excellent way to visualize the path of your chip shot through the air. Picture them following that "pipeline" for about a second, then falling toward their landing spot.

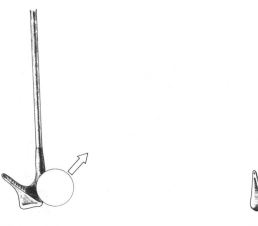

Figure 1.3   **Figure 1.4**

I use the phrases "hands ahead of clubhead" and "hands even with clubhead" several times. The position of the hands relates to *lofting* and *delofting*, which are skills you need to understand. You can magnify or lessen the loft angle of a wedge or any other club by the position of your hands relative to the ball. With hands ahead, you deloft, which makes the ball launch lower, spin less, and run more. With hands even, you add loft, which makes the ball launch higher, spin more, and run less.

The Little Angle That Gets You out of Sand

The other important equipment angle is bounce angle. Bounce angle is measured from the leading edge of your wedge's sole to the trailing edge (see figure 1.5). Bounce angle is a built-in factor that keeps your sand wedge from digging into the sand. If you're a confident, skilled bunker player, look for a wedge with 10 or 12 degrees of bounce. If you struggle in the sand, select a wedge with as much as 14 degrees of bounce.

One final equipment note is that lie angle (figure 1.5) in your wedges and other shorter clubs can affect both the flight of the ball and your

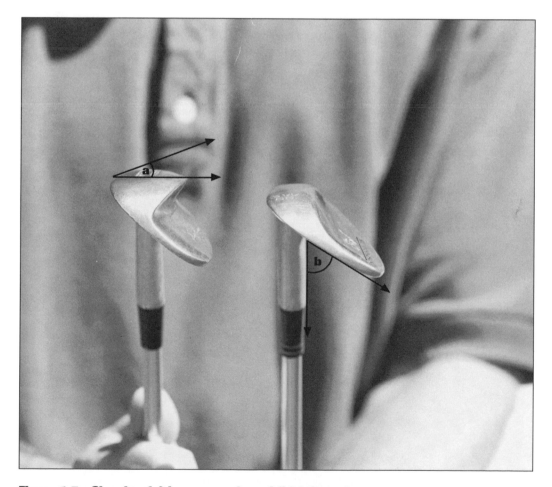

Figure 1.5 Showing (a) bounce angle and (b) loft angle.

swing. Have a golf professional tape the sole of your lofted clubs and let you hit some shots off a "lie board" or a hard, slippery surface, such as a plastic cutting board. The mark on the sole should be in the middle, not on the toe or heel.

If the mark is toward the toe or the heel, then your clubs are either too flat or too upright for your swing. As a result, you'll be getting some digging of the toe or heel, as well as some off-line directional orientation of your clubface. You'll also tend to miss the ball with the center of your clubface, hitting many toe and heel shots. This isn't good! So get your lie angle checked—it's important to good scoring.

Using this book effectively will require a little discipline. You need to follow its instructions step by step and practice the drills whenever you have a free moment. (Please note that the drills assume the player is right-handed.) But these pages should also inspire your creative talents as a shotmaker. Start by learning basic versions of the wedge shots, pitches, and chips, and then experiment. Feel free to develop your own style.

Chapter 2

Greenside Chip Shots

A chip is a shot that runs along the ground at least twice as far as it flies in the air. You can use any club from a 5 iron up to a pitching wedge or sand wedge, as long as you don't lob the ball in the air and put spin on the ball. (It should roll forward, not spin back.) A well-struck chip shot will carry in the air somewhere from 3 to maybe 20 feet, then run and run, all the way up to the hole.

How do you know how well, or poorly, you chip? Compare your chip shots to your long, lag putts. On a practice green, set up a chip starting 5-10 feet off the green, and a long putt, both about 20 paces from the hole. Try the putt twice, and see how close you get to the hole—they should be about 1 to 4 feet from the cup. Next, chip two balls. Did your chips get as close as the putts? Almost as close? Repeat this test a few times. The goal is to get your chip shots as close or nearly as close as your lag putts.]

Every chip you stand over will cause you to ask the same two questions: What club should I use? How hard should I hit it? The answers to those questions must come from practice—your sensory memory.

Watch the tour pros on television; they take *many* practice swings before they chip. These swings serve two purposes: to test the resistance of the grass and to answer the "how hard" question. The pros are trying to link the image of the practice chips with the "feel" of how long or fast a swing they took so they can execute the actual shot when it counts.

Practice these drills over and over to give you confidence in your chips. When you feel tension and doubt, pour your nervous energy into visualizing and practicing your swing. With each practice swing, say to yourself, "a little too hard" or "way too soft" or "a little faster," whatever thought will cue your hands and arms to create the right swing. Do this until you make a practice swing that causes you to say, "That's the one!" Then don't delay—step up and hit the ball.

1 Extended Club

SITUATION: Basic greenside chip. The pin is 30 feet away, and the ball will be moving slightly uphill.

STRATEGY:

You need to strike the chip cleanly with your club, which can be anything from a 7 iron to a pitching wedge. A clean hit will get the ball up and moving; and by choosing one of the lower-lofted chipping clubs, you limit backspin and encourage roll.

TECHNIQUE:

Use a basic chipping stance—feet close together, forward foot pointed slightly toward the target, weight slightly favoring the front foot, arms hanging straight down and close to your body.

CONCEPT:

You must learn to match swing length to the length of the shot and sweep the ball over the fringe to a point within four feet of the edge of the green. The idea is to create little spin, so the ball will roll like a putt to the hole. Little wrist hinging should occur during the backswing. The clubhead must not go past the hands—it must not "flip."

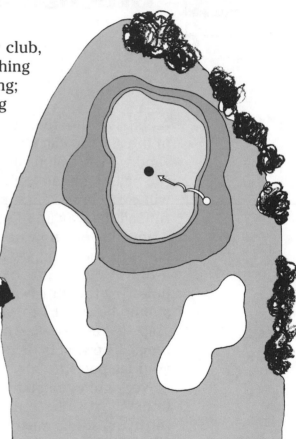

DRILL:

Find a discarded iron in the 7 iron to pitching wedge range. Cut off the cap of the grip so the shaft is open. Insert a wooden dowel or an old shaft firmly into the end of the open grip and cut it off about 18 inches past the end of the grip. Grip down at least to the middle of the grip and swing your shoulders and arms together, making sure the extension shaft does not hit your side. This will keep your wrists from flipping, which creates too much loft and inconsistent contact.

TIP: The secret is keeping your hands and wrists "quiet" instead of stiff. This will ensure better feel and touch. You will experience motion in your upper-back muscles. On the course you can refresh the feel of this drill by gripping down to the middle of the shaft and making practice swings.

2 Choke Down

> **SITUATION:** Basic greenside chip. The pin is 30 feet away, and the green is level.

STRATEGY:

With no break or slope to worry about, a clean chip at just the right force can leave you with a very short putt, maybe a tap-in. You have to dial in the feel of the correct stroke.

TECHNIQUE:

Use the setup for the basic chip shot described in Drill 1.

CONCEPT:

Developing feel is critical with all short-game shots. You can do this drill on the course as a rehearsal before the shot.

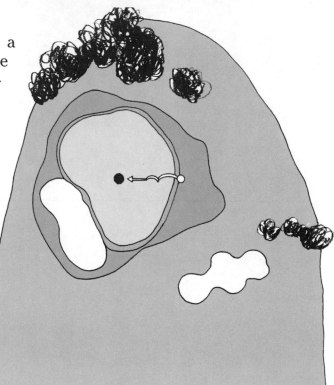

DRILL:

Choke down on the club you are using for the shot to a point below the grip, entirely on the shaft. Make your chipping motion, being careful not to let the grip end of the club hit you in the side. This will keep your hands quiet.

TIP: Because this is a rehearsal drill, focus on the motion and pace you need for the shot you are about to hit.

 **Sweep the Grass**

SITUATION: Chip shot from the fringe or fairway grass, with the pin at least 40 feet away, slightly uphill all the way.

STRATEGY:

The goal is to get the ball up and over the fringe, limiting spin so the ball runs on a steady pace to the hole.

TECHNIQUE:

Use the setup for the basic chip shot described in Drill 1. Your hands must lead the club through impact.

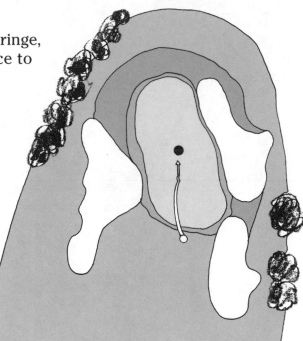

CONCEPT:

To succeed at this shot, you must trust the loft of the club to get the ball airborne. To do this, you will need to develop a motion that minimizes wrist activity and keeps your clubhead on a shallow descent, which will minimize spin.

DRILL:

This drill will help you learn to sweep the tips of the grass blades and use the loft of the club to get the ball in the air, instead of chopping the ground or trying to lift the ball with a scooping motion. The setup and motion are no different from what you would do to chip the ball, except in this drill there is no ball. You are sweeping the grass in the first cut of rough.

Place the ball in the first cut of rough just outside the fringe. The grass needs to be about one inch to one and a half inches tall. Practice just sweeping the tips of the grass instead of hitting the ball. You want to create a low back and low through motion by using your shoulders and arms, not your hands. Place a ball a few inches outside the spot where you are sweeping the grass. After 10 sweeps move immediately up to the ball and chip it, using the same motion.

TIP: You must trust the club's loft to get the ball up and over the fringe, so start this drill with a wedge.

 **4** **Chip off a Tee**

STRATEGY:

The goal is to get the ball up and over the fringe, limiting spin so the ball runs on a steady pace and finishes within three feet of the hole.

TECHNIQUE:

Use the setup for a basic chip shot described in Drill 1. Your hands must lead the club through impact.

CONCEPT:

This is another way to learn how to trust that the club's loft will get the ball airborne. With the ball off the ground, you'll be much less tempted to scoop it.

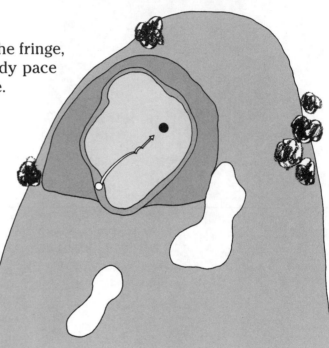

DRILL:

Tee up six balls in a row, six inches apart. Take your chipping setup and hit the shots one after another with no pause between shots. Focus on swinging your shoulders and arms together, keeping your hands quiet and ahead of the clubhead.

4

TIP: Keep the tempo and pace of the swing even, going back and forth like a pendulum or metronome.

5 Short Finish

STRATEGY:

This is a rehearsal exercise you can practice on-course to get the feel. You can also use it when practicing your chipping.

TECHNIQUE:

This drill will help you to know what it feels like to keep your hands ahead of the clubhead past impact.

CONCEPT:

The only way to stop the finish low and short is by maintaining the angle in your right wrist and keeping your left wrist and forearm in line.

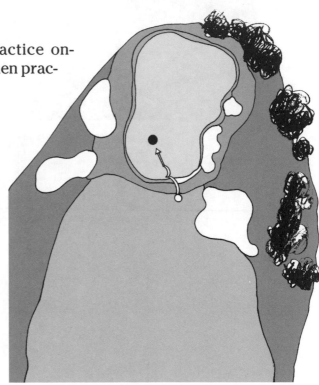

DRILL:

During practice place a club on top of two empty ball baskets and chip from a point about 18 inches behind this club's shaft. To keep from hitting the shaft, you must make sure the clubhead trails your hands. Once the clubhead gets past the hands it is difficult to stop it.

TIP: At the finish, you will feel some tension in the back of your left hand. This tension is what keeps you from flipping the clubhead forward with your right hand and wrist.

6 Hit the Side of Your Bag

STRATEGY:

You can do this drill on the course or during practice. It allows you to feel the firmness in your left wrist that shuts down the flipping motion created instinctively by your right hand.

TECHNIQUE:

Feel the hands and the grip end of the club leading the clubhead.

CONCEPT:

By putting the clubhead against the bag and pulling the handle to the target, you will retain the angle in your right wrist.

DRILL:

Practice hitting the side of your bag lightly or putting the clubhead against your bag and pulling the clubhead to the target. Feel the relationship and position of your wrists. The back of your left wrist will be straight and your right wrist will be bent.

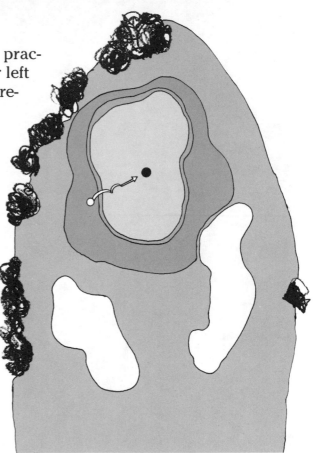

TIP: The motion must come from your arms and shoulders; keep the wrists quiet.

7 Change the Club

STRATEGY:

You first have to choose how far to advance the ball in the air and then how much it needs to roll after landing. The green itself is only a few feet away, but you detect little humps or a significant sideslope on that part of the green. Under these conditions, you need to be able to adjust the air-to-ground ratio of your shot.

TECHNIQUE:

Use the setup for a basic chip shot described in Drill 1. Your hands must lead the clubhead through impact.

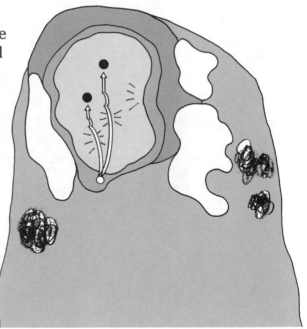

CONCEPT:

You will hit various clubs with the same motion to learn the reaction and distance. By learning how each club reacts you will club yourself on the course better. As a result, you'll avoid using a club that is too lofted (and coming up short) or a club that is not lofted enough (and going past the hole.)

DRILL:

Pick a spot five feet off the green. Set one club on the ground two and a half feet behind the ball and another club two and a half feet in front of your ball. With an identical swing, hit a chip shot with each of four clubs—your sand wedge, 9 iron, 7 iron, and 5 iron. You will notice each club will run farther as you move from the sand wedge to the 5 iron. Pick the club that will land two to four feet on the green and run the rest of the way to the hole. You must factor the slope and speed of the green into club selection.

 **Track**

SITUATION: Chip shot from the fringe or fairway grass, with the path to the hole bordered on each side by humps or swales that will cause the ball to drift far from the hole.

STRATEGY:

You need to keep the ball strictly on line to avoid these humps or swales.

TECHNIQUE:

Use the setup for a basic chip shot described in Drill 1. Your hands must lead the club through impact.

CONCEPT:

To hit chip shots on line, the clubface must be square and the path of the clubhead must be toward the target. Practicing inside a track will train you to keep the club on line and square, which again requires quiet hands.

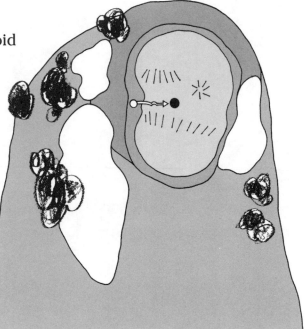

DRILL:

Place two clubs parallel to each other about eight inches apart. Make sure the track they create points directly at the target. Practice your chipping stroke, keeping the club inside the track. To hit chip shots on line, the clubface must be square and the path of the clubhead must be toward the target. Check that the clubface is at right angles to the two shafts that make up the track.

TIP: Hold your finish after the shot to check whether your club finished inside the track.

9 Chip Under the Target

STRATEGY:

Chipping means keeping the ball low so that it runs like a putt after it hits the green. This helps create low flight and a puttlike roll after landing.

TECHNIQUE:

To hit the ball low, you must deloft the club. Do this by keeping the grip end of the club in front of the clubhead.

CONCEPT:

Having a visual obstacle to hit under will help develop your delofting technique.

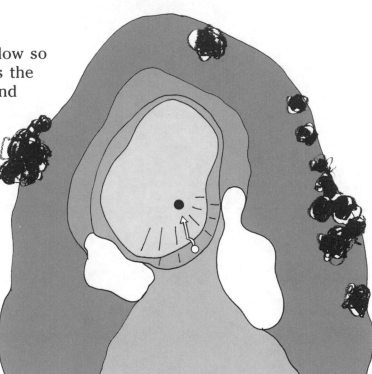

DRILL:

Place a club or bag on top of two buckets or chip from behind a bench. Having this obstacle in front of you will help you maintain your hand position relative to the clubhead.

Chip Under the Target

TIP: If props are not available, ask a friend to hold a club in front of you two feet off the ground to hit under.

10 Change the Target

SITUATION: Chip shot from the fringe or fairway grass onto an undulating portion of the green.

STRATEGY:

You must land your chip on a relatively small spot to keep the ball from being influenced by humps or swales that will cause the ball to drift far from the hole.

TECHNIQUE:

Use the setup for a basic chip shot described in Drill 1. Your hands must lead the club through impact.

CONCEPT:

With a single club, you can make small alterations in the shape and style of your chip shots by varying the length of the swing.

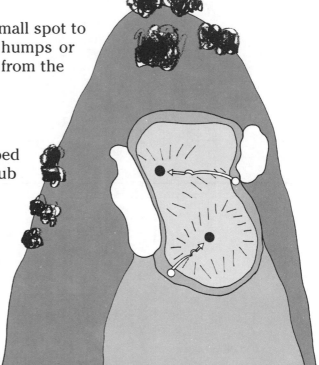

DRILL:

Hit your chip shots to different targets on the green. Make sure each time that the distance and line changes dramatically. This will refine your ability to change the size and pace of your stroke as your target changes. Be sure that you include uphill and downhill as well as right-to-left and left-to-right shots. The stroke remains the same but the target distance and line changes. Focus on changing the size of your stroke, not just the pace, for each shot. And don't be discouraged if your first efforts leave you way off target.

Symmetrical Swing

SITUATION: Steep uphill chip from off the green.

STRATEGY:

Your ball is in a place where getting close to the hole will be difficult. It's possible for the ball to take off and roll way past the hole. But it's also possible you might leave your shot short of the green in an even more difficult position than the original one.

TECHNIQUE:

Use the standard greenside chip setup and swing, with extra precision in how hard you strike the ball.

CONCEPT:

This is the no-target or different swing-sizes drill. It teaches you a straightforward greenside chip but applies to situations in which you must be precise about how hard to hit the ball—considering carry even more than roll.

DRILL:

Take your sand wedge and hit 10 chip shots, focusing only on a solid hit and where the ball lands. Do not consciously try to land it anywhere. Characterize the relative amount of force in each swing with words or numbers (for example, nine o'clock to three o'clock, eight o'clock to four o'clock; or short, medium, long). Keep the backswing and forward swing equal in length. Gradually increase the swing, then decrease it gradually. Remember that backswing must match forward swing.

TIP: Survey the landing spots and, in your mind, paint a row of stripes on the green.

12 Birdie Chip

SITUATION: Chip shot from off the green in a clean lie with plenty of green to work with and not more than 30 feet to cover.

STRATEGY:

This is a greenside chip where you want to be aggressive, maybe even try to sink it. Possibly you're in a match, and the other player has a makable putt.

TECHNIQUE:

Use the standard greenside chip setup and swing motion.

CONCEPT:

You are learning feel for how hard to strike your greenside shots. The connection you're making is between the natural feel of a throw and the less natural act of chipping.

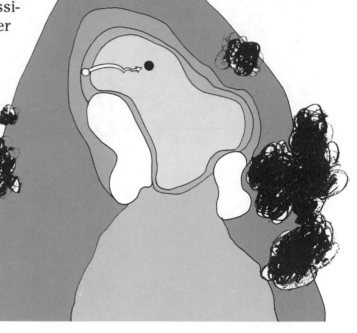

DRILL:

Take 10 balls and lay them in a situation like the one described above. Throw one underhand, then chip one. Repeat. On the third throw, try to hit the pin. On the fourth and fifth throws, try to get the ball to fall in the cup. When you're ready to be that precise with your chips, try to sink them.

TIP: Try some of these, both the throws and the chips, with your eyes closed. Play a game in which you don't quit until two of the throws and one of the chips go in.

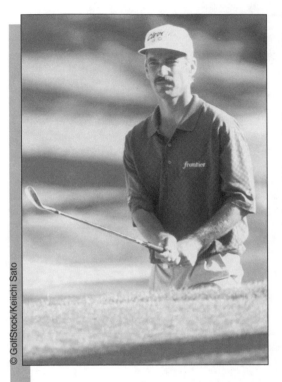

Corey Pavin:
Short-Game Whiz

Corey Pavin is a phenomenal athlete who happens to stand 5 foot, 9 inches and weigh only 150 pounds. His stellar golf career is a testament not to power golf but to Pavin's skills as a shotmaker. Among his principal credits are the 1995 U.S. Open championship and more than a dozen PGA Tour wins. Though we identify him here as a master of the chip, Pavin's most famous golf shot is the uphill, 230-yard 4 wood he hit on the 72nd hole of the '95 Open, which stopped 10 feet from the cup and secured Pavin his first major victory. And yet, even in that full 4 wood, we see some of Pavin's gifts for the short game. He played the shot to land some 10 yards short of the green, then skip onto the putting surface green and roll deep into the corner where the "Sunday pin" was cut.

Golf fans also remember Corey's brilliant chip-in from above the hole on No. 18 in the final afternoon four-ball match of the 1995 Ryder Cup. Playing with Loren Roberts against Nick Faldo and Bernhard Langer, Pavin made a perfect read and a beautiful stroke with his wedge to birdie the hole and seal his side's one-up victory.

A native of Los Angeles and a UCLA Bruin as well, Pavin takes as much pride in his two consecutive L.A. Open victories (in 1994 and 1995) as in any other career accomplishments. He is married and has two sons.

Chapter 3

Greenside Pitch Shots

In this chapter we will describe shots that either

- climb fairly high and land softly with little roll, or
- carry over 20 feet and stop quickly because of spin.

The second type of pitch shot is called for when you must clear an obstacle on the way to the green, or the pin is cut close to the edge of the green with little room to run it. The club used to hit most greenside pitch shots will be a gap, bunker, or lob wedge. These clubs have the most loft (between 52 and 60 degrees) and therefore hit the ball the highest with minimum roll. You must become friends with your wedges and learn how they react off different lies.

Some pitch shots will be straightforward, involving no obstacle. Others will be delicate, perhaps up a steep ridge to a pin cut close to the green's edge. In each case you will have some options about what club to use and how to play the shot. In most of the delicate situations you should make sure you *don't face the same shot again*, so be long rather than cute and way short. Leave yourself a putt instead of another pitch shot. You can change the loft of your shots in three ways:

1. Club face angle—open or square
2. Ball position—forward, middle, or back
3. Length of swing—long and smooth, or short and quick

These drills will help you learn how to open up the face of your wedges and how to play shots from different ball positions. In short, you will learn how to experiment and use your imagination.

13 Winner's Target

SITUATION: Chip shot from 30 to 60 feet off the green with a good chance to get it close if you can land your chip on the first 3 feet of the green.

STRATEGY:

The first few feet of green is a strip we call the winner's target. Controlling your chip shots from beginning to end means landing them early. That's what you'll try to do with this shot.

TECHNIQUE:

Use the stance and setup for a basic pitch shot.

CONCEPT:

You will understand and file away important information about club selection and how it affects distance. You'll also be getting more focused on accurate chipping to the winner's target just on the other side of the fairway, rough, or fringe you're hitting over.

DRILL:

Make a choice among sand wedge, pitching wedge, 9 iron, or 8 iron, depending on how far the hole is from the edge of the green. Hit to the same landing spot, substituting different clubs from your four most lofted. Hit the target with each and watch how the ball behaves after it lands. Pace off the roll distance and commit it to memory, allowing for the speed and slope of the green when you plan later shots.

13

 **Hit the Basket**

> **SITUATION:** Pitch shot from light rough, behind a bunker. The ball lies about 20 feet from the edge of the green. The pin is close to the near edge of the green.

STRATEGY:

Because you haven't got much green to work with, your shot must travel about 20 feet in the air, clear the bunker safely, then settle quickly, with limited roll.

TECHNIQUE:

The setup is for a basic pitch shot: a slightly open stance, weight slightly toward the forward foot, ball in the middle of the stance.

CONCEPT:

The key to having your pitch shots travel the right distance is landing them in the correct spot. Practicing hitting to a spot will help your touch and your ability to gauge distance. You can become skilled at landing your ball in a specific spot by repeating the same length swing but varying the tempo or pace of the swing. Slower-tempo shots will fly shorter distances, and faster-tempo shots will fly farther.

DRILL:

Place a range bucket, pail, small trash can, or box about 15 feet away. Try to hit your shots so that they hit or just clear the obstacle you have created.

TIP: To have more fun and make practice more productive, have a contest and count how many shots hit or land in the bucket.

Clubface Squared, Clubface Open

> **SITUATION:** Pitch shot that must travel about 15 feet in the air, clearing an obstacle such as a bunker, creek, or hill to reach the green. The pin is fairly close to the near edge of the green.

STRATEGY:

A soft, floating type of shot is required. But with the bunker in play, your swing cannot be tentative. The solution is to add loft to your sand wedge by opening the face and swinging faster.

TECHNIQUE:

Setup is the basic pitch shot setup, but you should aim a few degrees left of your target to compensate for the open-clubface angle.

CONCEPT:

Because your open-clubface shots will be higher and shorter, you can swing the club aggressively instead of trying to hit it perfectly. This will reduce your tendency to decelerate and come up short of your target.

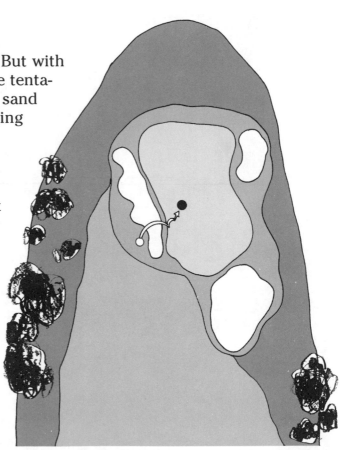

DRILL:

Place the club on the ground so it is 5 to 10 degrees open. You first turn the blade open, then grip the club. Hit five normal pitch shots with your sand wedge or lob wedge with the club square. Then hit with the clubface 10 degrees open. You will notice that the ball flight will be higher, shorter, and a little right of your target with the blade open. Do this again to learn to trust the effect of an open clubface versus a square clubface.

Clubface Squared, Clubface Open

16 One-Arm Swing

> **SITUATION:** Pitch shot from 20 to 60 feet off the green over an obstacle. The pin is cut very close to edge of the green.

STRATEGY:

Use the strategy described in Drill 11.

TECHNIQUE:

Use the basic pitch shot setup except the feet should be a few inches closer together.

CONCEPT:

Rather than adding loft by opening the clubface, you can also hit a high, soft shot by increasing the length of your arm swing. This method is preferable because contact is square and flush, rather than oblique and of a brushing nature. Usually a lob wedge or sand wedge is used for this shot.

DRILL:

With just your dominant hand on the club, swing the club away with your arm. Allow your wrist and elbow to hinge and use only a slight shoulder turn. On your forward swing, fling the clubhead through the impact area. Use no arm tension when you do this. You should flip and hinge your wrist through impact instead of rotating your arm and hand. The lie must be grassy. This shot is not recommended off a tight, firm lie. The clubhead must reach the ball ahead of the grip end to achieve the most loft. To repeat: right-handed golfers use right hand for this drill and left-handed golfers use left hand.

17 Full Swing, Slow Speed

SITUATION: Pitch shot from 20 to 60 feet off the green over an obstacle. The pin is cut very close to the edge of the green.

STRATEGY:

Use the strategy described in Drill 11.

TECHNIQUE:

Use a regular pitching setup with your stance narrowed.

CONCEPT:

Although this drill is similar to Drill 11, it uses a different physical cue to produce the necessary wrist hinging through impact. Because of centrifugal force, a full, wide swing arc keeps the clubhead moving briskly, even when the hands and arms feel like they're going at a deliberate pace. As long as you maintain full extension of your arms, slow, deliberate hand speed will allow gravity and centrifugal force to unhinge the wrists properly and let the clubhead go.

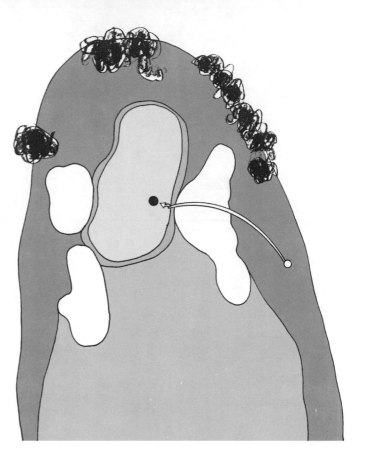

DRILL:

Take a lob wedge or sand wedge and set up for the basic shot. Open the clubface slightly more than usual and position the ball slightly farther forward in your stance than usual. Make a full arm swing without much lower-body turn. Your grip pressure should be light. The speed of the forward swing will be slow, not like molasses but at a leisurely pace. The combination of your wide swing arc and letting the clubhead go early in the forward swing will create the desired shot. The lie must be grassy with room under the ball. Experiment with different speed swings. Try to let momentum and gravity create the speed.

18 No-Pause Pitching

SITUATION: Basic pitch shot using a lofted wedge. The green is 20 to 60 feet away, and the pin is within 20 feet of the edge of the green.

STRATEGY:

This pitch shot can fly at a normal height and roll about 10 feet after it lands.

TECHNIQUE:

The basic pitch shot technique applies.

CONCEPT:

During a typical round, you'll probably get several chances to hit this shot. The key to hitting it successfully is simply to trust your fundamental approach.

DRILL:

Line up six balls in a row about six inches apart. Walk down the line hitting one ball after another without stopping between swings. Create a swinging motion without stopping. The pace of the swing should be the same back and forth. It will take some

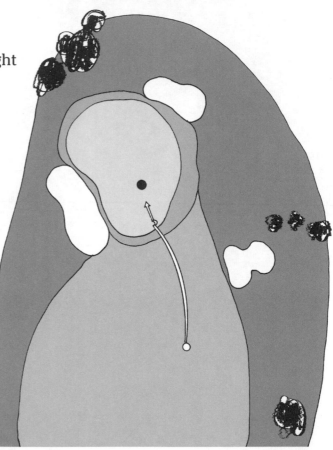

practice to get into the rhythm of walking and swinging, but you will discover quickly how easy it is to hit these shots. With the club swinging back and forth, you will not be able to freeze over the ball and tense up at or before impact.

TIP: Picture your best practice shots from this drill taking place on the 18th green when you need to get up-and-down to win the match or shoot a personal-best score.

19 Ball Position: Front-Middle-Back

SITUATION: Pitch shot that must clear a bunker but at the same time stay beneath a tree limb.

STRATEGY:

You will need to pitch the ball so that it flies slightly lower than usual.

TECHNIQUE:

Employ the basic pitching technique but lower the arc of this shot by adjusting the ball position forward in your stance.

CONCEPT:

Besides learning how to hit lower pitches by moving the ball back in your stance, you can also learn to hit higher, softer pitch shots by moving the ball forward in your stance. To develop a versatile short game you must become comfortable moving the ball forward and backward like this.

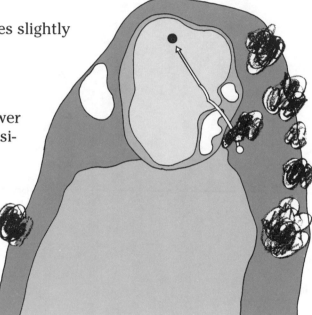

DRILL:

Play three pitch shots with the ball positioned off your forward foot, three shots with the ball positioned in the middle of your stance, and finally three shots with the ball positioned off your back foot. You will discover three different ball flights from high to low. Play all shots with the same stance and setup. The only variable is ball position. Do this repeatedly until you get comfortable with the ball positions and confident with the results.

Ball Position: Front-Middle-Back

TIP: Make sure your head position and weight remain the same on all shots. Your head will be behind the forward ball position and ahead of the back ball position. It may take time to become accustomed to this perspective.

20 Low and Short Finish

> **SITUATION:** The ball must clear a bunker with the pin 60 feet from the edge of the green.

STRATEGY:

Hit a low pitch shot that clears the obstacle, then runs back to the target.

TECHNIQUE:

Use the basic pitch shot stance and set up with the ball positioned middle to back.

CONCEPT:

To hit a low shot, you must learn to contact the ball with a descending blow.

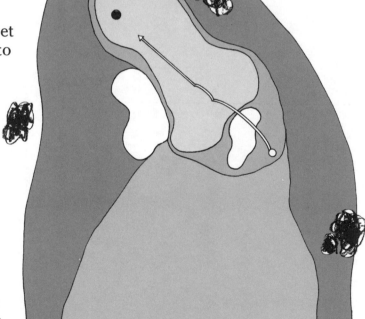

DRILL:

Using a sand wedge with the ball positioned in the middle of your stance, hit your pitch shot and break off your finish just after impact. Have a friend hold a club about waist high to your target side so that you have to stop before hitting his or her club. You will notice that your shots will fly low and, if the lie is fairly clean, check up (that is, halt due to backspin) slightly before running to the target. To execute this shot, you must contact the ball with a descending blow.

> **TIP:** Your target-side arm and hand must be firm to stop the finish and keep the handle in front of the clubhead.

21 Upslope Pitch

SITUATION: Your ball is on a steep greenside slope 20 feet from the green. The pin is 30 feet from the edge of the green.

STRATEGY:

You decide against trying to loft the ball all the way to the pin. Instead, you will land your ball on the green and run it up to the hole.

TECHNIQUE:

This pitch shot requires that you establish a balanced uphill stance, with the ball positioned toward your front (or uphill) foot.

CONCEPT:

Understand that the slope will add loft to the shot. Because the shot must travel a good 25 feet after it reaches the green, use a less-lofted club, such as a 9 iron or pitching wedge.

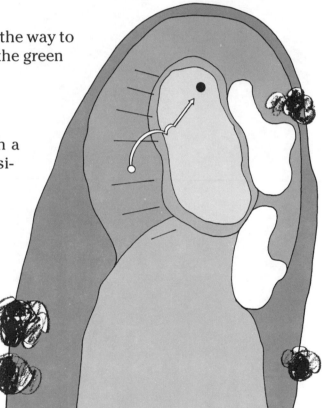

DRILL:

Practice with different clubs, from the 7 iron to the lob wedge, to discover the effect of the slope on loft. You want to choose the club that allows you to swing easily while not running on too far. A lob wedge will stop immediately, which requires you to swing too hard and fly the ball to the pin.

TIP: With the ball positioned forward and on an uphill slope, the shot will tend to go left slightly off the club. Learn to adjust your aim and trust this to happen.

22 Hardpan Lie

SITUATION: The ball is lying on hardpan or in very thin grass with firm ground underneath at a distance of 30 to 70 feet from the green.

STRATEGY:

If you're skittish about hardpan lies, use a strategy of simply hitting a clean shot to get the ball anywhere on the green. As you play and practice this shot, however, you may quickly become skilled at it and decide to play more aggressively for the pin.

TECHNIQUE:

Position the ball middle to back with weight decidedly on the forward foot and grip positioned ahead of the ball. Hit the ball cleanly just below its equator, while the club is still descending. Use a sand wedge.

CONCEPT:

Scooping or lifting the ball will not work here. You must develop a motion almost like chopping with a lofted club. You need loft but not bounce.

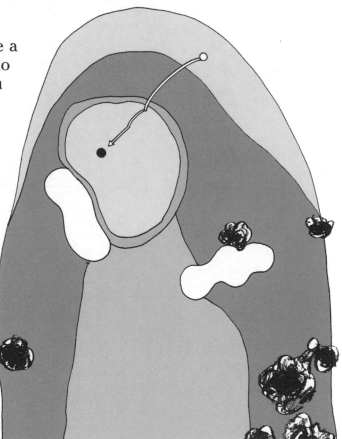

DRILL:

Find a similar situation around your practice green or elsewhere (look for a place that gets a lot of tire traffic). Use the setup described above without a ball. Practice sticking the club in the ground using a choppy up-and-down stroke instead of a low back-and-forth stroke. Without delay place a ball in position and hit it using the same motion. Repeat this until you hit clean shots. Don't worry about distance yet—you need to get comfortable seeing the ball go low and feeling the clubhead make impact with the ground.

> **TIP:** As the club descends, you must be turning onto your front foot. When playing from hardpan, be sure your weight never stays on your back foot.

© GolfStock/Pete Marovich

Phil Mickelson:
Tour Superstar

Many golf fans were introduced to Phil Mickelson when he appeared on the cover of *Golf Digest* in the spring of 1991, hitting a wedge shot off an uphill lie with his back to a green. The ball flew high in the air, over Mickelson's head and backward. An inset photo showed the ball landing on the green about eight feet from the hole.

Phil Mickelson is known not simply as a left-handed flop shot king, but as a tour superstar with incredible hands and a terrific record as both an amateur and a pro. He is the only golfer other than Jack Nicklaus to win the NCAA singles title and the U.S. Amateur in the same year. On the pro tour, he has been able to notch tournament wins at the rate of nearly two per season, an astonishing pace.

Mickelson's steep swing and his educated wrists enable him to hit high-lofted shots when most other pros would attempt a safer low, running chip. In Arizona, where Mickelson starred on the Arizona State golf team, most greens are elevated and many feature severe crowns. This style of architecture makes the high, floating pitch shot a requirement, and Mickelson made it his trademark. He used this technique in Phoenix to win himself a PGA Tour event, the 1991 Northern Telecom Open, while he was still an amateur.

Mickelson, recently married, is also an avid snow skier and water skier.

Chapter 4

Greenside Bunker Shots

The greenside bunker shot is probably the least understood and, therefore, the weakest shot in the repertoire of most players. In a properly hit explosion shot, the club never touches the ball—it extracts the ball and the sand around it together. To do this the club must bounce off, rather than dig into, the sand. This result requires a club with angle—a sand wedge—and usually an opened clubface. When the clubface is opened the bounce on the sole of the club increases and the width of the sole from toe to heel increases, making it easier for the club to slide through the sand. A closed clubface or a club with no bounce will dig into the sand, making it difficult for the club to extract the ball.

Newer golfers should approach these bunker shots with low expectations. The initial goal is to get the ball out and have a putt. Once you have learned to do this consistently, getting the ball out of the sand and close to the pin will depend upon your touch and overall skill level. The drills in this chapter will help you learn how to approach the ball at a steeper angle, how to trust the club to get through the sand, and how to hit consistently in the same place relative to the ball without aiming at a spot.

Have some fun learning and practicing these shots, and you'll soon be successful.

23 Line in the Sand

SITUATION: Greenside bunker shot from a level lie.

STRATEGY:

The bunker is quite deep, and your goal is to escape to the middle of the green.

TECHNIQUE:

Use an open stance and open clubface. The line of your toes should aim slightly left of the target, and the clubface should aim slightly right of your target.

CONCEPT:

Many poor bunker shots are the result of hitting either too far behind the ball or too close to the ball.

DRILL:

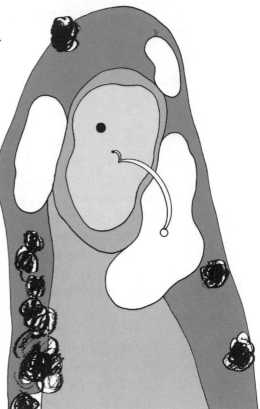

Draw a line in the sand perpendicular to the target line and about 15 feet long. Place 10 to 15 balls about three inches on the target side of the line and one foot apart. As you hit shots, walk down the line and examine where, relative to the line, your club enters the sand and how the shot responded. This will help you learn where to place the ball in your stance to achieve the most consistent results.

> **TIP:** If you have trouble hitting these shots well, go down the line trying to impact the sand on the line without a ball. Your left heel print should be very close to the line.

 **Board Under the Sand**

SITUATION: Greenside bunker shot from a level lie.

STRATEGY:

The bunker is quite deep, and your goal is to escape to the middle of the green.

TECHNIQUE:

Open your stance and open the clubface. The line of your toes should aim left of the target, and the clubface should aim right of your target. Remember, the clubface must be open to give you the effect of the bounce.

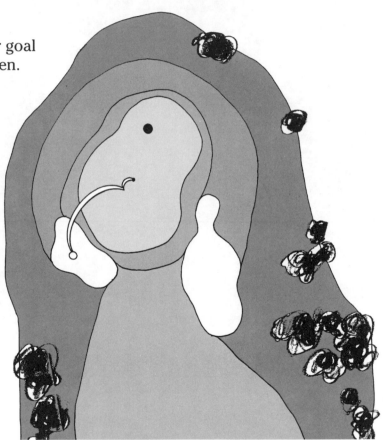

CONCEPT:

Most short iron shots take divots after impact. This drill will help you learn that a sand wedge will bounce through the sand and not dig.

DRILL:

Place a two-by-four in the sand and cover it with about one inch of sand. Practice hitting off the board without a ball to experience the bounce. After some practice place a ball on the board, cushioned by a one- to two-inch layer of sand and hit shots.

TIP: Make sure the board is buried solidly in the sand. First swings should be easy until you get the feel.

25 Head Cover Behind the Ball

> **SITUATION:** Difficult greenside bunker shot. Your lie is slightly downhill, the bunker is especially deep, and the green is not only small but also fairly fast.

STRATEGY:

Your goal is simply to stop the ball on any part of the green.

TECHNIQUE:

Use a basic bunker setup and swing, with an extra steep and somewhat harder swing.

CONCEPT:

With a steep angle of attack, you reduce your margin for error and can produce more consistent shots.

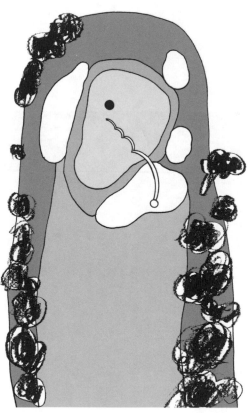

DRILL:

Place a head cover one foot behind the ball in a bunker. Take the club back without hitting the head cover. To produce this shot, you have to hinge your wrists early and swing your arms up rather than low and around. This creates a steep angle of attack to the ball. Try this a while, then try hitting some shots without hitting the head cover. This will help you learn to hit closer to the ball, something higher-handicap golfers have trouble doing.

Head Cover Behind the Ball

TIP: You may need to place the head cover more than one foot behind the ball but be sure to place it close enough to establish a steep angle of attack.

26 Change Clubs

SITUATION: The ball is in a bunker considered greenside but is at least 25 yards from the green and as much as 40 yards from the pin.

STRATEGY:

Instead of playing a sand wedge to this distant hole position, select a less-lofted club that will give you extra distance.

TECHNIQUE:

Your stance, clubface angle, and the path of your swing will vary slightly as you switch from club to club. Compared with the technique used with a sand wedge, these shots will require a more shallow angle of attack and a point of entry that is closer to the back of the ball. Remember, the less-lofted clubs will dig more than a sand wedge, so expect a different feel going into the sand.

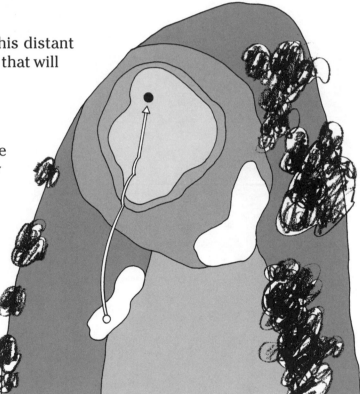

CONCEPT:

A less-lofted club will run more and spin less, which is necessary for a 20- to 40-yard bunker shot. Such a club, however, will be less forgiving of mistakes, such as hitting too far behind the ball, hitting thin, and so on.

DRILL:

In practice hit five bunker shots with your sand wedge, five with your pitching wedge, five with your 9 iron, and five with your 8 iron. You will discover that the ball will react differently with each club and that each club can extract the ball effectively from the bunker. The less-lofted clubs will run more, which is necessary on long bunker shots.

TIP: You will also need this shot when the pin is in the middle of a green that slopes downhill significantly toward your ball in the bunker.

27 One-Arm Swings

SITUATION: The ball is in a greenside bunker with fairly soft sand. Your lie is a semi "fried egg." The bunker is deep, and the pin is within 15 feet of the edge of the bunker.

STRATEGY:

You will have to lift the ball on a mostly vertical rise. Because of the fluffiness of the lie, your sand wedge will have to dig in a little deeper but not bury itself.

CONCEPT:

To be successful with this shot you must use the bounce on the sand wedge to get the club through the sand. The feel of using one arm (right arm for a right-handed player and left arm for a left-handed player) will let you swing the club up easier on the backswing and splash the sand by throwing the clubhead through the sand.

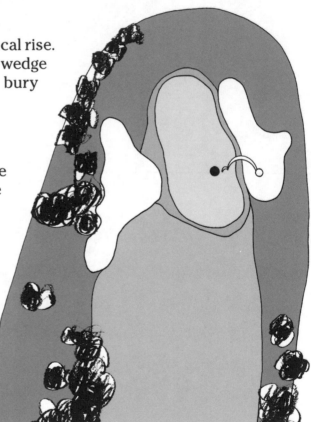

DRILL:

Hit bunker shots with one hand until the balls come out easily. You will need to make sure that you do not pull the handle down but rather throw the clubhead at the sand. The clubhead should go past the handle at impact so that you can use the bounce on the sole of the club.

Short-Finish, Full-Finish

> **SITUATION:** The ball is in a medium-deep greenside bunker. The pin is most of the way across the green, about 40 feet away. The green slopes slightly upward toward the pin and then sharply downward toward a pond whose bank is cut short, with no rough to keep balls out.

STRATEGY:

Your decision is a challenging one. You can hit a short escape shot that avoids the water but sets up a long, difficult putt, or you can try to hit over toward the pin and set up a possible makable putt.

TECHNIQUE:

The setup and placement of the ball remain the same for each shot.

CONCEPT:

You can use the length of your swing, particularly the forward swing and finish, to control distance on bunker shots such as these. The result will be a sense of control that will allow you to pursue either strategy.

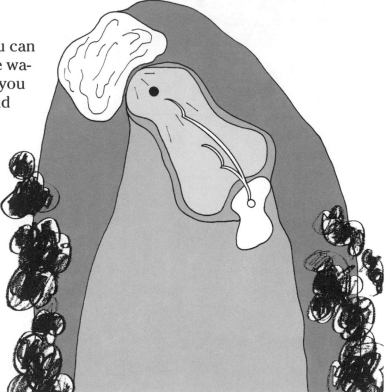

DRILL:

Alternate between a full finish and a dramatically short finish. Hit three or four bunker shots, stopping immediately after impact. Then hit three or four shots with a full finish. You should notice that the short-finish shots will fly only a short distance while your full-finish shots will travel much farther in the air. This is one of the elements used in hitting long and short bunker shots.

TIP: You will probably leave shots in the bunker and blade shots over the green. This is OK in practice and just part of learning this technique.

 **29** **Firm Sand**

STRATEGY:

By looking at the sand and feeling it under your feet, you can get a good sense of its consistency. You decide to make the proper adjustments and play aggressively for the pin.

TECHNIQUE:

Place the ball forward to ensure that the club does not enter the sand too steeply.

CONCEPT:

With a firm base of sand the club will bounce more dramatically out of the sand. You need to use a club with less bounce or square the face of your sand wedge to reduce bounce.

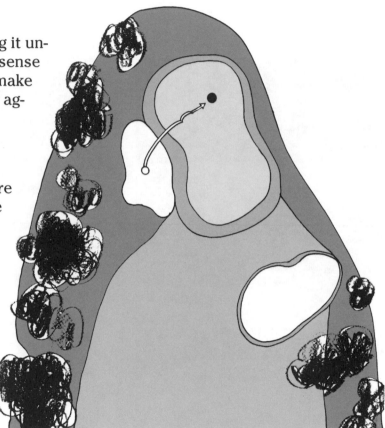

DRILL:

Alternate between your pitching wedge and your sand wedge with the face square to the line. Play the shots exactly the same and see how the ball reacts with each club. If the sand is extremely firm the pitching wedge might be the better selection. In either case the stroke should not be as hard nor will the finish be as full as a stroke in soft sand.

TIP: You must trust the club to bounce. The tendency will be to hit these shots too hard.

30 Chipped Bunker Shots

SITUATION: Your ball is in a clean lie in firm sand, in a fairly shallow bunker (not much lip) that is level or on a slight uphill tilt. The bunker fronts the green, and the pin is 20 yards away.

STRATEGY:

Because the lie is clean and the lip is low, you opt for the less risky route of chipping the ball—contacting sand minimally, in front of the ball—rather than blasting it.

TECHNIQUE:

Place the ball forward in your stance (to center). Your weight should be 70 to 80 percent on the forward foot, with the handle of the club positioned ahead of the ball. A level to descending blow is necessary on the forward swing, so your backswing is low and shallow.

CONCEPT:

In selecting a club, know that too much loft will at least get you out, even if the next putt is a long one. Too little loft, however, and you will hit the bank or lip, and have to play another shot from the sand.

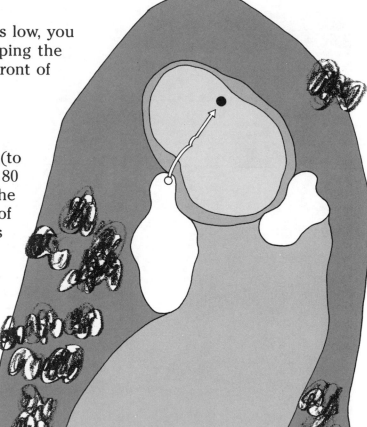

DRILL:

Hit the ball cleanly below the equator, using a club that has sufficient loft. Feel the handle of the club being swung back with little wrist hinge. With a tee in place of the ball, practice hitting sand in front of the tee. Practice descending-blow shots that brush sand in front.

TIP: Problems arise when you either hit too far behind the ball or hit the ball thin. You are better off hitting it thin.

31 Downhill Lies

SITUATION: Your ball and stance are on the downslope of a bunker.

STRATEGY:

Virtually any kind of escape from this situation in one stroke is a victory. Don't be too picky about where the ball comes to rest.

TECHNIQUE:

Position the ball in the middle of your stance. The clubface should be open. Angle your body with the slope and aim well left of the target.

CONCEPT:

To succeed with this shot, you must develop a stance and swing that will keep the club going down. This will ensure that you take the sand out well in front of the ball.

DRILL:

Draw a line in the sand. Using the setup described above, stand with the line in the middle of your stance. Practice taking sand out in front of the line. Your swing will have to be more vertical, and you will have to stay flexed longer into the swing. After you are able to consistently take sand out in front of the line, place a row of balls there and hit shots.

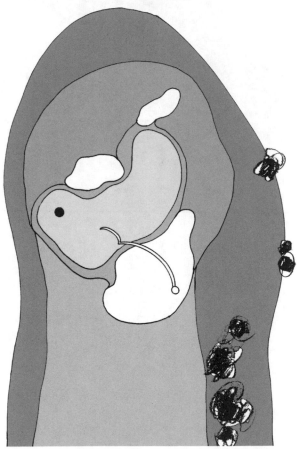

TIP: The ball will not come out high and soft. You must realize this and resist the temptation to lift the ball out. Doing so will only cause you to hit well behind the ball and either leave the ball in the bunker or skull it over the green.

 **32** # Putting From the Sand

> **SITUATION:** The ball is in a clean lie in a shallow bunker with a very slight lip. The pin is at least 15 feet from the edge of the bunker.

STRATEGY:

Because it's easier to strike the ball cleanly with a putter than a wedge, you decide to go the more conservative route and putt the ball. You can do this because you have plenty of green to run the ball along and because the lip of the bunker poses no obstacle to a putted ball.

TECHNIQUE:

Place the ball forward in your stance with your weight favoring your front foot. By placing the ball forward and your weight forward, you have moved the center, or bottom, of the swing arc forward. You will hit the ball cleanly with a level swing.

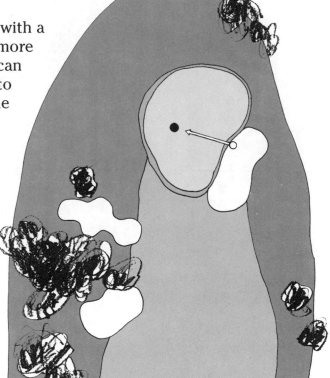

CONCEPT:

By using a putter, you avoid having to contact the sand, as you would with a wedge. But your part of the bargain is that you can't look up and you can't move as you make your stroke. The putter cannot touch sand at any time, and the stroke must be at least 50 percent more forceful than a putt of the same length along the green. The ball will come out of the bunker low and running.

DRILL:

Place five balls in a row in a clean lie. Carefully strike the ball with your putter, keeping your head still and your body rock solid. Drill by doing the Bellied Wedge Drill (see Drill 47), which will help you keep the club comfortably above the ground and will also help you strike the ball on the equator. Get this ball past the pin. Don't get cute and try to let it die right at the hole.

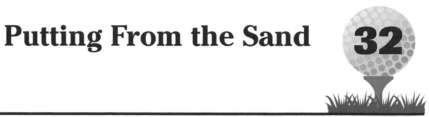

TIP: This stroke will always be stronger than a typical putt because it must roll through sand and fringe. Make sure you focus on speed rather than precision. Pick out a target beyond the cup, and tell yourself that's where the cup is.

© GolfStock/Larry Lambrecht

Ben Crenshaw:
Best Putter Ever?

Ben Crenshaw is known as one of golf's best putters ever, and this well-deserved reputation has obscured the fact that Crenshaw is also a wizard of the sand shot. In 1991, Crenshaw led the PGA Tour in sand saves with a 64.9 percent success rate that stood as one of the highest in tour history. A perennial top performer in the sand, Crenshaw came back with a 61.4 rating in 1995, better than all but four other professionals on the circuit.

His club of choice in the bunkers is a Wilson Staff 57-degree sand wedge. With it he can flip high-lofted explosion shots that settle softly, even on quick greens, or skim the sand to deliver low, running escape shots that check up near the hole or land short of it and "release" to make up the rest of the distance.

Crenshaw, a golf historian and collector, will go down in the books as a two-time Masters champion who won his second green jacket under extreme circumstances. It was 1995, and the 42-year-old Crenshaw was playing poorly. He was enduring physical problems ranging from bone spurs to calcium deposits to an incipient kidney stone, but his biggest blow would come with the death of his longtime teacher, Harvey Penick. Crenshaw traveled to Texas to serve as a pallbearer for the legendary Penick, flew immediately back to Augusta on the day before competition began, and won his second Masters with the spirit of his late friend and mentor carrying him forward.

Chapter 5

Intermediate and Full Wedge Shots

The drills in this chapter will help you learn to deal with conditions such as wind, tight lies, obstacles, and firm ground. You won't hit most of these shots with full power—these are scoring shots. When you play them you are trying to hit the ball close to the hole, not far from where you're standing.

By using some of the principles described in the early chapters, such as changing ball position and length of swing, you will learn to alter the ball's trajectory and distance. Some of the distances mentioned in the drills will vary, depending on your skill level and strength.

In golf, not all shots are played from level, clean lies with no wind and soft greens. By learning to read course conditions and adjust your shots, you can face adverse conditions with confidence.

33 Fairway Bunker Shot

STRATEGY:

A shot that leaves you anywhere on the green is more than acceptable. Select your club and plan your shot with the idea of reaching or coming up short but on the fairway.

TECHNIQUE:

You must brace your stance to reduce excessive lower-body movement and dig your feet securely into the sand.

CONCEPT:

This drill will help you learn to hit the ball cleanly, below the equator.

DRILL:

Place 10 striped balls in a clean lie within a bunker. Brace your stance. Start off by hitting short shots (10 to 20 yards). As you become more proficient, hit shots farther until you reach your target. If you take any sand it should be from *in front of the ball*. The ball will fly out low and fast.

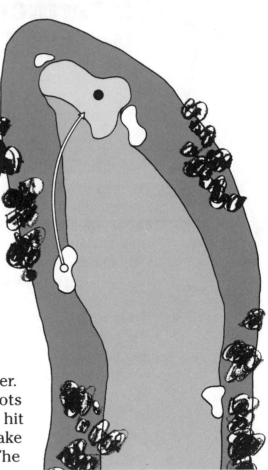

TIP: Swing aggressively through impact. Your ball will have lots of spin on it. Plan to fly the ball up to your target.

> **SITUATION:** You're in the fairway of a par 5 after two good shots. The green is about 80 yards away but significantly above your position on the fairway.

STRATEGY:

You've passed the distance test on this par 5. Now you have to demonstrate accuracy with your wedge. Because you can't see the green, however, your goal is just to get the ball on the green.

TECHNIQUE:

Set up for a one-half to three-quarter wedge shot. Place the ball in the center of your stance with your weight slightly favoring the forward foot.

CONCEPT:

Your tendency will be to take full swings and decelerate the downswing. Make sure you always accelerate your forward swing. Learn to regulate the distance of your less-than-full-swing wedges by varying the size of your swing instead of hitting with the same size swing at varying speeds.

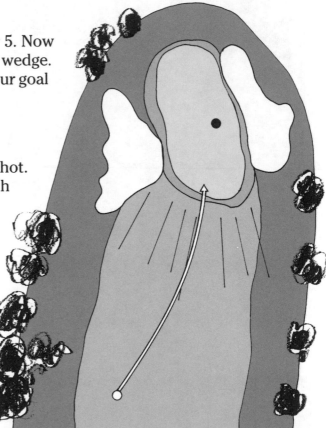

DRILL:

Hit shots by swinging your arms back and through from 9 o'clock to 3 o'clock, then from 10 o'clock to 2 o'clock, and finally from 11 o'clock to 1 o'clock. This will vary the distance of your shots. As you increase the size of your swing, the speed will naturally pick up without your conscious thought.

34

TIP: Remember, always accelerate your forward swing.

35 Strong Headwind

SITUATION: You are at your normal one-half to three-quarter wedge distance and hitting into a strong wind.

STRATEGY:

Hit the shot without the ball ballooning into the air and coming up short.

TECHNIQUE:

You will need to choke down to the bottom of the grip and place the ball in the middle of your stance with your weight favoring your front foot.

CONCEPT:

This drill will help you learn to lower the flight of the ball so the wind will have less effect.

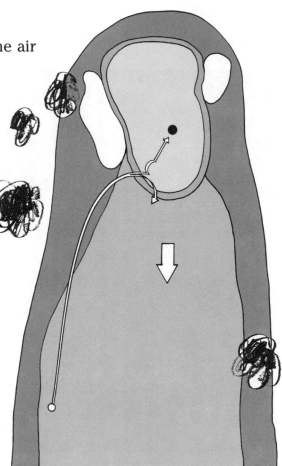

DRILL:

Place in the ground two sticks or shafts about three and a half feet tall and tie a string between them. Place this setup about three feet in front of your ball so that the string is across and perpendicular to your target line. Hit shots toward your target but stop your club before it hits the string. Make sure that your chest completely faces the target. This will help you learn how to hit the ball with your rotation instead of your hands and arms.

TIP: At first you will hit the string with little body rotation. You must feel as though you are leaving the clubhead at impact. Use more club and less swing.

36 Lofted Shot Over a Tree

SITUATION: Your ball is behind a tree that stands 50 to 80 yards from your target.

STRATEGY:

Hit a high-lofted shot and still get the carry distance you need to reach the green.

TECHNIQUE:

Play the ball far forward in your stance with the clubface wide open.

CONCEPT:

The setup and swing are designed to create height, not distance. Accuracy is not the goal with this shot. Extra body motion gives you the increased altitude you need.

DRILL:

Find a grassy area and set up using a range bucket or the end of your bag. Place your forward foot on the bucket. With the ball even with your forward foot and the clubface open, hit shots feeling your back shoulder stay low through impact. This drill simulates an uphill lie with your stance and keeps your weight on your back foot.

Lofted Shot Over a Tree

TIP: While playing this shot try to re-create the setup of an uphill shot by lowering your back shoulder and flexing your back leg.

 **37** **Bump and Run**

SITUATION: Your ball is in the fairway with a clear path to the green, about 80 to 110 yards out. The wind is either at your back or at your face, making a high shot impractical. The course is dry, not wet and slow.

STRATEGY:

You elect to play a long, low, running shot, known as the bump-and-run or run-up shot.

TECHNIQUE:

Use an 8 iron, 9 iron, or pitching wedge—a sand wedge will spin the ball too much. Take a closed stance, play the ball back, keep your hands forward and your weight slightly left (60 percent). Swing in a shallow, U-shaped arc.

CONCEPT:

The early part of this shot is shaped like the humpback line drive in baseball. There's a divot, but it's shallow and narrow. When it lands, the ball has enough energy to skip and run the last 30 to 50 percent of the way to the hole.

DRILL:

Drill by practicing the shot and holding your finish for two seconds. Concentrate on keeping your hands and the handle of the club leading the way. Release at impact but don't create a wristy feeling

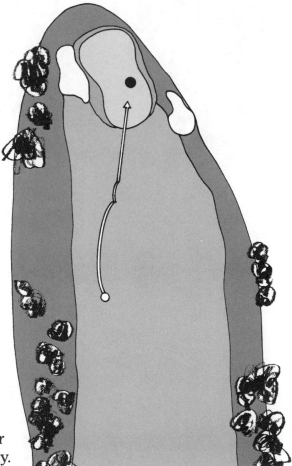

in this swing. The toe of the club must beat the heel in a race to the ball. This shot will need to run and run. At your finish, the toe of the club should be pointing to the sky.

38 Swing on a Chair

SITUATION: The ball is on a clean, level lie, and your target is one-half or one quadrant of the green. This shot requires extra precision.

STRATEGY:

You need to hit a specific half of the green. Just hitting the green won't be satisfactory.

TECHNIQUE:

Your stance should be open, with the left foot pulled back. This will result in less turn. Compared to other full wedge shots, this shot requires you to position your feet closer together and flex your knees and hips more.

CONCEPT:

This setup and shot dictate a tighter, more compact—though not rushed—swing. Think of coiling with your upper body, not transferring lots of weight and driving the legs.

DRILL:

Practice swinging on a chair or a bench, which inhibits hip turn. Swing with the heels down to restrain lower-body movement. The finish is not so full—think of the clubhead as the hand of a clock, which should be pointing toward one o'clock or two o'clock, not three o'clock, at top of backswing.

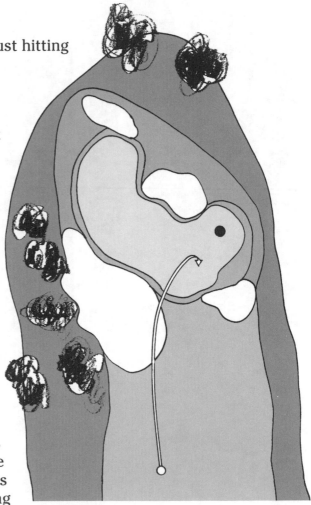

TIP: These three drills—38, 39, 40—are hit with your scoring clubs. You can and should learn to be sharp with them. The swing you use for this shot is not transferable to a full swing with middle irons or woods. The pitching wedge is presumed to have 47 to 49 degrees of loft.

39 Gap Wedge

SITUATION: The ball is on a clean, level lie, and your target is one-half or one quadrant of the green. This shot requires extra precision.

STRATEGY:

At this distance, you need to hit a specific quadrant of the green. Just hitting the green isn't satisfactory.

TECHNIQUE:

Your stance should be open, with the front foot pulled back. This will result in less turn. Compared to other full wedge shots, this shot requires you to position your feet closer together and flex your knees and hips more.

CONCEPT:

This setup and shot dictate a tighter, more compact—though not rushed—swing. Think of coiling with your upper body, not transferring lots of weight and driving the legs.

DRILL:

Same as Drill 38. Note that the ball's spin rate goes up as you switch from the pitching wedge

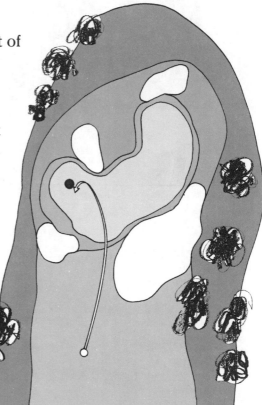

to the gap wedge. Remember to knock the ball closer to the hole with the gap wedge to offset extra spin. Expect reduced roll or even drawing back. (The gap wedge has 51 to 53 degrees of loft.)

40 Pin High

SITUATION: A three-quarter to full wedge shot from 75 yards with a sand wedge.

STRATEGY:

At this distance, barring any unusual conditions such as high wind, you should be aiming at the pin, trying to set up a one-putt for birdie.

TECHNIQUE:

Your stance should be open, with the left foot pulled back. This will result in less turn. Compared to other full wedge shots, this shot requires you to position your feet closer together and flex your knees and hips more.

CONCEPT:

This setup and shot dictate a tighter, more compact—though not rushed—swing. Think of coiling with your upper body, not transferring lots of weight and driving the legs.

DRILL:

Same as Drill 38. We assume a loft angle of 55 to 57 degrees on the sand wedge.

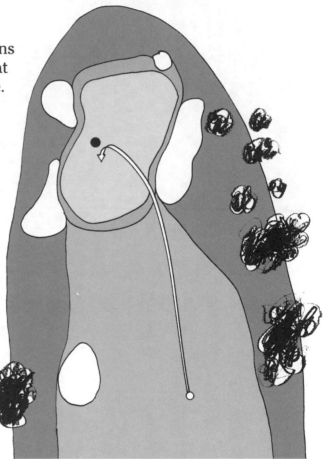

41 Uphill Lie

SITUATION: The ball is 110 yards from the green in a moderately uphill lie on the fairway or in light rough.

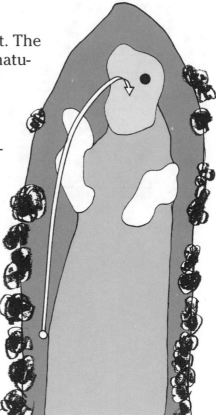

STRATEGY:

From this spot, you can certainly hit a fine approach shot. The center of the green is your goal. Trajectory of this shot is naturally high, so you may need to take one more club.

TECHNIQUE:

Play the ball slightly forward in your stance. Get your shoulders and hips sloping or tilting in line with the terrain to avoid sticking the club in the ground. Don't bend one knee more than the other.

CONCEPT:

You'll have the sensation of swinging more uphill. On these lies the contact must be clean.

DRILL:

Rehearse the shot by stepping to the side and sticking a tee in the ground. Nick or nip the tee one-half inch up without hitting the ground in front of it. Swing "with" the slope, not into the slope.

TIP: The tendency is this: downhill you top, uphill you hit fat. Keep that in mind.

42 Sidehill Lie: Ball Below Your Feet

SITUATION: The ball is 110 yards from the green in an uneven sidehill lie, slightly below your feet on the fairway or in light rough.

STRATEGY:

Some sidehill lies where the ball is below your feet are severe enough to be dangerous. Most are moderate, however, involving a difference of two or three inches. Still, any sidehill ball-below-feet lie is challenging. It's easy to have the shot fly off line to the right. Your goal is to reach the green safely. If you have water right and a bunker left, hitting this shot hole-high in the bunker is not a bad result.

TECHNIQUE:

Play the ball in the center of your stance. Create more flex in your knees and hips and maintain that flex to the finish. Aim slightly left to offset this shot's tendency to fade slightly right.

CONCEPT:

The adjustments you make in your drills and in your on-course rehearsal of this shot have the effect of *relocating the bottom of your swing* to a lower, more distant spot than you would swing to on a normal lie.

DRILL:

Rehearse the shot by stepping to the side and sticking a tee in the ground. Nick or nip the tee one-half inch up without hitting the ground in back of it or on the near side of it. Flex your knees down through the shot. Avoid the instinct to stand up as you move through impact and follow-through.

SITUATION: The ball is 110 yards from the green in a downhill lie, on the fairway or in light rough.

STRATEGY:

The downhill lie requires some adjustments, but once you make them you can play for a section of the green and swing away.

TECHNIQUE:

Play the ball back in your stance. Set up with a little more weight on your left side.

CONCEPT:

You never want to finish high with this shot. The ball comes off low and runs more, so throttle back or take less club.

DRILL:

Find a downhill lie and put a tee in the ground. Let your shoulders and your swing path follow the slope of the ground as you get into the impact zone. Clip the tee and scalp the grass in front of it. Take note of how much you have to stay down to clip and scalp. Stay with the shot longer to make sure you contact the ball cleanly.

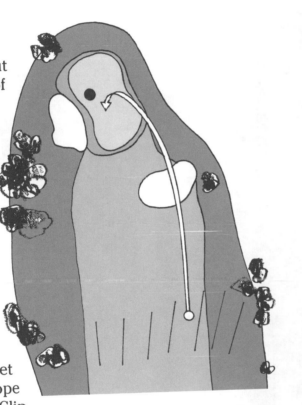

TIP: Keep rehearsing until you nick the tee a couple of times. Don't get the idea that you'll be able to adjust and hit the ball without at least one successful practice swing.

> **SITUATION:** The ball is 110 yards from the green in an uneven sidehill lie, resting slightly above your feet on the fairway or in light rough.

STRATEGY:

This situation, where the ball is above your feet, allows for more aggressive shotmaking than when the ball is below your feet. Pick a section of the green to which you'll play.

TECHNIQUE:

Play the ball in the center of your stance. Stand more vertically, with less hip bend. Aim slightly right of your target to offset this shot's tendency to hook left.

CONCEPT:

You'll be making a shallower and flatter swing than usual, because a V-shaped swing will cause a fat hit. Adjust your aim to a line slightly right of the actual target.

DRILL:

Get the feel for this shot by hitting balls (or just taking swings) off your knees. Do this to avoid hitting behind the ball. Take several swings, concentrating on a flatter swing plane. Rehearse the shot by stepping to the side and sticking a tee in the ground. Nick or nip the tee one-half inch up without hitting the ground in front of it. Keep rehearsing until you hit the tee a couple of times.

> **TIP:** If your rehearsal swings result in deep divots, choke down on the club about an inch.

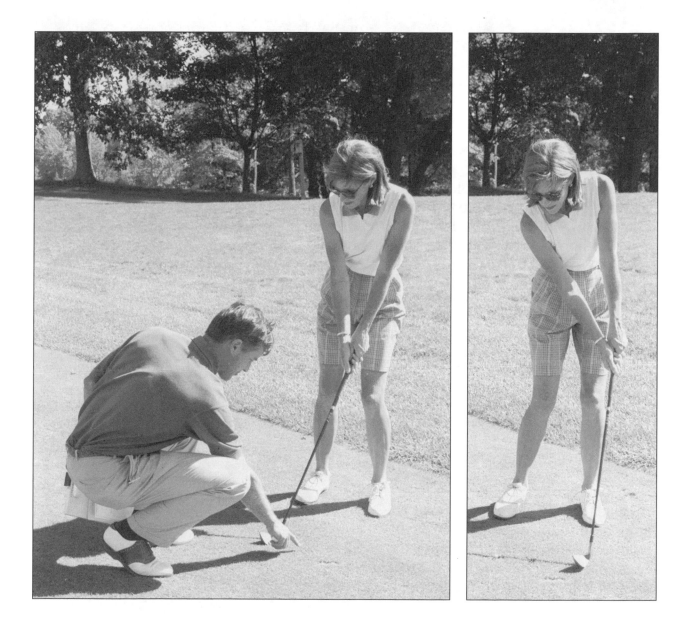

TIP: People who play on hilly courses will get better at this more quickly; flat-course people will take more time. The ball comes off low and runs more, so throttle back or take less club.

45 Hitting From a Divot

STRATEGY:

A key to success with this shot is to avoid becoming upset or irritated. Every golfer ends up in a divot occasionally. You may be able to turn this situation in your favor by hitting from the divot to the green, which will probably demoralize your opponent.

TECHNIQUE:

Use the same setup that you used for other full wedge or three-quarter wedge approach shots.

CONCEPT:

A thin hit here is much better than a fat hit.

DRILL:

Just as in the downhill lie shot, your hands will lead the clubhead through impact. Make sure to stay down longer than usual. Your finish is also lower—it's a break-off finish. Hit this shot without looking up for three full seconds. Finish with the clubhead pointing to the target, not wrapped around your body. An alternative drill is to put a tee in the ground and practice scraping the grass in front of the tee.

TIP: Hit balls out of divots on the range, creating pressure on yourself as though you were in competition.

46 The High-Spin Show-Off Shot

SITUATION: You have a clean fairway lie and less than 100 yards to the green. The pin is reasonably close to the center of the green.

STRATEGY:

You decide to try a high-spin shot that will make the ball stop on a dime, perhaps even back up. Some risk is involved, but you're ahead in the match and trying to psych out your opponent.

TECHNIQUE:

Play the ball back in your stance and open the clubface. Gauge the distance, then take a little less club and swing harder.

CONCEPT:

This is an enjoyable shot that you must hit with a pitching wedge or sand wedge. Clubhead speed is what you need to pull off the shot. Acceleration through impact is a must.

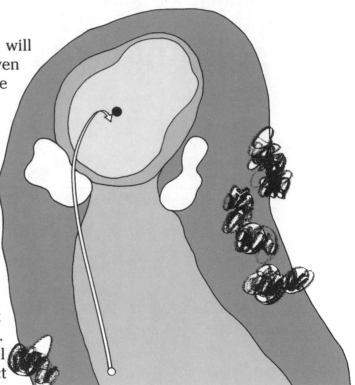

DRILL:

Hit down and across the ball to the left of the target. It must be a clean hit, if not slightly thin. Your ball will fly fairly low, and your swing will finish in a low, abrupt fashion.

The High-Spin Show-Off Shot

TIP: Try this shot on the range many times before you try it on the course.

© GolfStock/Pete Marovich

Paul Azinger:
Knockdown Style

The highlight of Paul Azinger's professional career is his victory in the 1993 PGA Championship at the Inverness Club in Toledo, Ohio. Dueling Greg Norman and Nick Faldo down the stretch, Azinger hit drives on the 71st hole of regulation and on the second hole of sudden death that left him in the 110- to 130-yard range he dearly loves. With his 9 iron on the penultimate regulation hole and his pitching wedge on the play-off hole, the wiry, Florida-bred pro hit two of his patented "low burner" shots. The first stopped three feet from the pin, and the second came to rest in easy two-putt range, allowing Azinger to win the '93 PGA over Norman.

Azinger puts his left hand on the club in an extremely "strong" position, such that he can see the knuckles of all four fingers. As a result, when he hits his wedge shots from the fairway, he keeps his wrists firm, delivering the club through a swift, swiveling motion of his hips and torso. Under pressure, this knockdown-style approach shot is very reliable, because it requires no precise or subtle movements of the hands and wrists.

With his first major victory, Azinger was primed to move on and become a true superstar. But 1993 brought serious illness as well as a major championship. Throughout 1994 and into 1995, Azinger battled lymphoma, eventually overcoming his disease through a successful radiation and chemotherapy regime. He has returned to solid form since, crossing the quarter-million mark in earnings for 1996.

Azinger lives with his wife and family in Bradenton, Florida. He does extensive volunteer work to help raise money for cancer research.

Chapter 6

Special Greenside Shots

A golfer doesn't have to hit a terrible drive or approach shot to end up in a disastrous situation. The shots and drills in this chapter will help you recover from places no golfer wants to be. Although many of these shots look unusual as the golfer prepares to play them, most are not really that difficult to execute. If you've practiced them even a few times, you have a good chance of pulling these shots off—as long as you aren't shy about attempting them.

Conventional pressure hardly exists with these shots because few people watching would expect you to hit them as planned. The only pressure you could feel is from embarrassment that you're even trying such an unorthodox shot. But execute these shots successfully even once, and you'll no longer feel bashful about trying them—you'll look forward to the challenge they present.

 **Bellied Wedge Shot**

> **SITUATION:** The ball is in a clean lie, backed up against a cut of rough or high grass collar. In this situation, you can't use your putter.

STRATEGY:

The percentages call for an intentionally skulled shot, known as a bladed wedge or bellied wedge.

TECHNIQUE:

Hold the wedge with your regular full-shot grip or your putter grip, but otherwise play the shot just like a putt. As you address your ball, the blade of the wedge will be suspended just above the collar grass, not resting on it. The shaft will be almost vertical, like a putter shaft, not setting on an angle.

CONCEPT:

Because of its weight and shape, your sand wedge is able to slide through the wall of grass that your ball is resting against. Don't try this shot with your pitching wedge. Thanks to the bounce angle on the sole (see page 5), the sand wedge has a unique ability to avoid catching in the grass as it's about to make contact.

DRILL:

Practice by setting up striped range balls so that the stripe is just at the equator of the resting ball. That's your target. You can also use the brand name of the ball as a target line. You'll be striking the ball with the leading edge of your sand wedge. Contact the ball right at its equator—too low and you'll flip it uselessly upward, too high and you'll only bump it forward a few feet. Remember: the edge of the blade meets the equator of the ball.

> **TIP:** You can practice this little shot whenever you have a wait on a tee, especially if the tee grass is cut short enough to let a ball roll.

48 Collection Bunker Chip

> **SITUATION:** The last decade or so has seen widespread use of a course-design feature called a collection bunker, and you've landed in one. A collection bunker is a bowl-shaped depression next to the green, with the grass cut at fairway height. Balls hit in that general area will collect into one low spot.

STRATEGY:

To solve this kind of short-game problem, players have come up with a new shot, using a metal wood as a chipping or putting club. Try this shot now, with the goal of getting within easy two-putt range.

TECHNIQUE:

This is a putt-type shot with your 3 wood. Choke down on the grip but don't try to stand as close to the ball as you would with your putter. Use your normal full-swing grip and just stroke the ball with a symmetrical motion.

CONCEPT:

You'll be learning how to get your ball to climb a hill under control without losing the momentum of its roll. Without taking the risks involved in a high pitch (flying it over the green, having it roll back down to you), you can escape the collection bunker and be putting on

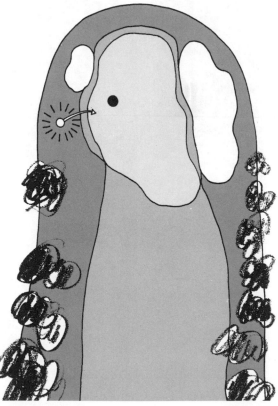

your next shot. The metal 3 wood is the best club to use because it has more loft and more mass than a putter but less loft than an iron. It also has a smooth sole, to avoid digging. Your putter would make the ball bore into the grass and die on the upslope. Your wedge or less-lofted iron would create spin that would slow the ball down, and any iron has a chance of digging or stubbing.

DRILL:

The drill aspect of this shot is simply to get a feel for how the ball behaves when a club designed to hit it 230 yards is used for a 40- or 50-foot shot. Think of making a pendulum stroke as you practice this. One good way to create a putter-type feel for the shot is to lean your 3 wood against your hip, address the ball with your putter in your hands, make a few phantom swings, and then drop the putter and grab your 3 wood. Don't change your position as you do this, except to back up slightly from the ball.

49 Wood Chip From Light Rough

SITUATION: The ball is in very light rough three to six feet off the green. You are playing over level or slightly sloped ground, not up a steep bank. The grass you have to get past is what I call "country-club rough," meaning that it's about two inches long.

STRATEGY:

Just as with the collection bunker shot, you're trying to avoid scuffing, stubbing, or digging in this medium rough. Likewise, you want the ball to keep its forward momentum.

TECHNIQUE:

Use the setup described in Drill 34.

CONCEPT:

Strike the ball harder than you would if you were putting from the same distance on the green.

DRILL:

Drill by practicing on the course. Chip one with your 7, 8, or 9 iron, then one with the 3 wood. Try to dial in the amount of force required.

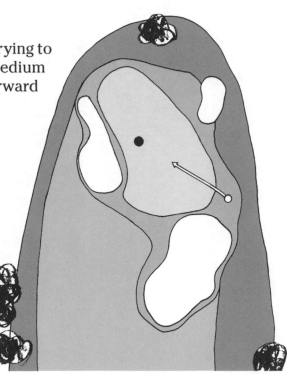

Wood Chip From Light Rough

TIP: There's a little bit of a slappy feeling to the impact on this shot—not a lot of follow-through.

50 Obstruction Shot

SITUATION: A right-handed player has the ball stuck against a tree, shrub, or wall. The only possible stance is on the "wrong" side of the ball.

STRATEGY:

Only one shot is possible—the back-to-target, one-handed backhand. It's more unorthodox than it is difficult. Learn the fundamentals, then approach the shot with a mix of confidence and that relaxed feeling of not having anything to lose.

TECHNIQUE:

Play this with the club (pitching wedge or 9 iron) in your right hand. The shaft is basically vertical. The line from the ball to your right toe extends straight through your left toe. Take a shallow, U-shaped swing and contact the ball in the center of the clubface.

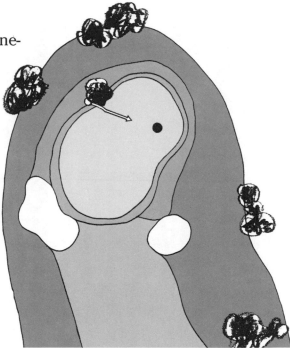

CONCEPT:

Although this is an unorthodox shot, you can feel fairly comfortable with it in a short time. What seems initially awkward will soon feel quite solid, especially if you focus on the relationship between the club handle and your forearm.

DRILL:

The only drill for this shot is to practice it, keeping the original elbow angle unchanged throughout your pendulum swing. Notice that the butt of the club separates from the forearm on the take-away, bumps into the forearm at impact, then remains pressed against the forearm as you complete the swing.

TIP: Expect your most solid contact to be slightly out toward the toe of the clubface.

51   **Fairway Putt**

> **SITUATION:** The ball is on the fringe or on short-cut fairway, a few feet to as many as 10 feet off the green.

STRATEGY:

The best option is to putt the ball, allowing for the resistance of the fringe, which will slow down your ball. The goal is to get in shape for a relatively short, makable second putt.

TECHNIQUE:

Execute this shot using the technique described in Drill 32. Add 10 or 15 percent more force.

CONCEPT:

With just a little practice, you can putt well enough from off the green to make putting a much less risky option than chipping. The most prudent option is to use your putter rather than chip with a wedge.

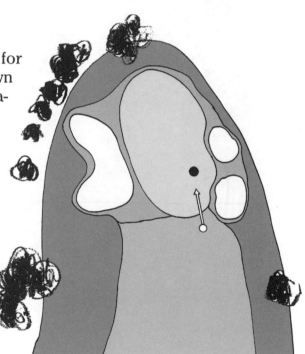

DRILL:

You can practice the stroke you need for this putt by doing the Bellied Wedge Drill (page 110). This is one short-game drill that is extremely easy to practice because most public golf courses have large no-chipping areas around their practice putting greens.

52 "Pop" Shot

SITUATION: Your ball is in a grassy or fluffy lie at the bottom of an embankment, with the green 5 to 20 feet above you. The ball is level with your shins or knees.

STRATEGY:

You have to hit a pop-up shot with a wide-open clubface.

TECHNIQUE:

The slope forces you to set up with your left foot above your right foot at address. Tilt your shoulders in line with the slope. Aim 5 to 10 feet right of the target and lay the clubface wide open.

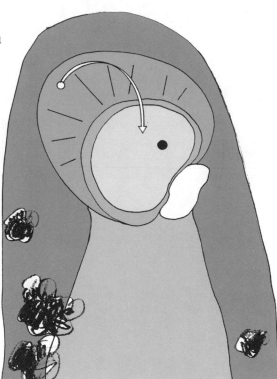

CONCEPT:

The shot is much easier than it looks because you can swing with widely varying force levels and have success. As long as you make square contact, the ball will go almost straight up, so the worst that can happen is that it stays in the air longer than you expected.

DRILL:

Your swing for this shot will be flat, like a baseball swing, and the ball will pop almost straight up. If you swing along the target line, your club and ball will just bank off the hill.

53 High-Low Sand Wedge

SITUATION: Your ball is 20 to 30 feet off the green with no obstacles in the way.

STRATEGY:

It is sometimes difficult to decide whether to chip or pitch certain shots. This drill equips you to make the borderline decision wisely and execute the shot.

TECHNIQUE:

Use basic chipping and pitching techniques.

CONCEPT:

This drill is an enjoyable five-minute exercise that helps you understand subtle differences between types of lies: grassy, tight, sitting up, sitting down, fluffy, and so forth.

DRILL:

Hit a regular chip shot with a sand wedge, then a regular greenside pitch shot. Alternate back and forth, using the sand wedge for all shots. Hit five low pitch shots, then five high ones. Follow this with five low chip shots, then five higher ones. Repeat four times.

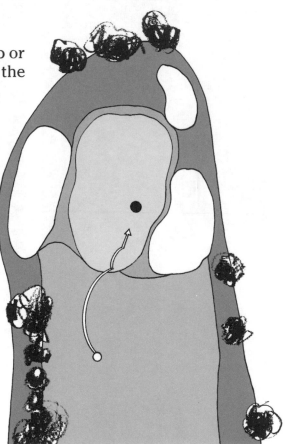

© GolfStock/Pete Marovich

Tiger Woods:
An Innovative Shotmaker

The name Tiger Woods conjures up images of booming drives and power-packed 1-iron shots. The other image we have of Woods involves long putts dropping in for birdie and a fist punching the air in celebration.

But the Tiger Woods you might enjoy watching most is the one who solves his greenside up-and-down challenges with some uniquely inventive shotmaking. During the 1997 U.S. Open, you might recall seeing Woods take out a 3 wood to sink his ball from a deep, close-cut "collection bunker" beside one of the Congressional Country Club's more elevated greens. The collection bunker is a grass bunker in the shape of a natural hollow (see drill 48 for details).

Tiger's 3-wood "bump" shot is an excellent way to roll the ball up to the green without risking an "air mail" mishap that would leave the ball in trouble on the opposite side. Woods, the three-time U.S. Amateur champion and the winningest PGA Tour rookie ever, has a few other greenside tricks up his sleeve. When he misses a green, which isn't too often, stay alert to see what club Tiger selects and how he chooses to play his recovery.

Originally from Cypress, California, Woods now resides in Orlando, Florida.

About the Authors

Jim Fitzgerald has been the head golf professional at the Chevy Chase Club in Chevy Chase, Maryland, since 1987. In nearly 20 years as a golf teacher and coach, he has given more than 12,000 lessons. In 1996 he was recognized by the Middle Atlantic PGA as Teacher of the Year.

An accomplished player as well as instructor, Fitzgerald relied on his excellent short game to win more than 30 professional events and set 3 course records.

Fitzgerald lives in Kensington, Maryland, with his wife, Jane, and his children. His favorite activities apart from golf include playing with his children, traveling, skiing, fishing, and running.

Dave Gould is a golf writer and editor with more than 14 years of experience covering the sport. He is a contributing editor for *Inside Golf* and a former executive editor of *Golf Illustrated*. Gould wrote his first book in 1993, and he has assisted well-known instructors such as Jim McLean and Craig Farnsworth with their books. He is an award-winning member of the Golf Writers Association of America.

Gould lives in Sandy Hook, Connecticut, with his wife, Rachel Basch. Along with golf, his favorite leisure activities are volleyball and snow skiing.